SIGMUND FREIHERR VON HERBERSTEIN

NOTES UPON RUSSIA:

BEING A TRANSLATION OF THE

EARLIEST ACCOUNT OF THAT COUNTRY,

TRANSLATED AND EDITED,

WITH NOTES AND AN INTRODUCTION,

BY

R. H. MAJOR

Volume 1

Elibron Classics
www.elibron.com

Elibron Classics series.

© 2005 Adamant Media Corporation.

ISBN 1-4021-0048-5 (paperback)
ISBN 1-4021-3376-6 (hardcover)

This Elibron Classics Replica Edition is an unabridged facsimile
of the edition published in 1851 by the Hakluyt Society,
London.

Elibron and Elibron Classics are trademarks of
Adamant Media Corporation. All rights reserved.

This book is an accurate reproduction of the original. Any marks, names, colophons, imprints, logos or other symbols or identifiers that appear on or in this book, except for those of Adamant Media Corporation and BookSurge, LLC, are used only for historical reference and accuracy and are not meant to designate origin or imply any sponsorship by or license from any third party.

THE HAKLUYT SOCIETY.

President.
SIR RODERICK IMPEY MURCHISON, G.C. St.S. F.R.S.
Corr. Mem. Inst. Fr., Hon. Mem. Imp. Acad. Sc. St. Petersburg, &c. &c.

Vice-Presidents.
THE EARL OF ELLESMERE.
CAPTAIN C. R. D. BETHUNE, R.N., C.B.

Council.

REAR-ADML. SIR F. BEAUFORT, K.C.B.	RICHARD FORD, ESQ.
CHARLES T. BEKE, ESQ., Phil. D., F.S.A.	JOHN FORSTER, ESQ.
THE LORD ALFRED S. CHURCHILL.	R. W. GREY, ESQ., M.P.
W. D. COOLEY, ESQ.	THOMAS HODGKIN, ESQ., M.D.
BOLTON CORNEY, ESQ., M.R.S.L.	JOHN WINTER JONES, ESQ.
THE RIGHT REV. LORD BISHOP OF ST. DAVID'S.	SIR CHARLES LEMON, BART., M.P.
	P. LEVESQUE, ESQ.
THE VISCOUNT EASTNOR.	THOMAS RUNDALL, ESQ.
SIR HENRY ELLIS, K.H., F.R.S.	THE HON. HENRY E. J. STANLEY.

Honorary Secretary.
R. H. MAJOR, ESQ., F.R.G.S.

Bankers.
MESSRS. BOUVERIE AND CO., 11, HAYMARKET.

THE HAKLUYT SOCIETY, which is established for the purpose of printing rare or unpublished Voyages and Travels, aims at opening by this means an easier access to the sources of a branch of knowledge, which yields to none in importance, and is superior to most in agreeable variety. The narratives of travellers and navigators make us acquainted with the earth, its inhabitants and productions; they exhibit the growth of intercourse among mankind, with its effects on civilization, and, while instructing, they at the same time awaken attention, by recounting the toils and adventures of those who first explored unknown and distant regions.

The advantage of an Association of this kind, consists not merely in its system of literary co-operation, but also in its economy. The acquirements, taste, and discrimination of a number of individuals, who feel an interest in the same pursuit, are thus brought to act in voluntary combination, and the ordinary charges of publication are also avoided, so that the volumes produced, are distributed among the Members (who can alone obtain them) at little more than the cost of printing and paper. The Society expends nearly the whole of its funds in printing works for the Members; and since the cost of each copy varies inversely as the whole number of copies printed, it is obvious that the Members are gainers individually by the prosperity of the Society, and the consequent vigour of its operations.

The Members are requested to bear in mind that the power of the Council to make advantageous arrangements, will depend, in a great measure, on the prompt payment of the subscriptions, which are payable in advance on the 1st January, and are received by the Secretary, R. H. MAJOR, Esq., 4, Albion Place, Canonbury Square, Islington; and by Mr. RICHARDS, 37, Great Queen Street, Lincoln's Inn Fields, who is the Society's agent for the delivery of its volumes.

It is especially requested, that all subscribers who shall not have received their volumes within a reasonable period after the payment of their subscription, will notify the same to the Secretary.

ALREADY PUBLISHED.

The Observations of Sir Richard Hawkins, Knt.

In his Voyage into the South Sea in 1593. Reprinted from the edition of 1622, and edited by Capt. C. R. DRINKWATER BETHUNE, R.N., C.B.

Select Letters of Columbus.

With Original Documents relating to the DISCOVERY of the NEW WORLD. Translated and Edited by R. H. MAJOR, Esq., of the British Museum.

The Discoverie of the Empire of Guiana,

By SIR WALTER RALEGH, KNT. Edited, with Copious Explanatory Notes, and a Biographical Memoir, by SIR ROBERT H. SCHOMBURGK, Phil. D., etc.

Sir Francis Drake his Voyage, 1595,

By THOMAS MAYNARDE, together with the Spanish Account of Drake's Attack on Puerto Rico, edited from the Original MSS., by W. D. COOLEY, Esq.

Narratives of Early Voyages

Undertaken for the Discovery of a Passage to CATHAIA and INDIA, by the Northwest, with Selections from the Records of the worshipful Fellowship of the Merchants of London, trading into the East Indies; and from MSS. in the Library of the British Museum, now first published, by
THOMAS RUNDALL, Esq.

The Historie of Travaile into Virginia Britannia,

Expressing the Cosmographie and Comodities of the Country, together with the Manners and Customs of the people, gathered and observed as well by those who went first thither as collected by William Strachey, Gent., the first Secretary of the Colony; now first Edited from the original manuscript in the British Museum, by R. H. MAJOR, Esq., of the British Museum.

Divers Voyages touching the Discovery of America,

And the Islands adjacent, collected and published by RICHARD HAKLUYT, Prebendary of Bristol, in the year 1582. Edited, with Notes and an Introduction, by JOHN WINTER JONES, Esq., of the British Museum.

A Collection of Documents on Japan,
With a Commentary, by THOMAS RUNDALL, Esq.

The Discovery and Conquest of Florida,
By DON FERDINANDO DE SOTO. Translated out of Portuguese by Richard Hakluyt; and Edited, with Notes and an Introduction, by W. B. RYE, Esq., of the British Museum.

The First Volume of Notes upon Russia,
Being a Translation from the Earliest Account of that Country, entitled RERUM MOSCOVITICARUM COMMENTARII, by the Baron Sigismund von Herberstein, Ambassador from the Court of Germany to the Grand Prince Vasiley Ivanovich, in the years 1517 and 1526. Translated, and edited with Notes and an Introduction, by R. H. MAJOR, Esq., of the British Museum.

Other Works in Progress.

THE SECOND VOLUME OF NOTES UPON RUSSIA.

REMARKS IN MANY VOYAGES TO HUDSON'S BAY, by Captain William Coats. To be edited, with additions, by JOHN BARROW, Esq., of the Admiralty.

DRAKE.—The *world encompassed* by Sir Francis Drake, 1577-80. Written by Francis Fletcher, Preacher, etc. Collated with a MS. To be edited by W. SANDYS VAUX, Esq., M.A.

SOFALAH.—The History of Eastern Ethiopia, by J. dos Santos, 1607. To be Translated, with Notes, by W. DESBOROUGH COOLEY, Esq.

THE EAST-INDIA VOYAGE OF SIR HENRY MIDDLETON IN 1604-5. From the rare Edition of 1606. Edited by BOLTON CORNEY, Esq.

A COLLECTION OF EARLY DOCUMENTS, to form a Supplement to the Narrative of Voyages towards the North West, by T. RUNDALL, Esq.

DE MORGA.—Sucesos en las Islas Filipinas.

Works suggested to the Council for Publication.

FRESCOBALDI.—The Travels of Frescobaldi in Egypt and Syria, in 1384. Translated from the Italian text as edited by Manzi.

BETHENCOURT.—A History of the Discovery and Conquest of the Canary Islands, made by Jean de Béthencourt, in 1402-25. From the French Narrative of his Chaplains, Pierre Bontier and Jean le Verrier.

CA DA MOSTO.—The Voyages of Ca da Mosto along the Western Coast of Africa in 1454. Translated from the Italian text of 1507.

VIRGINIA.—Virginia in the years 1584-1600; comprising the Narratives of Arthur Barlowe, Ralf Lane, Thomas Harriot, etc.

CADIZ.—A Brief and True Report of the Honourable Voyage to Cadiz, 1596. From the suppressed edition of 1598, with additions.

COLONIZATION.—Pamphlets on Colonization. By Sir William Alexander (afterwards Earl of Sterline), and James Hagthorpe.

JOAM DE CASTRO.—Rotiero em que se contem a Viagem que fizeram os Portuguezes no anno de 1541, partinando da Citade de Goa atre Soez.

CHINA.—The Historie of the great and mightie Kingdome of China and the situation thereof. Translated out of Spanish by R. Parke. London, 1588.

GALVANO.—Tratado dos descobrimentos antigos e modernos feitos até a era de 1550, composto pelo famoso Antonio Galvaô. Lisboa, 1731.

Laws of the Hakluyt Society.

I. The object of this Society shall be to print, for distribution among its members, rare and valuable Voyages, Travels, Naval Expeditions, and other geographical records, from an early period to the beginning of the eighteenth century.

II. The Annual Subscription shall be One Guinea, payable in advance on the 1st January.

III. Each member of the Society, having paid his subscription, shall be entitled to a copy of every work produced by the Society, and to vote at the general meetings within the period subscribed for; and if he do not signify, before the close of the year, his wish to resign, he shall be considered as a member for the succeeding year.

IV. The management of the Society's affairs shall be vested in a Council consisting of twenty-one members, namely, a President, two Vice-Presidents, a Secretary, and seventeen ordinary members, to be elected annually; but vacancies occurring between the general meetings shall be filled up by the Council.

V. A General Meeting of the Subscribers shall be held annually, on the first Thursday in March. The Secretary's Report on the condition and proceedings of the Society shall be then read, and, along with the Auditor's Report, be submitted for approval, and finally, the Meeting shall proceed to elect the Council for the ensuing year.

VI. At each Annual Election, six of the old Council shall retire; and a list of the proposed new Council shall be printed for the subscribers previous to the general meeting.

VII. The Council shall meet ordinarily on the 3rd Tuesday in every month, excepting August, September, and October, for the despatch of business, three forming a quorum, and the Chairman having a casting vote.

VIII. Gentlemen preparing and editing works for the Society shall receive twenty-five copies of such works respectively.

IX. The number of copies printed of the Society's productions shall not exceed the estimated number of Subscribers; so that after the second year, when the Society may be supposed to have reached its full growth, there shall be no extra copies.

X. The Society shall appoint Local Secretaries throughout the kingdom, empowered to enrol members, transmit subscriptions, and otherwise forward the Society's interests; and it shall make such arrangements with its correspondents in the chief provincial towns, as will insure to subscribers residing in the country the regular delivery of their volumes at moderate charges.

Rules for the Delivery of the Society's Volumes.

I. The Society's productions will be delivered without any charge, within three miles of the General Post Office.

II. They will be forwarded to any place beyond that limit, the Society paying the cost of booking, but not of carriage; nor will it be answerable in this case for any loss or damage.

III. They will be delivered by the Society's agent, Mr. THOMAS RICHARDS, 37, Great Queen Street, Lincoln's Inn Fields, to persons having written authority of subscribers to receive them.

IV. They will be sent to the Society's correspondents or agents in the principal towns throughout the kingdom; and care shall be taken that the charge for carriage be as moderate as possible.

LIST OF MEMBERS

OF

THE HAKLUYT SOCIETY.

Adam, Admiral Sir C., K.C.B., Greenwich Hospital
Admiralty (The), 2 *copies*
Ainslie, Philip Barrington, Esq., St. Colme
Allport, Franklin, Esq., 156, Leadenhall-st.
Army and Navy Club, 13, St. James's sq.
Arrowsmith, John, Esq., 10, Soho-square
Asher, Mr. A., Berlin
Ashton, J. Y., Esq., Liverpool
Atkinson, F. R., Esq., Manchester

Baillie, David, Esq., 14, Belgrave-square
Baker, William, Esq., Jun., 3, Crosby-sq.
Banks, W., Esq., Melina-place, Grove-rd.
Barrow, J., Esq., F.R..S, 7, New-st., Spring-gardens
Batho, J. A., Esq., 56, Lombard-street
Beatty, James, Esq., C.E., Southampton
Beaufort, Rear-Admiral Sir Francis, K.C.B., F.R.S., Admiralty
Beck, Dr., New York State Library, Albany
Beke, Charles T., Esq., Phil. D., 34, Cumming-street, Pentonville
Belcher, Captain Sir Edward, C.B., R.N., 22, Thurloe-square, Brompton
Bell, Reverend Thomas, Berbice
Bell, Robert, Esq., Norris Castle, East Cowes, I.W.
Bell, Robert, Esq., 33, Soho-square
Bell, W., Esq., Church-place, Clapham
Berlin, The Royal Library of
Betencourt, Alonzo, Esq., Philadelphia
Bethune, Captain C. R. Drinkwater, C.B. R.N., Admiralty
Bethune, Hon. J. E. D.
Biden, Captain
Blackie, Dr. Walter G., Villafield, Glasgow
Blackwood, Captain Fr. P., R.N., United Service Club
Blandford, Marquis of, 3, Wilton-terrace
Blunt, J., Esq., Mortlake
Blyth, James, Esq., 24, Hyde-park-gardens
Bombay Geographical Society
Bone, Mr. F. G., R.N.
Booth, B. W., Esq., Manchester

Boston Athenæum, The
Botfield, Beriah, Esq., Norton Hall, Northamptonshire
Bradshaw, Lieut. Lawrence, Woolwich
Brodhead, J. R., Esq., New York
Broughton, the Lord, 42, Berkeley-square
Brown, George, Esq., 41, Rochester-row
Brown, J., Esq., Newcastle-pl., Clerkenwell
Brown, W. H., Esq., Chester
Brown, John Carter, Esq., Providence, Rhode Island
Bruce, John, Esq., F.S.A., 5, Upper Gloucester-street, Dorset-square
Brussels, Royal Library of
Bullock, Capt. Frederick, R.N., Woolwich
Bunney, William, Esq., Hull
Burnett, W. F., Commander, R.N., Royal Naval College, Portsmouth

Campbell, R. H. S., Esq., 5, Argyle-place, Regent's-street
Cannon, Charles, Esq., British Museum
Carlton Club, Pall Mall
Chabot, Philip J., Esq., M.A., F.R.A.S., 61, Fashion-street, Spitalfields
Chapman, Captain, R.A., Athenæum
Chapman, William, Esq., Richmond
Chauncey, Henry C., Esq., New York
Chichester, J. R., Esq., 49, Wimpole-st.
Christie, Jonathan Henry, Esq., 9, Stanhope-street, Hyde-park-gardens
Churchill, Lord Alfred S., F.R.G.S., 6, Bury-street
Clarke, Thomas, Esq., Ordnance Office, Pall Mall
Clive, Robert, Esq., 53, Grosvenor-street
Colborne, the Lord, 19, Hill-st., Berkeley-square
Colledge, Dr., Lauriston House, Cheltenham
Collier, John Payne, Esq., F.S.A.
Colonial Office
Congress, Library of the, United States
Cooley, W. D., Esq., 33, King-street, Bloomsbury

Corney, Bolton, Esq., M.R.S.L., Barnes-terrace
Costello, Dudley, Esq., 54, Acacia-road, St. John's Wood
Cotton, R. A., Esq., Barnstaple
Cox, E. Wm., Esq., 3, Crown Office Row, Temple
Cracroft, Capt., R.N.
Cranstoun, G., Esq., Corehouse, Lanark
Cree, David, Esq., 23, Bush-lane
Croker, T. Crofton, Esq., 3, Gloucester-road, Old Brompton
Crowninschield, A., Esq.
Cunningham, Captain
Cunningham, Peter, Esq., 2, Madeley Villas, Kensington

Dalrymple, Arthur, Esq., St. Giles, Norwich
Daniel, G., Esq., F.L.S., St. John's Wood
De la Beche, Sir Henry, K.H., 28, Jermyn-street
De Lasaux, Miss
Dennett, W. H., Esq., Boston, U.S.
Dickens, Charles, Esq., 1, Devonshire-terrace, Marylebone
Dilke, C. Wentworth, Esq., 76, Sloane-st.
Dilke, C. W., Esq., Jun., 76, Sloane-street
Disbrowe, Sir Edward, K.C.B., St. Katherine's, Regent's-park
Drake, Samuel G., Esq., Boston, U. S.
Dry, Thos., Esq., 25, Lincoln's Inn Fields

East India Company, The Hon. the Court of Directors of the, 20 *copies*
Eastnor, the Viscount, 45, Grosvenor-pl.
Edmondston, James, Esq., 7, Trafalgar-square, Twickenham
Ellesmere, the Earl of, 18, Belgrave-square
Ellice, Rt. Hon. Edward, M.P., 18, Arlington-street
Elliot, J. B., Esq., Patna
Ellis, Sir Henry, K.H., F.R.S., &c., British Museum
Elphinstone, the Lord, 14, St. George's-pl.
Elphinstone, John F., Esq., 28, York-ter., Regent's-park
Elphinstone, Lieut., 3, Chesham-place, Belgrave-square
Enderby, Charles, Esq., East Greenwich
Ethersey, Commander, H.E.I.C.S.
Evans, Captain George, R.N.

Fayrer, Joseph, Esq., M.D., Royal Westminster Ophthalmic Hospital, Charing-cross
Fennell, James Hamilton, Esq., 4, Devereux-court, Temple
Force, Colonel Peter, Washington, U.S.
Ford, R., Esq., 123, Park-street, Grosvenor-square

Foreign Office
Forster, J., Esq., 58, Lincoln's Inn Fields
Franklin, Lady
Freer, W. E., Esq.

Galignani, M., Paris
Gawlor, Colonel, United Service Club
Gibraltar Garrison Library
Giraud, R. Hervé, Esq., Furnival's-inn
Gladdish, William, Esq., Gravesend
Glendening, Robert, Esq., 5, Britain-st., Portsea
Glenny, —, Esq., 152, Strand
Gordon, J. T., Esq., Sheriff of Mid Lothian, 18, Herriot-street, Edinburgh
Graham, Robert, Esq.
Gray, John Edward, Esq., British Museum
Greenwich Hospital, the Officers' Library
Greenwich Society for the Diffusion of Useful Knowledge
Grey, R. J. Moring, Esq., Trinity House
Grey, R. W., Esq., M.P., 16, Carlton-ter.
Guild, G. F., Esq., Boston, U.S.
Guise, W. V., Esq., Elmore-ct., Gloucester

Halliday, William, Esq., 14, Donegall-pl., Belfast
Hamilton, Robert, Esq., Charing Cross Hospital
Hanrott, P. A., Esq., Queen's-square, Bloomsbury
Harvey, Henry Martin, Esq., Leytonstone, Essex
Harvey, W. Brotherton, Esq., Salford, Manchester
Hawes, Benjamin, Esq., M.P., 9, Queen's square, Westminster
Hawkins, Edward, Esq., British Museum
Heath, Edward, Esq., Liverpool
Henderson, Dr., 6, Curzon-st., Mayfair
Henslow, Lieutenant Frederick, Windsor
Heywood, J., Esq., Acresfield, Manchester
Hertford Literary and Scientific Institution
Hobhouse, Edward, Esq., Twickenham
Hodgkin, Thomas, Esq., M.D., 35, Bedford-square
Hollond, R., Esq., M.P., Portland-place
Holman, Lieutenant, R.N.
Holmes, James, Esq. 4, New Ormond-street, Foundling, 2 *copies*
Holmes, John, Esq., British Museum
Home Office
Hull Subscription Library

Ibbs, Mr. J. C., H.E.I.C.S.

Jackson, H. Esq., St. James's-row, Sheffield
Johnston, Alexander Keith, Edinburgh
Jones, J. Winter, Esq., British Museum
Jukes, J. B., Esq., 28, Jermyn-street
Junior United Service Club, Pall Mall

Keith, T. Hilton, Esq., East India House
Kenyon, J., Esq., 39, Devonshire-place, New-road
Kerslake, Mr. T., Bristol
Keys, Mr. J. A., H.E.I.C.S.

Laird, John, Esq., Birkenhead
Laire, Fr. J., Esq., H. M. Dockyard, Chatham
Lardner, Leopold James, Esq., British Museum
Lane, H. Bowyer, Esq., 20, Suffolk-street, Pall Mall
Latham, R. G., Esq., M.D., 20, Upper Southwick-street, Hyde Park-square
Law, William, Esq., 103, Piccadilly
Lawrence, Abbott, Esq., 138, Piccadilly
Le Mesurier, R. Arthur, Esq., Corpus Christi College, Oxford
Lemon, Sir C., Bart., M.P., 46, Charles-street, Berkeley-square
Lenox, James, Esq., New York
Levesque, Peter, Esq., 29, Guildford-street
Little and Brown, Messrs., Boston, U.S.
Loftus, William Kennett, Esq., Newcastle-upon-Tyne
Logan, J. R., Esq.
London Institution, Finsbury Circus
London Library, 12, St. James's-square
Ludlow, J. M., Esq., 69, Chancery-lane

Mackenzie, Gen. Sir Alex., Bart., G.C.H. 4, Circus, Bath
Mackenzie, John W., Esq., Edinburgh
Mackenzie, C. A., Esq., Hyde Park-place
M'Leod, Miss, 4, Foley-place
Macready, W. C., Esq., 21, Suffolk-street, Pall Mall, East
Madan, Capt. Frederick, H.C.S., 5, Northwick-terrace, St. John's Wood
Madras Literary Society
Maidstone, the Viscount
Major, R. H., Esq., British Museum
Malcolm, W. Elphinstone, Esq., Burnfoot
Manchester Athenæum, The
Marsh, Hon. George P., Constantinople
Marsham, Robert, Esq., Stratton Strawless, Norwich
Massie, Captain T. L., R.N., Chester
Meek, Sir James, 14, Somerset-place
Milman, The Very Rev. H. H., Dean of St. Paul's
Milnes, R. Monckton, Esq., M.P., 26, Pall Mall
Mitford, Admiral
Montriou, Commander, H.E.I.C.S.
Montriou, W., Esq., Bombay
Muller, F., Esq., Amsterdam
Munich Royal Library
Munroe, James and Co., Boston, U.S.

Muquardt, —, Esq.
Murchison, Sir Roderick Impey, F.R.S. &c., 16, Belgrave-square
Murphy, H., Esq., Brooklyn, New York
Murray, the Lord, Great Stuart-street, Edinburgh
Murray, John, Esq., Albemarle-street
Murray, William, Esq., 2, John-street, Berkeley-square
Murton, George, Esq., Manchester

Nebyam, J. Moore, M.D., 16, Leeson-street, Dublin
Nelson, Thomas Wright, Esq., 23, Gloucester-place, New-road
Newcastle-upon-Tyne Literary and Scientific Institute
New York Mercantile Library
Nimmo, Thomas, Esq., Demerara
Norris, Edwin, Esq., Sec. Asiatic Society, 95, New Burlington-street

Oriental Club, Hanover-square
Oswald, Joseph, Esq., 29, Mitre-terrace, Downham-road, Kingsland
Ouvry, F., Esq., F.S.A., 49, Oxford-terrace, Hyde Park

Parker, J. W., Esq., West Strand
Pasley, Major-General Sir C. W., K.C.B., 12, Norfolk Crescent, Hyde Park
Pemberton, Mrs.
Pennington, John, Esq., Philadelphia
Pennsylvania, Historical Society of
Penton, Henry, Esq., 8, Park-st., Grosvenor-square
Petit, Rev. J. Louis, the Uplands, Shiffnal
Petit, Lieut.-Colonel C. B., 9, New Square, Lincoln's Inn
Pollington, Viscount, 2, Bolton-row
Porter, G. W., Esq., British Museum
Porter, Thomas, Esq., Manchester
Porteus, John, Esq., Manchester
Portsmouth, the Royal Naval College
Pourtales, Count Albert, Berlin
Powis, the Earl, 45, Berkeley-square
Platt, G. Clayton, Esq., Philadelphia
Prescott, Rear Admiral H., C.B., Portsmouth Dockyard
Pringle, William, Esq., 3, King's-road
Proby, John Joshua, Esq., 19, Eaton-square
Putnam, G. R., Esq.

Raymond, Geo., Esq., 18, Pall Mall East
Read, William, Esq., Rathmines, Dublin
Reed, F. J. Esq., Friday-st., Cheapside
Rendell, J. Esq., 8, Great George-street
Renouard, Rev. G. Cecil, Swanscombe, Dartford
Rhodes, R., Esq., 9, Circus, Greenwich

Rhys, Thomas, Esq., Royal Ordnance, Woolwich
Richards, Mr., 37, Great Queen-street
Richardson, Sir John, M.D., F.R.S., Haslar, Gosport
Richardson, Ralph, Esq., Greenfield Hall, Holywell, Flintshire
Riggs, G. W., Washington, U.S.
Ritter, Professor Karl, Berlin
Robinson, Lieut. Walter F., R.N., F.R.G.S., Junior United Service Club
Rose, Wm., Esq., Coalport, Shropshire
Royal Society, Somerset House
Royal Geographical Society, Waterloo-pl.
Rumbold, C. E., Esq.
Rundall, Thomas, Esq., East India House
Rutherford, Andrew, Esq., M.P., Lord Advocate of Scotland, St. Colm.-st., Edinb.
Rye, Arthur B., Esq., Banbury
Rye, W. B., Esq., British Museum

Sanders, Captain, H.E.I.C.S.
Saunders, Trelawney, Esq., 6, Charing-cr.
Schomburgk, Sir Robert, St. Domingo
Sedgwick, the Rev. Adam, Woodwardian Professor, Cambridge
Simmonds, the Rev. J. D., M.A., Chilcombe, Winchester
Simpkinson, Sir F., Knt., 21, Bedford-pl.
Simpson, Lieutenant
Singapore Library
Smith, Andrew, Esq., M.D., 7, Pelham-crescent, Brompton
Smith, Edmund, Esq., Hull
Smith, George, Esq., 20, Finsbury-square
Smith, G., Esq., Hague-ter., Kingstown, Dublin
Smith, J., Esq., Alscot-place, Grange-road, Bermondsey
Smith, J., Esq., Bombay
Sotheby, S. Leigh, Esq., the Woodlands, Norwood
Stanley of Alderley, The Lord
Stanley, Hon. Henry E. J., 2, Grosvenor-crescent
Staunton, Sir G. T., Bart., F.R.S., M.P., 16, Devonshire-street, Portland-place
St. Andrew's University
St. David's, the Bishop of, Abergwili, Carmarthenshire
Stevens, H., Esq., Boston, United States
Stirling, Wm., Esq., of Keir, 128, Park-st.
Sunderland Literary and Philosophical Society
Swan, the Rev. R. C., Hothfield, Kent

Talbot, the Earl
Taylor, R., Esq., Red Lion Court, Fleet-st.
Taylor, T. Esq., F.T.C.C.
Ternaux Compans, Mons. H., Paris
Thomas, Rev. Vaughan, High-st., Oxford
Thomas, W. A., Esq., 50, Threadneedle-st.
Thompson, Thos., Esq., Town Clerk, Hull
Titchfield, Marquis of, 19, Cavendish-sq.
Todd, R. B., Esq., M.D., F.R.S., 3, New-street, Spring Gardens
Trade, Board of
Travellers' Club, 106, Pall Mall
Trinity House, Tower Hill

United Service Institution

Vidal, Captain, R.N.
Vienna Imperial Library
Von Bach, Johann Friedrich, Esq., British Museum
Von Siebold, Col. Ph. Fr., Leyden

Waite, Henry, Esq., Church-street, Stoke Newington
Walker, H. Esq., Cheltenham
Walker, J., Esq., 47, Bernard-st. Russell-sq.
Walker, Joshua, Esq., Jun., 2, Park-place, Harrow-road
Washington, Captain J., R.N., Wood-street, Woolwich
Waters, J. S., Esq., Baltimore, U.S.
Watts, Thomas, Esq., British Museum
Weir, William, Esq., 30, Great Coram-st.
Whateley, William, Esq., Q.C., 6, Park-street, Westminster
Whewell, the Rev. W., D.D., Master of Trinity College, Cambridge
White, the Rev. James, Bonchurch, Isle of Wight
Whiteman, J. C., Esq., East India House
Wilkinson, John, Esq., 3, Wellington-st., Strand
Williams, T., Esq., Northumberland-house, Strand
Willson, the Rev. J., 1, Raymond's Buildings, Gray's Inn
Wilson, Edward S., Esq., Hull
Winstanley, E. N., Esq., 7, Poultry
Wolff, H. Drummond, Esq., 44, Half-moon-st., Piccadilly
Woodd, T. Basil, Esq., 108, New Bond-st.
Wood, Lieutenant John, H.E.I.C.S., 137, Leadenhall-street
Wright, H., Esq., Cheltenham
Wyld, James, Esq., M.P., Strand

Young, G. F., Esq., South Sea House

HONORARY LOCAL SECRETARIES.
EDINBURGH..........MR. T. J. STEVENSON, 87, Princes Street.
GLASGOW...........MR. D. BRYCE.
OXFORD ....MR. J. H. PARKER.
PLYMOUTH ....LLEWELLYNN JEWITT, ESQ.
ST. HELIER'S, JERSEY..MR. LEFEUVRE.

WORKS ISSUED BY

The Hakluyt Society.

NOTES UPON RUSSIA.
VOL. I.

M.DCCC.LI.

Etched by Sarah E. Major.

THE BARON SIGISMUND VON HERBERSTEIN.

In his STATE DRESS, *as Ambassador from the Emperor Maximilian to the Grand Duke Vasiley Ivanovich.*

From an Original Drawing in the Grenville Library.

NOTES UPON RUSSIA:

BEING A TRANSLATION OF THE

Earliest Account of that Country,

ENTITLED

RERUM MOSCOVITICARUM COMMENTARII,

BY THE BARON

SIGISMUND VON HERBERSTEIN,

AMBASSADOR FROM THE COURT OF GERMANY TO THE GRAND
PRINCE VASILEY IVANOVICH, IN THE YEARS
1517 AND 1526.

TRANSLATED AND EDITED,
With Notes and an Introduction,
BY
R. H. MAJOR,
OF THE BRITISH MUSEUM.

VOL. I.

"— if thou list to know the Russes well,
To Sigismundus booke repayre, who all the trueth can tell."
Turbervile, 1568.

LONDON:
PRINTED FOR THE HAKLUYT SOCIETY.
M.DCCC.LI.

LONDON:
RICHARDS, 37 GREAT QUEEN STREET, LINCOLN'S INN.

THE HAKLUYT SOCIETY.

SIR RODERICK IMPEY MURCHISON, G.C.St.S., F.R.S., Corr. Mem. Inst. Fr., Hon. Mem. Imp. Acad. Sc. St. Petersburg, &c., &c., PRESIDENT.

THE EARL OF ELLESMERE.
CAPT. C. R. DRINKWATER BETHUNE, R.N., C.B. } VICE-PRESIDENTS.

REAR-ADMIRAL SIR FRANCIS BEAUFORT, K.C.B.
CHARLES T. BEKE, ESQ., Phil. D., F.S.A.
THE LORD ALFRED S. CHURCHILL.
WILLIAM DESBOROUGH COOLEY, ESQ.
BOLTON CORNEY, ESQ., M.R.S.L.
THE RIGHT REV. LORD BISHOP OF ST. DAVID'S.
THE VISCOUNT EASTNOR.
SIR HENRY ELLIS, K.H., F.R.S.
RICHARD FORD, ESQ.
JOHN FORSTER, ESQ.
R. W. GREY, ESQ., M.P.
THOMAS HODGKIN, ESQ., M.D.
JOHN WINTER JONES, ESQ.
SIR CHARLES LEMON, BART., M.P.
P. LEVESQUE, ESQ.
THOMAS RUNDALL, ESQ.
THE HON. HENRY E. J. STANLEY.

R. H. MAJOR, ESQ., F.R.G.S., HONORARY SECRETARY.

TO

SIR HENRY ELLIS, K.H.

ETC. ETC. ETC.

AS TO HIS EARLIEST SURVIVING FRIEND,

AND THE SUGGESTER OF THIS TRANSLATION,

THE FOLLOWING PAGES ARE INSCRIBED,

WITH EVERY SENTIMENT OF

GRATEFUL AFFECTION AND RESPECT,

BY

THE EDITOR.

PREFACE.

THE Editor has found it necessary, on account of the length of his work, to divide it into two volumes. The second volume, however, is already at press, and will, unless unforeseen obstacles occur, be very shortly completed.

Should the large space allotted to dry bibliography in the Introduction be objected to by some, the Editor hopes that his anxiety to afford what he considered to be useful information, will protect him from too severe a reproof; while to the more curious student he trusts it will prove far from unacceptable.

It is possible, that occasionally sentences may be found in the translation somewhat too harshly turned, or too unwieldy from their length or involved construction, to please a well-attuned English ear; the translator can only plead in excuse, that the original, though in Latin, is written by a German, and naturally exhibits much of that involution of style peculiar to the German language; while it is certainly not the more lucid from having been written three centuries ago.

R. H. M.

INTRODUCTION.

WHEN the following "Notes upon Russia" are presented to the reader as the *earliest* description of that country, the statement, though substantially and for all essential purposes correct, must not be allowed to pass without a word of modification. As we shall presently take occasion to show, the Baron Sigismund von Herberstein was preceded by numerous travellers to Russia, the record of whose peregrinations could scarcely have been handed down to us without some slight allusion to the character of the country they visited; yet from none of them have we received anything that could with reason be referred to as an authentic description of the country and its people, derived, as all such descriptions should be, from lengthened personal observation and industrious inquiry. The present work, however, which embodies the experience and observations of a sagacious and pains-taking man, during two periods of residence, in all about sixteen months, in Moscow, as ambassador from the Emperor of Germany to the Tzar, has won for its author so high a reputation for correctness and minuteness of detail, that he has been thought by many (and one of the number is the learned historian, August Ludwig Schlözer himself) worthy of the designation of the "Discoverer of Russia". The "Rerum Moscoviticarum Commentarii" has been a standing book of reference for all subsequent historians of the great empire of the north; and it is not without good reason that the distinguished biographer of Herberstein, Friedrich Adelung (to whose works, as quoted below,[1] the editor is mainly indebted for the materials of this introduction) expresses his surprise that a work of such importance should so long have remained untranslated, either into the Polish, the French, the Dutch, or the English languages. Especially is this expression of astonishment applicable, as he justly observes, to England and Holland,—countries which have for nearly three centuries maintained commercial relations with the Russian empire. The scope of the work comprises brief but interesting, and in many cases highly amusing, sketches of the history, antiquities, geography, and productions of the country, with the religion, form of government, peculiarities in matters of warfare, trade, domestic habits, and amusements of the people.

The advantages possessed by Herberstein for collecting all the materials requisite for the supply of this extensive range of information, were various and im-

---

[1] Siegmund Freiherr von Herberstein mit besonderer Rücksicht auf seine Reisen in Russland. St. Petersburg, 1818, 8vo.

Kritisch Literärische Uebersicht der Reisenden in Russland bis 1700. St. Petersburg, 1846, 4to.

portant. In the first place, may be mentioned the clear-sightedness and experience which his residence in foreign courts had superadded to his own naturally keen understanding; add to this, the intercourse which his position as ambassador at Moscow enabled him to cultivate with the best informed and most intelligent people of the metropolis. Independent of these advantages, which enabled him to sift and scrutinize the accounts which might be supplied to him from the descriptions of others, he possessed a fund of information in the men who were assigned to him as interpreters. These persons, named Gregor Istoma, Vlas, and Dmitrii, had themselves made considerable journeys in their native country, and the results of their several observations in these journeys were communicated to Herberstein by the first-mentioned of the three in writing. Our author likewise had the benefit of being acquainted with several foreigners who had long resided in Russia, among whom should especially be mentioned the minister and confidant of the Grand Duke, often spoken of in his work under the name of George the Little. Another source of information may also be mentioned as proving serviceable to Herberstein in the composition of a work which has conferred immortality upon his name; namely, a considerable number of manuscript annals, to which he makes especial reference, under the title of " Literæ cujusdam Warlami Prioris Huttiniensis Monasterii", anno 7034 [A.D. 1525].

Before we proceed to give an account of the bibliography of the work before us, it may be desirable to vindicate its value by laying before the reader a list of the various travellers to Russia who preceded Herberstein, and more especially of those authors, whether travellers or otherwise, who anticipated him, in making allusion, however slightly, to the history, geography, natural history, or customs of the country.

Although a bibliographical account of the narratives of these early travellers will occupy a considerable space in this introduction, and though in some cases their travels only partially refer to Russia, it is hoped that the details we are about to give will not be considered inappropriate, and that by members of the Hakluyt Society at least they will be regarded as both interesting and important.

They are principally derived from the researches of Adelung, as given in his "Kritisch Literärische Uebersicht der Reisenden in Russland bis 1700" (St. Petersburg, 1846, 4to.), but have received considerable additions and alterations from the editor of the present volume. The first traveller in the list is—

(1.)

OHTHERE. 890.

Ohthere, a northman, of whom we know little more than that he was born in Helgoland, was a man of substance, and undertook several voyages, one of which was from Norway towards the extreme northern coasts, in the course of which he became acquainted with the Finns and Bjarmier, or Permians, in the north-east of European Russia. In one of these voyages he must have reached the shores of England, which was at that time governed by Alfred the Great. This famous prince collected[1] all the attainable geographical accounts of the then known world, which, together with the narration of Ohthere's voyages and that of Wulfstan (who, it is possible, became acquainted with Ohthere in the course of his voyages, or resided with him in England), he included in his valuable Anglo-Saxon translation of the *Hormista* of Paulus Orosius. The beautifully written and well-preserved original of this work is to be found in the Cottonian collection of manuscripts in the British Museum. It was published under the title—

The Anglo-Saxon version from the historian Orosius, by Alfred the Great. Together with an English translation from the Anglo-Saxon. By Daines Barrington; London, 1773; 8vo.

Dr. Joh. Reinh. Forster, who gave a German translation of the narratives of Ohthere and Wulfstan, in his *Geschichte der Entdeckungen*, under the title, *Erdbeschreibung vom nördlichen Europa nach König Alfred*, etc., with many valuable comments and explanations,[2] says that Alfred's account of the two voyages of Ohthere and of that of Wulfstan, which is

---

[1] See "Asserus de rebus gestis Alfredi in Anglica, Hibernica, etc., scripta, ex bibliotheca Camdeni. Auctore Silvestro Giraldo (properly Giraldus de Barry, but better known as Giraldus Cambrensis, born 1146, in Wales). Francf. 1602, fol., p. 5.

[2] Very circumstantial accounts of King Alfred's work, and Ohthere, will be found in Beckmann's Litter. d. ält. Reisebeschr. Th. i, p. 450, etc.

both exact and authentic, is exceedingly valuable, as it contains the best information in regard to the geography of the northern regions of the ninth century.

Ohthere's voyages have also been printed in the following works.

In the first volume of Hakluyt's Principal Navigations, etc., of the English nation, 1599-60, there is a translation from the Anglo-Saxon of the "Voyages of Octher, made to the east parts beyond Norway, reported by himself unto Alfred the famous king of England, about the year 890." Following this is "The voyage of Octher out of his countrey of Halgoland into the Sound of Denmarke, unto a part called Hetha, which seemeth to be Wismar or Rostoke"; and in the page following we have an account of "Wolstan's navigation within the East sea (within the Sounde of Denmarke), from Hetha to Trussa, which is about Dantzic." This English translation is said to have been made for the work by Dr. Caius; but it has never been highly estimated as an accurate translation, and is now considered valueless.[1]

Aelfredi magni Anglorum Regis vita tribus libris comprehensa a Jo. Spelman anglice conscripta, dein Latine reddita et annotationibus illustrata ab Aelfredi in collegio magnæ aulæ universitatis Oxoniensis alumnis. Oxonii, 1673, fol., p. 205, *et seq.*

Scriptores rerum Danicarum. Ed. Langebek, Hafniæ, 1773, fol., vol. ii, p. 106, *et seq.* In the original Anglo-

---

[1] See Petheram's "Anglo-Saxon Literature in England". London, 1840; p. 46.

Saxon, with a Latin translation, and an excellent commentary.

The best edition, however, that has yet appeared, is that published by the celebrated Anglo-Saxon scholar Rasmus Rask, accompanied by a Danish translation and critical remarks.—See " Samlede tildels forhen utrykte Afhandlinger af R. K. Rask". Del. 1. Köbenhavn. 1834; 8vo.

(2.)
IBN-FODHLAN. 921.

Ibn-Fodhlan, or to give him his name fully and correctly, Ahmad Ben-Fodhlan Ibn al Abbas Ben-Assam Ben-Hamad, was, in the year 921 of our era, sent by the Abasside khaliph Almuktsadir Billah as companion to an ambassador to the king of Wolga-Bulgharia, or according to Yakut,[1] to the Sclaves. In this journey he met with the Wolga Russians, who had come hither in ships to trade; and his narrative contains a remarkable and circumstantial representation of the manners and customs of these Russians.

Ibn-Fodhlan's account indeed, as could not fail to be the case, was known to other ancient Arabian authors; and, as we now discover on nearer comparison, was used by them, but is only completely preserved in Yakut, through whose medium he was first made known to Europeans in the following publications—

---

[1] Author of the well-known "Muajim Albuldan", a very valuable alphabetical dictionary of countries.

Die ältesten arabischen Nachrichten über die Wolga-Bulgharen aus Ibn-Foszlan's Reise-Berichte. In the Mémoires de l'Acad. Imp. des Sciences de St. Pét. VI. ser. t. i. St. Petersb. 1832, p. 527, etc.

Ibn-Foszlan's und andere Araber Berichte über die Russen älterer Zeit. Text und Uebersetzung mit kritisch-philologischen Anmerkungen; nebst drei Beilagen über sogenannte Russen-Stämme und Kiew, die Warenger und das Warenger-Meer, und das Land Wisu, ebenfalls nach Arabischen Schriftstellern, von C. M. Frähn, etc., Herausgegeben von der Kaiserlichen Akademie der Wissenschaften. St. Petersburg, 1823, 4to.

(3.)
BENJAMIN OF TUDELA. 1160.

Rabbi Benjamin of Tudela (a town in Navarre) made himself famous by visiting all the synagogues of his religion in the east, in order to become acquainted with the customs, ceremonies, and rabbis of each. He set out from Spain in 1160, and travelling by land to Constantinople, proceeded through the countries to the north of the Euxine and Caspian Seas, as far as Chinese Tartary. Thence he turned southwards, crossed several provinces of the further India, and embarking on the Indian Ocean, visited several of its islands. After an absence of thirteen years, he returned by way of Egypt to Europe, bringing with him much information concerning a vast tract of the globe, then almost entirely unknown to the people of the west. He left a curious narrative of his travels, the authority of which, however, has been questioned, though many of its errors are attributed to the incorrect versions that have been given of it. Be this as it may, we accept with confidence the statement made by one of such extensive learning in philology and bibliography as Mr. A. Asher, the eminent bookseller of Berlin, who has edited the latest and infinitely the best edition of this traveller's Itinerary (*vide infra*), " that it was in order to remedy a defect of which he complains, namely, an almost total want of research upon the geography of the middle ages, and to furnish materials for such a study, that he selected the Itinerary of the Rabbi Benjamin of Tudela, not only," he says in his preface, " because it contains *more facts and fewer fables* than any other cotemporary publication which has come down to us, but also because it describes a very large portion of the earth known in the twelfth century."

In the bibliography of the work given in the first volume of Mr. Asher's edition, and which we here transcribe, is an explanation of the origin of many of the corruptions which have tended to detract in some measure from the reputation of this most interesting narrative.

1. The first edition was printed at Constantinople, Soncini, 1543, 8vo.; sixty-four pages, in the Rabbinic character.

This edition is so extremely rare, that notwithstanding the most diligent search, Mr. Asher has not been able to meet with any complete copy. It *has been* in the Bibliothèque Royal, at Paris, but upon the closest inquiry could nowhere be found. The

Oppenheim division of the Bodleian library contains an incomplete copy of this rare book, being deficient of the first fourteen pages, or one quarter of the whole work. Like most other Hebrew books which issued from the early Constantinople presses, this is but a very poor specimen of correctness and typography. All mistakes of this "princeps" have unfortunately crept into the editions noticed below, Nos. 3, 4, and 10, and have led the translators into error. The rarity constitutes its only value.

2. *Hebrew.* Travels of R. Benjamin of blessed memory; printed at Ferrara in the house of Abraham Ben Usque, in the year 316 [1556]; small 8vo.; sixty-four pages, in the Rabbinic character.

This second edition is perhaps rarer still than the first, and having evidently been printed from another manuscript, is indispensably necessary for a critique of the work. The text is much purer than that of the former, and in many instances its readings give a sense, where the former is too corrupt to be understood.

Unfortunately, this edition was unknown to the early translators, B. Arias Montanus and l'Empereur, who would have made fewer mistakes and formed a more correct judgment of our author, had they been able to compare it with that of Constantinople. It forms the groundwork of Mr. Asher's edition and translation. No public library in France or Germany,—most of which that gentleman personally visited or inquired at by correspondence,—possesses a copy; and the only one now known to exist is in the Oppenheim division of the Bodleian library at Oxford.

3. *Hebrew*. Travels, etc.; printed in the country of Brisgau, in the year 343 [1583], by the Siphroni; small 8vo., thirty-two pages, in the square character.

This is a reprint of the first (Constantinople) edition; it repeats faithfully all the mistakes of that edition. This is one of the rarest of the rare books printed in Brisgau.

4. *Hebrew*. Itinerarium D. Benjaminis F. M. Lugduni Batavorum apud Elzivirios, 1633; 24mo., 203 pages, square character.

This edition was probably reprinted from that printed in Brisgau, and formed (as well as that quoted below, No. 13) part of the "Respublicæ Elzevirianæ", a collection well known to the amateurs of those *bijoux* of the celebrated Dutch printers. Constantin l'Empereur, the learned editor, changed but very few words in the text, and reserved his emendations for the notes, with which the edition quoted under No. 10 is enriched.

5. *Hebrew*. The Travels of Rabbi Benjamin the Physician, of blessed memory, who travelled in three parts of the world—in Europe, in Asia, and in Africa. Printed at Amsterdam in the year 458 [1698], in the house of Caspar Sten; 24mo., 65 pages.

There are some pretended ameliorations in this edition, but they are founded upon mere suggestion, and at best upon the translations of Arias Montanus and l'Empereur.

6. *Hebrew*. Travels, etc.; s. 1. 1734.

This edition, which Mr. Asher had not seen, is quoted by Dr. Zunz, in "Zeitschrift für die Wissenschaft des Judenthums." Berlin, 1823, p. 130.

7. *Hebrew.* Travels of R. Benjamin. Printed under the direction of John Andrew Michael Nagel, for the use of his scholars at this celebrated university. Altdorf, 1762, printed by John Adam Hessel; small 8vo., 56 pages, square character.

A correct reprint of No. 4 of this list, containing every mistake of its original. This edition is so rare, that Meusel doubted its existence.—See his "Lexicon deutscher Schriftsteller"; vol. x, 1810.

8. *Hebrew.* Travels, etc.; printed at Salzbach, 542 [1782]; small 8vo., 32 pages, square character.

A very poor reprint of l'Empereur's edition, upon wretched German blotting-paper, full of mistakes, and without the least literary value.

9. *Hebrew.* Travels of R. Benjamin; printed at Zolkiew, in Austrian Gallicia.

An edition quoted by the celebrated scholar, the Rev. Rabbi Salomon L. Rapoport, in his geographical preface to Shalom Cohen's "Kore Haddoroth". Warsaw, 1838.

10. *Hebrew* and *Latin.* Itinerarium D. Benjamin, cum versione et notis Constantini l'Empereur ab Oppyck S. T. D. et S. L. P. in acad. Lugd. Batav. Lugd. Batavorum. Ex officina Elzeviriana, 1633; small 8vo., of 34 (unnumbered) and 234 (numbered) pages.

This edition, as far as the text and translation are concerned, is composed of Nos. 4 and 12 of this list;

the dissertation and the notes contain a vast deal of antiquated learning.

11. *Latin.* Itinerarium Benjamini Tudelensis : in quo Res Memorabiles, quas ante quadringentos annos totum fere terrarum orbem notatis itineribus dimensus vel ipse vidit vel a fide dignis suæ ætatis hominibus accepit, breviter atque dilucidè describuntur; ex Hebraica Latinum factum Bened. Aria Montano Interprete. Antwerpiæ, ex officina Chr. Plantini, Architypographi regii, MDLXXV, 8vo.

The celebrated Arias Montanus was the first to introduce this work to the learned Christians, who, although they might understand the Scripture Hebrew, were strangers to the Rabbinic style, in which these travels were written. In many instances, he has rather guessed at, than faithfully translated, the text; but notwithstanding this, his labours deserve respect, and his suggestions in many instances are nearer the truth than those of later translators.

12. *Latin.* Itinerarium Benjaminis. Lat. redditum: Lugd. Batav., 1633; 24mo.

This neat little volume, which forms part of the " Respublicæ", is one of, if not *the* rarest of that series. The text is that of No. 10 of this list.

13. *Latin.* Itinerarium Benjaminis Tudelensis ex Versione Benedicti Ariæ Montani. Helmstadi in typographeo Calixtino, excudit Henningus Mullerus, MDCXXXVI; sm. 8vo.

14. *Latin.* Benjaminis Tudelensis Itinerarium ex Versione Benedicti Ariæ Montani. Lipsiæ apud Joann. Michael. Ludov. Teubner. MDCCLXIV; 8vo.

This is a corrected reprint of all the contents of the volume just noticed under No. 13.

15. *English.* The Peregrinations of Benjamin, the sonne of Jonas a Jew; written in Hebrew; translated into Latin by B. Arias Montanus. Discouering both the state of the Jews and of the world, about foure hundred and sixtie yeeres since.

For this first English translation, see Purchas's "Pilgrimes". London, 1625; fol., vol. ii, liv. 9, chap. 5, p. 1437; it is divided into five paragraphs.

16. *English.* The Travels of R. Benjamin, the son of Jonas of Tudela, through Europe, Asia, and Africa, from Spain to China, from 1160 to 1173. From the Latin versions of B. A. Montanus and Constantine l'Empereur, compared with other translations into different languages.

This extract of the "Itinerary" will be found in Harris's "Collection of Voyages and Travels". London, 1744; fol., vol. i, p. 546 to 555; and the introduction, which is prefixed, as well as the notes, are not devoid of interest.

17. *English.* Travels of Rabbi Benjamin, son of Jonah of Tudela, through Europe, Asia, and Africa, from the ancient kingdom of Navarre, to the frontiers of China. Faithfully translated from the original Hebrew, and enriched with a Dissertation and Notes, Critical, Historical, and Geographical. In which the true character of the author and intention of the work are impartially (!) considered.

By the Rev. R. Gerrans, lecturer of Saint Catherine Coleman, and second master of Queen Elizabeth's Free Grammar School, Saint Olave, Southwark. This author, says the editor, Mr. Gerrans, flourished about the year 1160 of the Christian era, is highly prized by the Jews and other admirers of Rabbinical learning, and has frequently been quoted by the greatest orientalists that this or any other nation ever produced; but was never before (to the editor's knowledge) wholly translated into English, either by Jew or Gentile. London, MDCCLXXXIV, 8vo.

The absurdities of this editor have been ludicrously exposed by Mr. Asher, in his edition of 1840.

18. *English.* The Travels of R. Benjamin of Tudela, from the Latin of B. Arias Montanus and Constantine l'Empereur, compared with other translations into different languages.

This abridgment will be found in Pinkerton's "General Collection of the best and most interesting Voyages and Travels of the world." London, 1808-14; 4to., vol. vii.

19. *French.* Voyage du célèbre Benjamin, autour du Monde, commencé l'an 1173 (*sic*) contenant une exacte et succincte description de ce qu'il a vû de plus remarquable dans presque toutes les parties de la Terre; aussi bien que de ce qu'il en a appris de plusieurs de ses Contemporains dignes de foi. Avec un détail, jusques ici inconnu, de la conduite, des Sinagogues, de la Demeure et du nombre des Juifs et de leurs Rabins, dans tous les endroits où il a été, etc., dont on aprend en même tems l'état où se trouvaient alors diférentes Nations avant l'agrandissement des Turcs. Ecrit premièrement en Hebreu par l'auteur de ce Voyage, traduit ensuite en Latin par Benoit Arian Montan; et nouvellement du Latin en François. Le tout enrichi de Notes, pour l'explication de plusieurs passages.—In Bergeron's "Collection de Voyages, faits principalement en Asie, dans le 12, 13, 14, et 15 siécles, à la Haye," 1735; 2 vols., 4to.

Neither the notes nor the map which accompanies this poor piece of work, are of any value.

20. Voyages de Rabbi Benjamin, fils de Jona de Tudele, en Europe, en Asie, et en Africa, depuis l'Espagne jusqu'à la Chine. Traduits de l'Hebreu et enrichis de notes et de Dissertations Historiques et Critiques sur ces Voyages. Par J. P. Barratier, Etudiant en Théologie. A Amsterdam, aux dépens de la Compagnie, 1734; 2 vols., small 8vo.

21. Voyages de Benjamin de Tudelle autour du monde, commencé l'an 1173. De Jean du Plan-Carpin en Tartarie, du Frère Ascelin et de ses compagnons vers la Tartarie. Du Guillaume de Rubruques en Tartarie et en Chine en 1253, suivi des Additions de Vincent de Beauvais et de l'Histoire de Guillaume de Naugès, pour l'Eclaircissement des précédentes Voyages. Paris, imprimé aux Frais du Gouvernement pour procurer du Travail aux ouvriers Typographes. Août, 1830, in 8vo.

A reprint of No. 18, and (as Mr. Asher says) curious only on account of the occasion, which procured Master Benjamin the honour of being called forth again from oblivion.

22. *Dutch.* De Reysen van R. Benjamin Jonas Tudelens. In de drie Deelen der Werelt. Tut Nederdyts overgeschrieben door Jan Bara. Amsterdam, Jonas Rex, 1666; 24mo., 117 pp.

This translation having been made from l'Empereur's Latin version, offers nothing new or valuable to the critical reader.

23. *Jewish-German.* These are the voyages of R. Benjamin Tudeleus, the Physician (!), which he has travelled through three corners of the world. Amsterdam, 451 [1691]; 8vo.

This translation by Chaim Ben Jacob, was made from l'Empereur's text; and although the editor was a Jew, he was too illiterate to correct any of the errors of l'Empereur.

24. *Jewish-German.* These are the voyages, etc. Francfort on the Mayne, 471 [1711]; 8vo.

A mere reprint of the former edition, and consequently as worthless in a critical point of view.

Adelung quotes another edition, with the following title—

Les voyages de Benjamin de Tudèle, traduits en Français accompagnés du texte, corrigé et complété d'après un manuscrit du xive siècle, et suivis de notes historiques, géographiques, et littéraires, par E. Carmoly. Paris, 1839; 8vo.

But the editor has been informed that Mr. Asher, who had also met with the title, but not with the work, doubted its existence, and wrote to M. Carmoly requesting information respecting it. His application received no answer, and it may therefore be fairly supposed that such an edition never had existence.

We have finally to mention the completest edition of all, entitled—

The Itinerary of Rabbi Benjamin of Tudela, translated and edited by A. Asher. London and Berlin, 1841; 8vo. Hebrew and English.

(4.)
ANONYMOUS ENGLISHMAN. 1243.

We have an account of the travels in Tartary, of an English traveller, whose name is unknown, which will be found printed in the following collections.

In the first book of Hakluyt's collection, under the title—

The Voyage of a certain Englishman into Tartary, and from thence into Poland and Hungary, anno 1243.

And from thence transferred into the—

Collection of Voyages by Robert Kerr: Travels of an Englishman into Tartary, and thence into Poland, Hungary, and Germany, in 1243.—See tom. i, p. 114.

(5.)
JOANNES DE PLANO CARPINI. 1245.

Joannes de Plano Carpini, an Italian minorite, together with five other brothers of the order, the minorite Benedict of Poland, and the friars-preachers Ascelin, Simon de St. Quentin, Alexander, and Albert, were chosen to undertake a journey into the country of the Mongolians. As the devastations committed by these conquerors of Europe became more and more alarming, Pope Innocent IV, at the council of Lyons, in 1245, resolved to send the above-named monks as ambassadors to these formidable enemies of Christianity, in order to pacify them, or, if possible, to divert them from Europe, and to instigate them rather to a war against the Turks and Saracens. At the same time they were to endeavour to persuade the Mongolians to embrace the Christian faith, and in any case to gather every possible information respecting a people so little known.

Plano Carpini, together with Benedict, travelled through Bohemia and Poland to Kiev, and thence by the mouth of the Dnieper to the camp of Korrensa, a general of the Mongolians, whence crossing the Don and Wolga, they came to the encampment of Batu Khan, who sent them to Kajuk Khan, called also Cuyne, the emperor of the Mongolians.

Carpini was absent sixteen months, and after having done his best to carry out the instructions he had received, he returned to Europe.

"He had the merit of being the first to publish in Europe a rational description of the Mongol nation; though ignorant, bigoted, and credulous, he was not altogether destitute of talent and observation; and his prudent deportment procured him opportunities which the monastic austerity of Ascelin and his companions could never have expected."[1]

Of this journey we have a detailed and also an abbreviated account, both in Latin, and of these there are several, in part contemporaneous, copies. The Imperial Library of Vienna possesses of the larger narrative three copies, two of which are on parchment, of the thirteenth century. The one in quarto, and marked, *Hist. prof.*, No. DCLI, bears the title—

Relacio fratris Joannis de Plano Carpini, ordinis fratrum minorum, de Tartaris; *and begins with the words :* Anno Domini M°.CC°. XL. V°. Frater Johannes de ordine minorum fratrum dictus de Plano Carpini a domino papa missus ad Tartaros cum alio fratre ejusdem ordinis.

The folio MS. is marked *Hist. prof.*, No. XCIV, and has the title—

[1] Cooley's "History of Maritime and Inland Discovery," i, 254.

Carpini Plano libellus de moribus bellicis Tartarorum, 1245. It commences with the prologue : Omnibus Xpi fidelibus frater Johannes de Plano Carpini, etc.

The third Vienna copy is in folio, and on paper, marked No. 651, and bears the title—

Carpini Plano legatio in Tartariam.

Another copy is to be found in the Vatican library, with the title—

Libellus historicus Joannis de Plano Carpini, qui missus est legatus ad Tartaros anno Domini 1246 ab Innocentio IV Pontifice Maximo.

The following copies are farther known. In Cambridge two, one in the University library, No. 61, 3 ; the other, in that of Corpus Christi College, No. 181.

In Tournai, in the library of St. Martin.

In Leyden, in the University library. This MS. belonged formerly to the celebrated Paul Petau.

In the British Museum is a copy which formerly belonged to Lord Lumley, and which was used by Hakluyt for his "Principal Navigations".

In the Bibliothèque Royale, Paris, No. 686, in the collection presented by Jacques Dupuy, and another MS., No. 2477, written on parchment in the fourteenth century, which formerly belonged to the minister Colbert.

The work is divided into two distinct parts, of which the first contains the narrative of the journey itself, the rest treating of the manners, customs, etc., of the Tartars.

The printed travels may be found in the following works :—

Italian. Vincent de Beauvais has inserted an ample abridgment, which occupies thirty-one chapters of his "Speculum Historiale"; first printed, Nuremberg, 1473; a French translation of which was published 1495. The same abridgement of the voyages of Brother John and Brother Simon had been translated into Italian, and published separately at Venice, 1537, 8vo., under the title—

Opera dilettevole da intendere, nel qual si contienne doi itinerarij in Tartaria, per alcuni frati del ordine minore, e di S. Domenico (cioe frate Giovanni e frate Simone) mandati da Papa Innocentio IIII nella detta Provincia de Scithia per Ambasciatori, non piu vulgarizata.—Stampata in Vinegia, per G.—Aut. de Nicolini da Sabio, M.D.XXXVII, small 8vo.

This was reprinted in Ramusio's "Collection of Navigationi et Viaggi," 1574; vol. ii.

English. Hakluyt gave a fraction of the original narrative after a MS. of Lord Lumley; republished likewise the abrégé of Vincent de Beauvais, and added an English translation.

French. A translation from Hakluyt, with additions, was given in Bergeron's "Voyages en Tartarie", 16mo., under the title "Relation des Voyages en Tartarie de Fre Guillaume de Rubruquis, Fr. Jean du Plan Carpin"; and in a subsequent edition of Bergeron by Vander Aa (Leyden, 1729; 4to., vol. i), under the following title—

Voyages très-curieux faits et écrits par les R.R. P.P. Jean du Plan Carpin, Cordelier, et N. Ascelin, Jacobin:

Envoyez en qualité de légats apostoliques et d'ambassadeurs de la part du Pape Innocent IV vers les Tartares et autres peuples orientaux : avec ordre exprès de décrire de bonne foi ce qui regarde les Tartares, comme la situation tant de leur pays que de leurs affaires ; leur vêtement, boire et manger, leur gouvernement politique et civil, culte de religion, discipline militaire, enterremens, et autres points les plus remarquables ; dont l'observation était le sujet de leur ambassade. Le tout raporté fidèlement par ces religieux. Avec des notes, tables, observations, une carte très-exacte de ces voyages et de très-belles figures pour l'explication des choses.

In 1725, this narrative was published by Bernard, at Amsterdam, in vol. vii of " Recueil des Voyages au Nord."

Relation du voyage de Jean du Plan Carpin en Tartarie. In the Recueil des Voyages au Nord, t. vii. Printed in the Voyages de Benjamin de Tudèle. Paris, 1830, 4to.

Finally, a critical and most elaborate edition appeared under the title—

Relation des Mongols ou Tartares, par le Frère Jean du Plan de Carpin, de l'ordre des Frères Mineurs, legat du Saint Siége Apostolique, Nonce en Tartarie pendant les années 1245, 1246, 1247, et Archévêque d'Antivari. Première édition complète, publiée d'après les manuscrits de Leyde, de Paris, et de Londres, et précédée d'une notice sur les anciens Voyages en Tartarie en général, et sur celui du Plan de Carpin en particulier, par M. d'Avezac. Paris, 1838; 4to. This important work forms the fourth volume of the Recueil de Voyages et de Mémoires publiés par la Société de Géographie de Paris, p. 399-779.

Russian. Moscow, 1795; 8vo. :—also, by Jasykow. St. Petersburg, 1825 ; 8vo.

Dutch. Seer aanmerkelyke Reysebeschryvingen van Johan du Plan Carpin en Br. Ascelin, beyde als legaten van den H. Apostolischen stoel, en voor gesanten van den Paus Innocentius de IV afgesonden na Tartaryen en andere oosterche volkeren. Nu aldereest getrouwelijk na het egte handschrift vertaald door Salomon Bor predikant tot Zeyst. Leyden, 1706, 8vo.

This forms the first part of the first volume of a collection of Dutch translations of remarkable travels, which the well known bookseller Van der Aa published in 1706, under the title of: " Naaukerige versameling der gedenkwaardigste zee en land Reysen na Ost en West Indien."

Respecting the travels of Plano Carpini, see Sprengel's " Gesch. d. geogr. Entdeck.", p. 278-288, where the same are accompanied by many learned explanations, as also Murray's " Discoveries in Asia", vol. i, pp. 84-109.

(6.)
ASCELIN. 1245.

Nicolas Ascelin, a Dominican, was despatched by Pope Innocent IV to the Mongolians, at the same time that Plano Carpini was sent by way of Poland and Russia to the court of the Khan. He was accompanied by the monks Alexander, Albert, and Simon de St. Quentin. His entire journey lasted only for a short time; and as he speaks chiefly in his narrative of his reception in the camp of Bajothnoi (Bajunovian?), he gives but few disclosures respecting the countries he travelled through. His route seems to have been by the south of the Caspian Sea, through Syria, Persia, and Khorasan. Ascelin's narrative, moreover, has not reached us entire; we know of it only from the accounts received by Vincent de Beauvais from Ascelin's companion, Simon de St. Quentin.

The account of Ascelin's journey will be found in the following works, as already more fully described.

Speculum historiale Vincentii Bellovacensis. Venetiis, 1499, fol. L. 31, C. 40, *et seq.*

Opera dilettevole ad intendere la qual si contiene dei Itinerarii in Tartaria. Venezia, 1537, 4to.

Voyage du P. Ascelin. In Bergeron, Voyages, éd. de P. van der Aa; vol. i. Together with the Travels of P. Carpino.

In Murray's Discoveries and Travels in Asia, vol. i, p. 75-84.

Voyage du Frère Ascelin. Printed in Voyage de Benjamin de Tudèle, etc. Par. 1830, 4to.

Russian: In Jasykow, as alluded to in the notice of Plano Carpini.

(7.)

SIMON DE SAINT QUENTIN. 1245.

Simon de St. Quentin, a Dominican monk, accompanied the embassy sent to Tartary by Pope Innocent IV, and prepared an account of this journey in Latin. The complete original of the journey has not been found; the dominican Vincent de Beauvais, Simon's contemporary, gives, however, in his "Speculum Historiale", in book XXVII, a great part, viz., nineteen chapters, of the " Itinerarium Fratris Simonis"; and from this source Reinerus Reineccius has received it into his " Historia Orientalis".

This portion of the "Itinerarium" is also found in MS. No. 686, in the Royal Library of Paris, which bears the title—

Itineraria in Tartariam Fr. Joannes de Plano Carpino, ord. Minorum, et Fr. Simonis de S. Quintino ord. prædicatorum, etc.

These extracts are also found in Hakluyt's "Collection", vol. i, p. 25-29: "Libellus Historicus", etc., but where Simon's travels are mixed up with Plano Carpini's narrative.

They are also found in Italian, in the now very rare work entitled—

Opera dilettevole da intendere, etc. Venez., 1537, 8vo., and again in Ramusio Raccolta di Viaggi, vol. ii of the edition of 1574, under the title, Due Viaggi in Tartaria.

(8.)

RUBRUQUIS. 1253.

Wilhelm von Ruysbroeck, Rusbrock, or Rubruk, commonly known by the Frenchified name of De Rubruquis, was a friar of the minorite order. He was sent to the Mongolians by the French king Louis IX, 1253, then in his crusade against the Saracens, when the rumour had spread in Europe that the Mongolian chief, Mangu Khan, had embraced the Christian religion. In the year just mentioned, he set out on his journey, with a fellow traveller, Bartholomæus of Cremona, went to Constantinople, over the Black Sea, through the Crimea,[1] and finally arrived after many difficulties in the district of the city of the Caraci, in the Gobi desert, where Mangu Khan was then residing. His accounts of the countries he passed through are more circumstantial than those of his predecessors, which were unknown to him. He introduces, however, a number of cities under names which cannot yet be identified. We have to thank him, among other things, for the first accounts collected from personal experience respecting China, which he derived from a Chinese ambassador in the Mongolian camp. Rubruquis tarried five months in the neighbourhood of Mangu Khan, and passed then by Saraï, Astrachan, and Derbent, through Georgia, Armenia, and Turcomania, across the Mediterranean to Cyprus, Antioch, and Tripoli, from which latter place he transmitted the narrative of his travels to the King of France. From this latter circumstance he is sometimes called William of Tripoli.

Sprengel says of these travels:—"Rubruquis, by his journal, certainly widely extended the knowledge of the period with respect to northern Asia and the countries around the Caspian and Black Seas; and it is the more valuable inasmuch as he has conveniently inserted all manner of useful observations,

---

[1] The following observation is made by Adelung in a note:— "Ruysbroeck spoke first of Goths in the Crimea, and Barbaro and Busbeck confirmed his accounts. It is known that no remains of them are to be found there at the present day, as Pallas informed me in 1810, in reply to my request for information thereupon."

which travellers at that time seldom thought worth recording"; and accompanies this opinion with many examples, at pp. 295-299 of his work.

Rubruquis wrote his travels in Latin, and several copies of the original still exist.

There is a copy in manuscript in the Royal Library of Paris, in the codex No. 686, which bears the title: "Itineraria in Tartariam". — See d'Avezac's Plan Carpin, p. 50.

It has only been once printed in the language of the original, and that in Hakluyt's Collection, vol. i, pp. 71-79, but from a manuscript of Lord Lumley's, imperfect at the end.

Purchas found a perfect copy of the travels in Benet College Library at Cambridge, with the inscription: "Historia Monogallorum sive Tartarorum".— See d'Avezac, p. 52. He translated it into English, and inserted it into his "Pilgrimes", vol. iii, p. 1. Roger Bacon has likewise inserted extracts from Rubruquis, in his "Opus Majus".

Bergeron translated it from this English version into French, under the title—

Voyage remarquable de Guillaume de Rubruquis, envoyé en Ambassade par le Roi Louis IX en differens parties de l'Orient, principalement en Tartarie et à la Chine, l'an de notre Seigneur 1253. Contenant des recits très singuliers et surprenans. Ecrit par l'Ambassadeur même. Le tout orné d'une Carte de voyage de tailles douces, et accompagné de Tables. Traduit de l'Anglais par le Sr. de Bergeron.

In Bergeron's Voyages, etc., vol. i, collated, says Bergeron, with two Latin MSS.

It was again reprinted under the title: "Relation

du Voyage en Orient de Guillaume de Rubruk", in vol. iv of the publications of the Geographical Society of Paris, " Recueil de Voyages et de Mémoires", pp. 205-296.

Here, and to both the foregoing journeys, belongs the following—

Quelques observations du Moine Bacon touchant les parties septentrionales du Monde, avec les relations touchant les Tartares; tirées de l'histoire de R. Wendover et de Mathieu de Paris, avec quelques lettres sur le même sujet; où l'on fait voir l'inhumanité, les mœurs sauvages, la rage et la cruauté des Tartares; leurs invasions, par lesquelles ils menacent de détruire la Chrétienté; avec une lettre de l'Empereur pour demander du secours au Roi d'Angleterre contre les Tartares dont on fait voir les rapines, les cruautez, et les meurtres; mais ils y sont courageusement repoussez. In P. Bergeron's Voyages, etc., vol. ii.

Both Forster, " Gesch. d. Entdeck", p. 127-146, and Sprengel, " Gesch. d. Entdeck", p. 288-299, have supplied explanatory and very learned remarks upon the travels of Rubruquis.

(9.)
MARCO POLO. 1271.

Marco Polo, on whom Malte Brun has bestowed the inappropriate[1] appellation of the " créateur de la géographie moderne, l'Humboldt du treizième siècle," was descended from a noble family of Venice. His father Niccolò Polo, and his uncle Matteo Polo,

[1] We say inappropriate, because with all the merits of Marco Polo he could lay no claim to an acquaintance with science and philosophy, while in these the illustrious Humbolt even at this day stands preeminent.

had many years before made a trading journey to Tartary; and when afterwards in 1271, the two set out on a similar journey to the east, they took young Marco, then seventeen or eighteen years old, with them. The journey was again into Tartary, to the court of Kublai Khan, where Marco found opportunity to develope speedily his rare capacity, learnt several oriental languages, was frequently employed by the prince just named to undertake distant journeys and important business, and collected at the same time the materials of his work on the east, which, as Sprengel says, " was long the general manual of Asiatic geography throughout entire Europe, especially after the voyages of the Portuguese had confirmed many of his supposed rodomontades."

He is said to have acquired great wealth from this journey, through trading and the generosity of Kublai Khan, on which account his countrymen gave him the surname of *il Millione;* and even down to the time of Ramusio, the house in which Marco Polo had lived at Venice was called *la corte del Millioni*.[1] He finally returned to Europe in 1295, but was soon after named commander of a division of the Venetian fleet against the Genoese, and as such, fell into the hands of the hostile admiral Lampa Doria. He was now carried prisoner of war to Genoa, where, although

[1] Ramusio, "Raccolta", vol. ii, p. 6, says, Marco Polo may have obtained this name on account of the great wealth of the Asiatic court, which he mentions in his travels (*e.g.*, the income of Kublai Khan from Kinsai, with its districts, alone amounted to 23,200,000 Venetian ducats), at first as a kind of nickname, but afterwards given by the Venetian government itself.

treated with great kindness and sympathy by the principal inhabitants, he nevertheless spent four years in prison. Here his famous work was composed, which will further be noticed in detail.

On account of the unstable life which Marco Polo led during his long sojourn in the east, it is not likely that he should have kept a detailed journal. He appears farther to have brought with him[1] only the short notices, which he collected for Kublai Khan on his route, and with the help of these dictated his narrative to his friend and fellow-sufferer, Rustichello, a native of Pisa, in his prison at Genoa.

With respect to the language in which the work was originally composed, Mr. Marsden, in his important and learned work presently to be quoted more at length, adduces evidence to show that it was not written in Latin, as Ramusio erroneously understood, but in a dialect of Italian; and in this conclusion he is warranted by the decided opinion of the celebrated Apostolo Zeno, who expresses himself as follows:—
"Io sono persuaso che il Polo la scrivesse primieramente, non come vuole il Ramusio, in lingua *latina*, ma nella *volgar* sua natia, e che poco dopo da altri fosse translatata in Latino."

With all the apparent improbabilities and inconsistencies of Marco Polo's narrative, there is still enough in it to convince the most sceptical of its general accuracy; while, as Mr. Marsden justly observes, the numerous descriptions and incidents afford

---

[1] Ramusio says: "Fece venir da Venezia le sue scritture e memoriale che avea portato seco."—See Zurla, vol. i, p. 18.

unobtrusive proofs of genuineness. Many of these details, which for centuries had excited either ridicule or suspicion, have been shown to be correct by the discoveries of modern times, while others less generally comprehensible have been elucidated and explained by the learning and research of Mr. Marsden.

Before we proceed to give the bibliography of the work, we would quote that part which treats of various countries which belong to modern Russia, which occurs at the end of the third book. According to the text of Ramusio, it reads thus:—"DELLA PROVINCIA DI RUSSIA. La provincia di Russia è grandisima, et divisa in molte parti, et guarda verso la parte di Tramontana, dove si dice essere la regione delle tenebre. Li popoli di quella sono Christiani, et osservano l'usanza de' Greci nell' officio della chiesa. Sono belissimi huomini, bianchi e grandi, et similmente le loro femine bianche et grandi, con li capelli biondi et lunghi, et rendono tributo al Ré di Tartari detti di Ponente, con il qual confinano nella parte di loro regione che guarda il Levante. In questa provincia si trovano abondanza grande di pelli di Armelini, Ascolini, Zebellini, Vari, Volpi, et cera molta; vi sono anchora molte minere, dove si cava argento in gran quantità. La Rossia è region molto fredda, et mi fù affermato cha la si estende fino sopra il Mare Oceano, nel qual (come abbiamo detto di sopra) si prendono li Girifalchi, Falconi pellegrini in gran copia, che vengono portati diverse regioni et provincie."

Ramusio says in reference to Marco Polo's account

of the climate of Russia: "Vltimamente nel fine del terzo libro, ove parla della Rossia, et del Regno delle Tenebre, come quello che in varij mappamondi antichi, è posto per fine del nostro habitabile sotto la Tramontana, non s'inganna punto del sito del detto regno, nelli mesi però ch'egli scrive dell' inverno."

All the texts of Marco Polo are defective, uncritical, and incorrect. The testimony of Purchas on this point is as follows:—"Multos auctores corruptos vidi, sed nullum corruptiorem quam Latina Pauli Veneti editio est. Ramusius edidit Italicam versionem, quæ aurea est si cum Latina comparetur."

The first Latin translation appears to have been made about the year 1320, by a monk of the Order of Preachers, named Francesco Pipino (called also Pepuri), of Bologna, to the performance of which task he was invited by the superiors of his order.

The following MSS. of Marco Polo are known:—

In Venice. *Latin.* Ramusio says of it: "Una copia di qual libro scritta la prima volta latinamente, di meravigliosa antichità e forse copiata dall' originale di esso Messer Marco, molte volte ho veduta e incontrata con questa che al presente mandiamo in luce."

This MS., which Apostolo Zeno also saw in the library of the senator Giacomo Soranzo, is lost; or, at least, we no longer know where to find it.[1]

In Paris. *Latin.* In the Bibliothèque Royale, No. 8392. A beautiful MS. in folio, on parchment, with many miniatures. By the monk Fra Pipino of Bologna,

[1] See Zurla, vol. i, p. 19.

translated again into Latin from an Italian translation made from a Latin copy. Copies of this MS. are also found in the public libraries of Rome, Padua, Modena, Ferrara, Berlin, and Wolfenbüttel. That in the British Museum is supposed by Sir Henry Ellis to have been written about 1400.

In Mentz. *Latin.*

See Recensus codd. Moguntiæ in R. Capituli Metropolitani Bibliotheca latitantium, pars prima. In Val. Ferd. de Guden Sylloge variorum diplomatariorum Monumentorumque veterum ineditorum adhuc, et res germanicas imprimis Moguntinas illustrantium. Francof., 1728; 8vo.; pages 377-385.

In Giessen, in the University library, *Latin*, under the title—

Marcus Polus de Venetiis: de conditionibus et consuetudinibus orientalium regionum: bound up with Cod. 218, a MS. of Eusebius. See Catalogus Codd. Mspt. Bibliothecæ Academ. Gissensis. Auct. J. Valent. Adrian. Francof. ad Mœn. 1840, 8vo.

In Florence. *Italian.* This MS. is generally called by the epithet of Marco Polo, *il Millione*, and under this name is entered in the Dictionary of the Academia della Crusca.

In Brit. Mus. (Sloane MSS.), bearing date 1457.

In Berne. *French.* Of the fourteenth century, on parchment, in folio. In the library of Bongars.— See Sinner, " Catalogus Codd. MSS. Bibliothecæ Bernensis annotationibus criticis illustratus; addita sunt excerpta quam plurima et præfatio, curante J. R. Sinner" (Bernæ, 1770; 3 vols., 8vo., t. ii, p. 419), where the history of this translation is given. In the year 1307, Thibault, Seigneur de Capoy, passing through Venice on his way to Constantinople, had here the honour to receive a copy of his travels from Marco Polo himself, "desirans," as Thibault says, "que ce qu'il avoit veu fus sceu par l'univers monde, et pour l'onneur et reverence de tres excellent et puissant princ Monseigneur Charles fils du Roy de France et Comte de Valois, bailla et donna au dessus dit Seigneur de Cepoy la premiere copie de son dit livre." A French MS. of 1300, is in the Royal Library of Paris. Other older French translations, which are probably copies only of this, are cited in "Montfaucon Biblioth. MSS. nova," p. 895.

A manuscript extract from the travels, under the title: "De magnis mirabilibus mundi et de Tartaris", cap. XXI, is found in a codex of the fourteenth century, in the Ambrosian library of Milan, bearing the title: "Imago Mundi pars II, seu chronica Fratris Jacobi ab Aquis (Giacomo d'Aqui), in Lombardia ord. Præd. usque ad annum 1296."

Respecting the manuscripts of Marco Polo's travels, see "Ricerche critico-biografiche sui testi di Marco Polo", in Zurla's work hereafter quoted, vol. i, p. 13, and in Purchas's "Pilgrimes".

The most remarkable editions of Marco Polo in both languages of the original, are the following—

Incipit prologus in libro domini Marci Pauli de Veneciis de consuetudinibus et condicionibus orientalium regionum. Rome or Venice, between 1484 and 1490 (but according to Brunet, 1490-1500); 4to.

M. Paulus Venetus de regionibus Orientalibus. Zwoll, 1483, 4to.

Marco Polo da Veniesia delle meravigliose cose del Mondo da lui vedute, da Giambattista Sessa. In Venetia, 1496; 8vo.

Again reprinted, Brescia, 1508; 8vo. This is a kind of extract in the Venetian and Tuscan dialects, and is now scarcely anywhere to be found.

Marco Polo Venetiano, in cui si tratta le maravigliose cose del Mondo per lui vedute, del costume di varii paesi, etc. Venetia, s. a. Small 8vo.

These Italian editions were repeated: Venetia, 1508, fol.; 1533, 8vo. Treviso, 1590, 8vo. Venetia, 1597, 8vo; 1611, 8vo.; 1626, small 8vo.; Trevigi, 1672, small 8vo.

Paulli Veneti, de regionibus orientalibus Libri III, in the Orbis novus regionum et insularum veteribus incognitarum, etc. of Simon Grynæus. Basil, 1532, fol.

Marco Polo, gentilhuomo Venetiano, delle cose de' Tartari et delle Indie Orientali, con la vita et costumi di que' popoli, descrittione di que' paesi, et molte altre cose notabili et meravigliose: in tre libri descritte, non prima che hora cosi interi et copiosi publicati. In the Raccolta di Ramusio, vol. ii, p. 1-60 (1559).

This is the best and most correct Italian text of Marco Polo.

Marcus Polus de Mirabilibus Mundi in latinum conversus, prohemio addito. Venetiis, 1583, 4to. Apud Juntas.

Appears to have been printed after the Latin translation of Frà Pipino.

Marci Pauli Veneti de regionibus orientalibus Libri III, ex editione Reineri Reineccii. Helmstadii, 1585, 4to. Also 1602, 4to. Amstelodami, 1664, 4to.

M. Pauli Veneti de regionibus orientalibus Libri III, cum Cod. Msto. Bibliothecæ Electoralis Brandenburgicæ collati, exque eo adjectis notis plurimum tum suppleti, tum illustrati. Accedunt Haithoni Armeni, Historia Orientalis, quæ et de Tartaris inscribitur. Itemque Andreæ Mülleri Greiffenhagii de Chataja disquisitio, inque ipsum Paulum Venetum præfatio et indices. Coloniæ Brandeb., 1671, 4to.

"Voyages de Marco Polo." Paris, 1624; 4to. *Latin* and *French*. This forms the first volume of "Recueil de Voyages et de Mémoires publiés par la Société de Géographie de Paris," of which, up to the present time, seven volumes in 4to. have appeared.

Viaggi di Marco Polo illustrati e commentati, preceduti dalla Storia delle Relazioni vicendevoli dell' Europa e dell' Asia, da Baldelli. Firenze, 1827, 4 vols. in 4to, and atlas in folio.

Il Milione di Marco Polo, testo di lingua del secolo XIII, ora per la prima volta publicato ed illustrato dal Conte Giov. Batista Baldelli Boni. Firenze, 1827; 4to, 2 vols.

I viaggi in Asia, in Africa, nel mare dell' Indie, descritti nel secolo XIII da Marco Polo, testo di lingua detto il Milione, illustrato con annotazioni. Venezia, 1824, small 8vo., 2 vols.

It is said that Klaproth had collected rich materials for a new edition. It is much to be regretted that it was never published.

It was natural that a work of such extraordinary contents as Marco Polo's travels should soon be translated into several languages. These translations are here arranged according to their dates.

German. The oldest German translation was printed at Nürnberg by Fricz Creussner. Its title is as follows—

Hie hebt sich an das Puch des edelñ Ritters vñ Landtfarers Marcho Polo. In dem er schreibt die grossen wunderlichen Ding dieser Welt. Sunderlichen von den grossen Künigen vnd Keysern die da herschen in den selbigen landen, vnd von irem volck vnd seiner gewonheit da selbs. Disz hat gedruckt Fricz Creüszner zu Nurmberg Nach cristi gepurdt Tausent vierhundert vñ im sibenvñsibenczigtñ iar (1477); fol.

First edition, of extreme rarity, in the Grenville Library. The following note is in Mr. Grenville's handwriting: "The volume agrees with Dr. Dibdin's description of Lord Spencer's copy (see *Bibl. Spenc.*, vol. vi, p. 176), having fifty-seven leaves of text; but the wood-cut, representing a full length figure of Marco Polo on the reverse of the first leaf, is supplied in this copy by an admirable fac-simile. The present is a very fine rubricated copy. When Mr. Marsden published his translation of this work, the only known copy of this first German edition was in the Imperial Library at Vienna, and I had a literal transcript made from it: since that time a second copy was found, and sold by Payne and Foss to Lord Spencer: and now I have purchased from Leipsic the present beautiful copy. I know of no fourth copy. The copy at Vienna wants the portrait."

See also respecting this edition, Panzer's "Annalen der älterem deutschen Litteratur," i, 99-100.

A reprint of this German translation appeared at Augsburg, 1481, by Anthonius Sorg, in the "Historia von Hertzog Leuppold und sein Sohn Wilhelm, von Osterreich," in fol.

Another version by Mich. Herr, appeared in the German translation of the "Novus orbis regionum" of Simon Grynæus, etc. Strassburg, 1534; fol. A version equally distinct from the other was made from the Italian of Ramusio, and entitled as follows—

Marcus Polus; wahrhafte Beschreybung seiner wunderlichen Reise in die Tartarey, zu dem grossen Can von Chatai verrichtet. Aus dem Italiänischen verteutscht durch Hieron. Megiserum. Leipzig, 1609, 8vo; 1611, 8vo.

Marco Polo's Reise in den Orient während der Jahre 1272 bis 1295, in's Deutsche übersetzt nach den besten Ausgaben des Originals und mit einem Commentare begleitet von Felix Peregrin. Ronneburg und Leipzig, 1802, 8vo.

Portuguese. Marco Paulo de Veneza das condições e custumes das gentes e das terras e provincias orientaes. Ho livro de Nycolao Veneto [Niccolò di Conti]. O trauado da carta de hull genoves das ditas terras. Imprimido per Valentym Fernandez Alemaão. Lyxboa, 1502; fol.

This is a translation from Pipino's Latin version.

Spanish. Libro del famoso Marco Paulo Venetiano de las cosas marvillosas que vido en las partes orientales, conviene saber, en las Indias, Armenia, Arabia, Persia, e Tartaria, e del poder del Gran Can, y otras reys; con otro tratado de Micer Poggio Florentino e trata de las mesmas tierras y islas. Traducido por Rodriquez (Arcediano), canonico de Sevilla. Sevilla, 1520, fol.; and Logrono, 1529, fol.

Historia da las gradezas y cosas maravillosas de las provincias orientales, sacada de Marco Polo Veneto, y traduzida de Latin en Romance, y añadida en muchas partes, por D. Martin Abarca de Bolea y Castro. En Zaragoça por Angelo Tauano, 1601, 8vo.

English. The most noble and famous travels of Marcus Paulus, one of the nobilitie of the State of Venice, in the east partes of the world, as Armenia, Persia, Arabia, Tartary, with many other kingdoms and provinces. No lesse pleasant than profitable, as appeareth by the table or contents of this booke. Most necessary for all sortes of persons, and especially for travellers. Translated into English (by John Frampton). London, 1579; 4to.

A translation by Samuel Purchas, in his "Pilgrimes," from the text of Ramusio.

Another, in the "Bibliotheca Navigantium" of Harris, likewise from the text of Ramusio.

We have next to quote the excellent and well known edition of Mr. Marsden, likewise translated from Ramusio, entitled—

The travels of Marco Polo, a Venetian, in the thirteenth century. Being a description, by that early traveller, of remarkable places and things in the eastern parts of the world. Translated from the Italian, with notes, by William Marsden, F.R.S., etc. With a map. London, 1818, 4to.

And finally, an edition entitled—

The Travels of Marco Polo, greatly amended and enlarged from valuable early manuscripts, recently published by the French Society of Geography, and in Italy by Count Baldelli Boni. With copious notes, illustrating the routes and observations of the author, and comparing them with those of more recent travellers. By Hugh Murray, F.R.S.E. Two maps and a vignette. New York, 1845; small 8vo.

Dutch. Translated from the Latin edition of R. Reineccius, under the title—

Marcus Paulus Venetus: Reisen en Beschryving der Oostersche Lantschappen, etc. Beneffens de Historie der Oostersche Lantschappen door Haithon van Armenien te zamen gestelt. Door J. H. Glazemaker. Amsterdam, 1664, 4to.

French. We have already spoken of the very ancient French translation of Thybault de Cepoy.

A translation of the Latin text in the "Novus Orbis," was published anonymously at Paris. 1556, 4to.; with the title—

La Description géographique des provinces et des villes les plus fameuses de l'Inde Orientale, avec les mœurs, loix, et coutumes des habitans d'icelles, mesmement de ce qui est soubz la domination du grand Cham, empereur des Tartares. Par Marc Paule, gentilhomne Vénitien, et nouvellement reduict en vulgaire François. Paris, 1556, 4to.

Les Voyages très-curieux et fort remarquables achevés par toute l'Asie, Tartarie, Mangi, Japon, les Indes Orientales, Iles adjacentes, et l'Afrique, commencés l'an 1252. Par Marc Paul, Vénitien, Historien recommandable par sa fidélité. Qui contiennent une relation très-exacte des Païs Orientaux. Dans laquelle il décrit très-exactement plusieurs païs et villes, les quels lui-même a voiagés et vus la pluspart : et où il nous enseigne brièvement les mœurs et coutumes de ces peuples, avant ce temps là inconnus aux Européens ; Comme aussi l'origine de la puissance des Tartares, quand à leurs conquêtes de plusieurs Etats au Païs dans la Chine ; ici clairement proposée et expliquée. Le tout divisé en III Livres ; conféré avec un manuscrit de la Bibliothèque de S. A. E. de Brandebourg, et enrichi de plusieurs notes et additions tirées du dit manuscrit, de l'édition de Ramuzio, de celle de Purchas, et de celle de Vitriaire.

In Bergeron's Collection, à la Haye, 1735; 4to.

Detailed accounts of Marco Polo will be found in the following works—

Sur la chorographie de Marc Paul, Vénitien. Preface d'André Müller Greiffenhag. Bergeron's Voyages, vol. ii.

Témoignages et jugemens de plusieurs savans touchant la relation de Marc Paul, Vénitien, entre lesquels ils s'en trouvent quelques uns qui contredisent à ces Relations, mais dont la pluspart sont favorables et très dignes de Foi. Bergeron, vol. ii, p. 26.

Terrarossa Riflessioni Geografiche circa le Terre incognite. Padova, 1687, 4to. Treats chiefly of Marco Polo.

Ab. Renaudot des anciennes Relations des Indes et de la Chine, de deux Voyageurs Mahométans qui y allèrent dans le IX siècle, trad. de l'arabe avec des remarques. Paris, 1718, 8vo.

The following works may also be quoted:—

Murray's Discoveries and Travels in Asia, vol. i, pp. 151-182.

Tiraboschi Storia della Letteratura Italiana. Defends Marco Polo especially from the charges of error brought against him.

Saggi di Studj Veneti, di Toaldo. Venez., 1782, 8vo. Contains, among other things, an Elogio de' Poli.

Dissertazione intorno ad alcuni Viaggiatori eruditi Veneziani poco noti; dal Abbate Morelli. Venezia, 1803; 4to.

Vita di Marco Polo. In the Collezzione di Vite e Ritratti d'illustri Italiani, da Dottoni. Padova, 1816; 8vo.

Notice sur la rélation originale de Marc Pol, par Paulin-Paris. Paris, 1823, 8vo.

Vies de plusieurs personnages célèbres des temps anciens

et modernes. Par M. Walckenaer, Laon, 1830, 2 vols., 8vo. Tom. ii, p. 1-34.

Very valuable accounts of Polo are found also in " Joh. Reinh. Forster's Gesch. d. Entdeck. im Norden," p. 151-182.

A very important work respecting Marco Polo and his travels is—

Di Marco Polo e degli altri Viaggiatori Veneziani più illustri: Dissertazione del P. Ab. D. Placido Zurla; con appendice sopra le antiche mappe lavorate in Venezia, e con quattro carte geografiche. In Venezia, 1818; large 4to., 2 vols.

This work, the whole of the first volume of which is occupied with Marco Polo, contains a very detailed investigation respecting the text of his travels, as well as a thorough analysis of the countries he travelled through. This survey is divided into the following sections:—1. Geography, p. 87-206; 2. Natural History and Physical Geography, p. 207-241; 3. History, p. 242-266; 4. Religion, p. 267-303; 5. Manners and Customs, p. 304-324; 6. Arts and Sciences, p. 325-349; 7. Commerce and Navigation, p. 350-368.

Forster says, in his " Gesch. d. Entdeck." p. 152: " It were to be wished, that a man of extended reading would compare all these translations with the Wolffenbüttel manuscript, and prepare and publish a new edition of this useful, and, for the geography of the Middle Ages, highly important book." This wish appears to have been in great measure fulfilled by Marsden's work.

(10.)
GIOVANNI DI MONTE CORVINO. 1288.

Giovanni di Monte Corvino, a Franciscan monk of Calabria, was despatched as ambassador by Pope Nicholas IV, in 1288, to Arghun, to the Mongolian Khan of Persia, He spent some time at Tauris, and left that city in 1291 for India, where he made several conversions. He then proceeded further east to Khan-Balyk, or Cambalu, the capital of the Tatars, the modern Peking, where he died, holding the honourable position of archbishop of the missions in that city. Regarding his travels in Tartary, we have only two of his letters, dated respectively 1305 and 1306, which are found printed in the following works—

Wadding, Annales Minorum. Romæ, 1732, fol., vol. vi, p. 69 sq.

Mosheimii Historia Tartarorum Ecclesiastica. App. xliv et xlv, p. 114-120.

Marsden, the Travels of Marco Polo, a Venetian, in the thirteenth century. London, 1818, 4to., p. 243-245.

See also, respecting this monk, " Nouveaux mélanges Asiatiques," par M. Abel Remusat; vol. ii, p. 193-198.

(11.)
HAITHO. 1290.

Haitho, Hatto, or Hayton, was a prince of the royal family of Armenia. Having long followed the profession of arms under his uncle Haitho II, king of Armenia, he retired in 1305, in fulfilment of a vow which he had formerly made, to Piscopia in Cyprus, where he entered a convent of Premonstrants. He subsequently came to Poitiers in France, and there, by the desire of Pope Clement V, dictated to Niccolò Salconi, in the French language, the history of the East, from the time of the appearance of the Mongolians; which the latter translated in 1307, into Latin, under the title, "Liber Historiarum partium Orientis."

Haitho's work consists—1, of accounts of the Tatars, from Jenghis Khan to Mango Khan; 2, of narrations from Haitho I, king of Armenia, respecting his life and travels; 3, of the monk Haitho's narrative of the events of his own time.

Haitho was not a traveller; but deserves mention here, inasmuch as in his work he frequently touches on northern Asia, and several countries pertaining to modern Russia.

Haitho's work is found both in Latin and French, in manuscript, in the Imperial Library of Vienna, viz.—

Haithon, la flor des Histoires de l'Orient, par Nicolas Faucon, in 4to., Hist. prof., No. 39.

Haitoni flos Historiarum Orientis. Fol., Hist. prof., No. 73.

Likewise, in the celebrated manuscript of Marco Polo, at Bern; and in the Bibliothèque Royale of Paris, No. 7500 and 8392.

The printed editions of this work are the following—

Here begynneth a lytell Cronycle, translated and imprinted at the cost and charge of Rycharde Pynson, by the commaundement of the ryght high and mighty prince Edwarde duke of Buckingham, yerle of Gloucester, Staffarde, and of Northampton. Imprinted by the sayd Richarde Pynson, printer unto the kinges noble grace. (No date.) Fol. B.L.

In the Grenville collection. The volume consists of forty-eight leaves. On the verso of fol. 35, "Here endeth the boke of thistoris of thorient partes cōpyled by a religious man frere Hayton, frere of Premonstre order, somtyme lorde of Court and cosyn german to the kyng of Armeny, upon the passage of the holy lande. By the commaundement of the holy fader the apostle of Rome, Clement the V, in the citie of Potiers: which boke I, Nicholas Falcon, writ first in French, as the frere Hayton sayd with his mouth, without any note or example; and out of French I have translated it in Latyn for our holy fader the pope. In the yeere of our lorde god 1307."

Mr. Grenville, in his manuscript note, says: "The present is the only translation into English, and from the circumstances of its being printed by Pynson, and having been (when in Mr. Heber's collection) bound with two other works (Mirrour of good Maners and Sallust), both translated by Barclay, was probably also translated by him. It is a book of extraordinary rarity, no perfect copy that can be traced having previously occurred for public sale."

The earliest French edition was printed at Paris, in 1529, with the title—

L'Hystore merveilleuse, plaisante et recreative du grand

Empereur de Tartarie, seigneur des Tartares, nommé le Grand Can, etc. Paris, pour Jehan Sainct Denys, 1529; fol.

On the first leaf of the text of the volume it is stated, that the work was originally written in Latin in the year 1310, by the very noble Monsieur Aycon, Seigneur de Courcy, in the abbey of the Epiphany, whither he had retired: and that in 1351, it was translated into French by Brother Jehan Longdit. This edition is very rare; but a copy is in the Grenville Library.

Les fleurs des hystoyres de la terre dorient. Compilees par frere Haycon seigneur du core et cousin germain du roy d'Armenie par le commandement du pape.

This edition, without date, is also in the Grenville Library.

Histoire orientale, où des Tartares, de Haiton, parent du roi d'Armenie; qui comprend premièrement une succincte et agréable description de plusieurs royaumes ou païs orientaux, selon l'état dans lequel ils se trouvoient environ l'an 1300; secondement une relation de beaucoup de choses remarquables, qui sont arrivées aux peuples de ces païs et nations. Le tout décrit par la main de Nicolas Salcon, et traduit suivant l'édition latine d'André Müller Greiffenhag. In Bergeron's Voyages, vol. ii.

Latin. Haithoni Armeni, Liber historiarum partium orientis, sive passagium terræ sanctæ, scriptus anno Redemptoris nostri MCCC. Haganoæ, 1529; 4to.

This first edition, in Latin, was edited by Men. Molther.

Haithoni Armeni, Liber de Tartaris. In the Orbis novus regionum et insularum veteribus incognitarum, etc., of Simon Grynæus. Basileae, 1537; fol.

Historia orientalis Haythoni Armeni et huic subjectum

Marci Pauli Veneti Itinerarium: item fragmentum e Speculo historiali Vincentii Belvacensis ejusdem argumenti. Auctore Reinesio Reineccio. Helmæstadii, 1585, 4to.

Haithoni Armeni Historia orientalis, quae et de Tartaris inscribitur. In Andr. Mülleri M. Pauli Veneti de regionibus orientalibus, libri III. Coloniae Brandeb. 1671, 4to.

Italian. Ayton Armeno, dell' origini et successione di Gran Cani Imperadori Tartari, et come aggrandirono l'Imperio loro, et della vita, religione, costumi et conditione de' Tartari. In Raccolta di Ramusio, vol. ii, p. 60-66, is divided into two sections, viz., Discorso sopra il libro del signor Hayton Armeno, p. 60-62; and Parte seconda della Historia del signor Hayton Armeno, che fù figliuol del signor Curchi, parente de' Rè di Armenia, p. 62A-64A.

Compendio della Storia de' Tartari scritta dell' Armeno Aitone, fatto da Gio-Boccaccio in Latino, trovato e tradotto in volgare, e pubblicato da Sebast. Ciampi. In Monumenti di un manuscritto autografo e lettere inedite di Mes. Giovanni Boccaccio, il tutto trovato ed illustrato da Sebastiano Ciampi. Milano, 1830, 8vo.

It was also translated into Dutch by J. H. Glazemaker, and printed with his translation of Marco Polo. Amsterdam, 1664; 4to.

(12.)

RICCOLDO DA MONTECROCE. 1296.

In 1296, Riccoldo da Montecroce, or Ricaldus de Monte Crucis, a Dominican of Florence, Sanctius de Bolea, Guillelmus Bernardi, Bernardus Guille, and several other monks, were sent by Pope Boniface VIII to the Saracens, Bulgarians, Kumans, Alans, Chazars, Goths, Russians, Nestorians, Georgians, Tatars, and other oriental and northern people; and Riccoldo left an "Itinerarium peregrinationis" of his travels,— the original text of which is not, however, extant. Jean Lelong, a Benedictine monk of Ypres, translated the work into French in 1351, and through this translation we are acquainted with Riccoldo's travels.

Four copies of Lelong's translation are known, which correspond with each other pretty well. One, which contains, with the travels of Haitho, those of Oderic, Boldensel, and the archbishop of Sultanieh, in folio, adorned with miniatures, is to be found in the Royal Library of Paris, marked No. 7500 C. A copy of this was made by the Chancellor Baron Rumänzow, which is to be found in the library of the Rumänzow Museum, under No. 40. This translation bears the following title—

> Cy commence le livre de peregrinacion de l'itineraire et du voyage que fist ung bon preu d'omme des freres precheurs qui ōt nom frère Riculd, qui par le commendement du Saint Pere ala oultre mer pour prechier aux mescreans la foy de Dieu, et sont en ce traictié par ordonnance contenuz les royaumes pays et provinces, les manieres diverses des gens, les loys, les sectes, les creances, etc. Et fut ce livre translatez du Latin en François en l'an de grâce mil ccciI fait et compilé par frere Jehan Lelong d'Ypre, moine de l'eveschée de taroenne. Folio.

It was printed with Haitho's work, entitled—

> L'hystore merveilleuse plaisante et recreative du grand empereur de Tartarie, seigneur des Tartares, nommé le grand Can, etc. Paris, 1529; sm. fol.

The second copy of Lelong's translation is to be

found in the City Library of Berne, in the same manuscript containing Marco Polo.

The third, in the Cotton Collection of manuscripts, British Museum, with the press-mark, Otho D. II.

The fourth, in the Archiepiscopal Library of Mentz An extract of the "Peregrinacion" will be found in Murray's "Discoveries and Travels in Asia," vol. i, p. 197, etc.

Ricold de Montecroix, voyageur et missionnaire en Asie. In Nouveaux Mélanges Asiatiques par M. Abel-Rémusat, vol. ii, p. 199-202.

(13.)
ODERICO DI PORDENONE. 1317.

Oderico Mattheussi, a Franciscan monk, born about 1285, at Pordenone, in Friuli, on which account he is generally called Oderico of Friuli, Odericus de Forto Julii, also Odericus de Portenau. He undertook in 1317 a journey through Tartary by Trebisond to India, and returned by Thibet to Europe. In 1330, he dictated, in Padua, to Guglielmo di Solagno, a monk, his travels in Italian, and then went to Udine, where he died in 1331.

Copies of the travels of Oderico exist in manuscript in the Arundel Collection, British Museum (press-mark, 13 f. 38 b.), under the title, "Itinerarium fratris Odorici de ordine Minorum de Mirabilibus Indie"; and in the Royal Collection (press-mark, 14 c. 13, fol. 216), under the title, "Itinerarium fratris Odrici Ordinis fratrum Minorum de Mirabilibus orientalium Tartarorum." These manuscripts are pronounced by good authority to be in the early half of the fourteenth century, and most probably a short time after the death of the author. The following also are known; viz., one under the title, "De Mirabilibus Mundi", after the Latin translation of the monk Heinrich von Glatz, in Udine, in the Royal Library of Paris, Nos. 2584 and 3195; in Corpus Christi College, Cambridge, No. 407; and in the Cathedral Library of Mentz, No. 52. The French translation of Jean le Long of Ypres, is found in manuscript in the Royal Library of Paris, No. 7500 C, and No. 8392, on parchment, and with many miniatures, in the City Library of Berne, and in the Cottonian Collection, British Museum.

Oderico's journey is printed—

In the Acta Sanctorum, and Wadding's Annales.
Latin and English. By Hakluyt, t. ii, p. 39-67.
Italian. By Ramusio, in the Appendix by Tommaso Giunti, vol. ii, fol. 237-248; and in: Elogio storico alle geste del Beato Oderico dell' ordine de' Minori conventuali, con la storia da lui dettata de' suoi viaggi Asiatici, illustrata da un religioso dell' ordine stesso, e presentata agli amatori delle antichità (Dal Fr. Giuseppe Venni). Venezia, 1761, 4to.

French. Printed with Haitho's work, entitled—

L'hystore merveilleuse, plaisante et recreative du grand empereur de Tartarie, etc. Paris, 1529, fol.

Sprengel gives in his "Gesch. der geog. Entdeck." p. 348-9, a comparison of the names of various places found in Oderico's travels.

See further the article drawn up by De la Renaudière : Oderic, in the " Biographie Universelle", t. xxxi, p. 499.

(14.)
IBN BATUTA. 1324.

Ibn Batuta, an Arabian author, left an account of a journey, in which the Russians are incidentally mentioned.

See respecting him, Frähn's Ibn Foszlan, p. 229.

His work first appeared in an English translation entitled—

The Travels of Ibn Batuta : translated from the abridged Arabic manuscript copies, preserved in the public library of Cambridge. With notes, illustrative of the history, geography, botany, antiquities, etc., occurring throughout the work. By the Rev. Samuel Lee; 4to. London (printed for the Oriental Translation Committee), 1829.

A Portuguese translation of the entire work was published under the title—

Viagens extenses e dilatadas do celebre Arabe Abu-Abdallah, mais conhecido pelo nome de Ben-Batuta. Traduzidas por Jose de Santo Antonio Moura. Tom. i, 4to. Lisboa (published by the Acad. Real das Sciencias), 1840.

A particular account of Ibn Batuta and his travels will be found in the " Roosskiee Viestneek", 1841; No. 2, p. 462.

(15.)
JEAN DE COR. 1330.

Jean de Cor, a Franciscan monk, was sent in 1330, by Pope John XXII, as missionary into Tartary, and for his zeal in the work of conversion was by him nominated Archbishop of Sultanieh. He left a narrative of his travels, which bears the following title—

De l'Estat et de la Gouvernance du grant Kaan de Cathay, souverain empereur des Tartres, et de la disposition de son empire et de ses autres provinces; interprété par un arcevesque que on dit l'arcevesque Saltensis, par le commandement du pape Jehan, vingt deuxiesme de ce nom, et translaté de Latyn en Françoys par frère Jehan le Long, né de Yppre, moine de Sainct-Berthin en Sainct-Omer.

This narrative is found in the Royal Library of Paris, in a fine manuscript (No. 8392), adorned with many miniatures.

See D'Avezac, Relations des Mongoles ou Tartares, page 25.

(16.)
JOURDAIN CATALAN. 1330.

Jourdain Catalan, commonly called Jordanus Catalani, a French Dominican monk of Séverac, made several journeys into Asia in the beginning of the fourteenth century; and in 1330 was sent by Pope John XXII to Sultanieh in Tartary, as the bearer of the pallium to Jean de Cor, the archbishop of that see. He left several documents, more particularly his "Memorabilia", a copy of which was in the possession of Walckenaer, from which it was printed in the "Recueil de Voyages et de Mémoires" of the Geographical Society of Paris, vol. iv, page 1-65.

The narrative bears the title—

Description des Merveilles d'une partie de l'Asie par le P. Jourdan Catalani.

See d'Avezac, already quoted, pp. 25-26.

(17.)
SIR JOHN MANDEVILLE. 1322-56.

Sir John Mandeville belonged to an ancient and distinguished English family. He was born at Saint Alban's, and received a careful education. His favourite studies were mathematics, surgery, and theology. His busy spirit urged him at the same time to inquire into the nature and condition of foreign countries; and with this intention he went, in 1322, through France on a journey to the Holy Land, served several years under the Sultan of Egypt and the Grand Chan of Cathay. After thirty-three years' wanderings in Asia, he returned to Europe, and died, in 1371, in Liège, where his monument is still to be seen. In the year 1356, as he says himself, in the thirty-fourth year after his departure, he drew up a narrative of his travels, in the French language apparently, but translated it himself soon after into Latin. This narrative, according to his own acknowledgment, included many of the chronicles, adventures, and romances of chivalry, so much admired in that age; but in almost every allusion to such romances he refers to them as merely matters of hearsay. This acknowledgment, we conceive, ought to be allowed to clear this early traveller from the charge of wilful falsification, which the manifest exaggerations occurring in his story have caused to be thrown upon him. With respect to the marvels which he asserts to have fallen under his own observation, they, like those of Herodotus and Marco Polo, have been mainly, if not entirely, verified by the researches of more recent travellers. This twofold ground of exculpation we hold to be an acquittal for Mandeville, on the score of veracity. In England there are several copies of an English version of his narrative, the original of which is dedicated to Edward III, and said to have been written by Mandeville himself.

His work belongs to this place, on account of his details respecting the Tatars and the countries ruled by them.

Of the English manuscripts, there are nineteen copies in the British Museum, according to Mr. Halliwell. "So numerous," he says, "indeed, are they, owing to its great popularity, that it would be an endless labour to collate them all, though scarcely any two copies agree to any extent."

Besides the English manuscripts, there is a very ancient one in the French language in the Municipal Library of Berne; one in the Grenville Library, upon vellum, of the fourteenth century; and another very fine one in the Royal Library of Paris, also on vellum, with many miniatures.

The various editions of his travels are the following—

English. Here begynneth a lytell treatyse or booke

named Johan Maūdeuyll, knyght, borne in Englonde, in the towne of Saynt Albone, and speketh of the wayes of the holy londe towarde Jherusalem and of marueyles of ynde and of other dyuerse coūtrees. Emprynted at Westmynster by Wynken de Worde, anno dñi, MCCCC.LXXXXIX; 8vo.

This edition contains one hundred and nine chapters, exclusive of the introduction, and has several wood-cuts.

In the Grenville Library is an undated edition, "emprented by Rychard Pynson", entitled—

The boke of John Maunduyle, knyght, of wayes to Jerusalem, and of marueyls of ynde and of other countrees; 4to.

Mr. Grenville, in his manuscript note, says:— "Dibdin seems to agree with Sir F. Freeling, in considering this book as of the fifteenth century, and therefore prior to that of W. de Worde of 1499, which was esteemed the first edition. No other copy being as yet ascertained, I readily purchased it, though it wants four leaves. The text varies very much from Este's edition; but I have never found that of W. de Worde, to collate it with that edition."

Other English editions are—

1503, 8vo; 1568, 4to; 1670, 4to; 1696, 4to; 1722, 4to; and lastly, the most perfect edition, under the title: The voiage and travaile of J. de Mandeville, which treateth of the way of Hierusalem, and of marvayles of Inde, with other islands and countryes. London, 1725, 8vo.

This last edition was reprinted "with an introduction, notes, and glossary, by J. O. Halliwell, Esq." 8vo.; London, 1839.

Latin. Itinerarius domini Johannis de Mandeville militis. (Without place, date, or name of printer.) 4to.

This is the first of the Latin editions, being probably printed about 1480.

It was also printed in the first edition of Marco Polo.

In Purchas's "Pilgrimes", a Latin extract.

French. Ce livre est appelé Mandeville, et fut fait et composé par Jehan de Mandeville, chevalier natif d'Angleterre de la ville de St. Albain, et parle de la terre de promission, c'est a dire de Jerusalem, etc. Lyon, 1480, small fol.; and again, 1487, 4to.

Maitre Jehan de Mandeville, lequel parle des grandes aventures des pays étranges où il s'est trouvé, ensemble la terre de promission, et du saint voyage de Hierusalem. Paris (no date), 4to; also, 1517 and 1542.

By Bergeron, from the Latin translation of the extract in Purchas, under the following title—

Recueil ou Abrégé des Voiages, et Observations du Sr. Jean de Mandeville, Chevalier et Professeur en Médecine, faites dans l'Asie, l'Afrique, etc. Commencées en l'an MCCCXXXII [1322]. Dans lesquelles sont compris grand nombre de choses inconnues. Par Monsieur (John) Bale.

So attractive a book would not fail of being translated into other languages. We are aware of the following translations—

Italian. Tractato delle piu maravigliose cosse e piu notabili, che si trovano in le parte del mondo vedute ... del cavalier J. da Mandavilla. Milano, 1480, 4to; Bologna, 1488, 4to; Venezia, 1491, 4to; Firenze, 1492, 4to; Venezia, 1496, 4to; Milano, 1497, 4to: Bologna, 1497, 4to; Venetia,

1504, 4to; Venezia, 1515, 4to, and 1534, 8vo; 1537, 8vo; 1564, 8vo; 1567, 8vo.

German. Das buch des Ritters von Montevilla. Augspurg, 1481, fol., with wood-cuts; and 1482. fol., with woodcuts. This translation is by Michelfelser.

Johannes von Montevilla, Ritter, Strassburg, 1484, folio, with wood-cuts; translated by Otto von Demeringen. Also 1488, 4to; 1499, fol., with wood-cuts; 1501, with woodcuts; 1507, fol.

Des Ritters Johannes von Montevilla Reyss und Wanderschaft durch das gelobte Landt, Indien und Persien. Francof. 1580, 8vo; 1600; 1608.

The same in "Reisebuch des Heiligen Landes," etc. Franckf. 1629; fol. Th. I, p. 759.

Des Ritters Johannes von Montevilla Curieuse Reissbeschreibung, 1690, 8vo; 1692; 1696.

Spanish. Valencia, 1540; fol.

Dutch. Antwerpen, 1494; fol.

(18.)

Francesco Balducci Pegolotti. 1335.

Francesco Balducci Pegolotti, of Florence, made a journey into the east in the service of the Florentine Trading Company, and collected, especially in Tana (Asow), very useful accounts concerning the route of the caravans which went to China through the interior of Asia. He wrote in 1335 a work on the subject, a kind of commercial geography, remarkable for its time, bearing the title—" Libro di divisamenti di paesi et di misure di mercatanzie e d'altre cose bisognevoli di sapere a' mercatanti di diverse parti del mondo." This was afterwards printed from a manuscript in the Riccardi Library, at Florence, under the above title, with the false imprint "Lisboa e Lucca", but at Florence in 1766.

It is also contained in the third volume of the work—

Della decima e delle altre gravezze imposte dal comune di Firenze, della moneta et della mercatura dei Fiorentini fino al secolo XVI. Opera di Gian Francesco Pagnini del Ventura. In Firenza, 1766, 4to, 4 vols.

Of this extract, for which the work deserves a notice here, the first chapter bears the title—" Avisamento del viaggio del Gattajo per lo cammino della Tana ad andare et tornare con mercatanzie"—which is translated in Forster's " Gesch. d. Entd." p. 187-189, with explanations.

Franz Balducci Pergoletti's Reise-Route von Asof nach Peking.

With the corresponding text of the original. In Sprengel's " Gesch. d. geog. Entd." p. 257, etc. With many observations and explanations.

(19.)

Luchino Arigo. 1374.

The still unpublished narrative of an expedition of the Genoese Luchino Arigo, to the Don and Caspian in 1374, is to be found in a manuscript of the beginning of the fifteenth century, bearing the title, " Itinerarium Antonii Usus Maris," preserved in the public library of Genoa.

(20.)

PETER SUCHENWIRT. 1377.

Peter Suchenwirt, probably of Austrian parentage, flourished between the years 1356 and 1395, and left a collection of poems, which consist partly of historical relations, partly of allegorical and didactic poems. In the first we find several poems collected, for the most part, on the spot; short indeed, but for the period to which they belong very valuable relations respecting Russian countries and regions, and for the historical occurrences which they touch upon. On this account, Suchenwirt is here deserving of a place. Two manuscripts are known of the entire collection of his poems, one of which, the Palatine, was long preserved in the Vatican, and is now deposited at Heidelberg; the other is in the Imperial Library of Vienna. They were first published by the learned Primisser, at Vienna, in 1827, under the following title—

Peter Suchenwirt's Werke, aus dem vierzehnten Jahrhunderte. Ein Beitrag zur Zeit-und Sittengeschichte, mit einer Einleitung, historischen Bemerkungen und Wörterbuche. Wien, 1827; 8vo.

In the historical poems, Suchenwirt touches on the history, exploits, etc., of the heroes of his time, but chiefly those of his own countrymen both at home and abroad. Some of these knights-errant, and among others more particularly Friedrich von Chreutzpeck and Hans von Traunn, proceed on their various and distant campaigns into Russian countries, and both were present at the battle of Isborsk, 1348, and at the storming of this city by the German Orders. Isborsk is here called Eysenburk and Eysenwurch, and receives the appellation of *die gehewer*, or *the famous*.

That which we have more especially to refer to occurs in the fourth poem of Suchenwirt's work, which bears the inscription, "Von Herzog Albrecht's Ritterschaft". In 1377, the young duke Albrecht III, son of Albrecht II, of Austria, undertook, in company with many nobles, an expedition to Prussia, in which Suchenwirt attended him as officer of the court (hofdiener), *that thence he might be able, from personal observation, to describe the countries through which they passed*. The soldiers of Duke Albrecht advanced from Insterburg, in Prussia, at the same time with the German Orders, towards the Samaiten (Samogitia), and penetrated from thence into the Russian territories, which, in later times, under Polish rule, was called Black Russia. Suchenwirt relates, v. 360, etc.

" Des dritten tages chom daz her
Vroleich in ein ander lant
Daz waz Russenia genannt,
Da sach man wuhsten prennen,
Slahen, schiezzen und rennen,
Haid ein, pusch ein, unverzagt," etc.

Afterwards, at verse 427, etc., we are told—

" Daz her wuchst drew gantze lant
Die ich mit namen tue bechannt;
Sameyt, Russein, Aragel.
Wint, regen und der hagel
Begraif uns da mit grozzen vrost,
Da fault uns harnasch und die chost," etc.

The crusaders then returned (v. 441), and hastened towards Memel (" und eylten zu der Mymmel,"), making their way through a trackless country, and experiencing many discomforts on account of the bad weather. They passed through, v. 473, etc.—

> " Ein Wildung heist der grauden,
> Gen westen noch gen sauden
> So poz gevert ich nye gerayt,
> Daz sprich ich wol auf meyn ayt," etc.

They then reached Königsberg, of which it is said, v. 483—

> " Tzu Chunigezperch so waz uns gach
> Do het wir rue und gut gemach."

The three districts here introduced, Russein, Aragel, and Grauden, Primisser explains by White Russia, Carelia, and Graudenz. These districts, however, are so far distant from Insterburg, the point from which the army of the Orders started, and so remote from each other, that this supposition is exceedingly improbable. The following explanation would appear to be more natural, whereby the accuracy and truthfulness of Suchenwirt, in his names of districts, places, and rivers, are more clearly established. The army of the Orders proceeded from Insterburg into Samogitia, penetrated on the third day into Russenia, *i. e.*, Black Russia, the district of Novogrodek in the modern government of Grodno, on the Upper Niemen, laid waste a portion of this province and of Aragel, pushed on to Memel, and then retreated through the waste of Graudenz into the country of the Orders; when Suchenwirt, in consequence of fatigue, stayed behind at Königsberg. Aragel, according to Schlözer, in his "Geschichte von Litthauen", is the Germanised name of the Lithuanian province Aragola, or Aragallen, and the waste of Grauden is the district on the Niemen, north-west of Grodno, which city is well known to lie on the Niemen, and at that time was well built. The country lying thence north-west towards the Prussian boundary is still little known in our times, and might easily have been designated a waste by Suchenwirt. Such an expedition, from Insterburg through Samogitia to the district of Novogrodock, and from thence to the Niemen through Grodno, back to the Prussian boundary, could be well accomplished in a short time.

Finally, the observation has still to be made, that Suchenwirt appears to have known the diversity of the Russian countries mentioned by him. The most remote north-eastern Russia to which the Livonian expedition went, he calls White Russia (Weizzen Reuzzen). Isborsk lies in White Russia (s. xviii, v. 205 and 506). The Russian districts, which in a strict sense form the frontier of Lithuania, he calls Russenia, or Russein (s. vi, v. 362 and 429); they comprise the territories subsequently called Black Russia. Red Russia, on the other hand, or those Russian districts which first came under Polish rule, which lay nearest to our poet's description, and hence the best known to him, he simply calls Russia (Reuzzen).[1]

[1] The following note, bearing reference to this narrative, is given by Price in his edition of Warton's "History of English Poetry,"

(21.)

JOHANN VON SCHILDBERGER. 1394.

Johann von Schildberger, born in Munich, accompanied the army of King Sigismund of Hungary, in 1394, against the Turks; but in the following year was taken prisoner at the battle of Nicopolis by the Turks, and by order of Bajazet I (or, as he names

1824, vol. ii, p. 167, and is inserted here from its interesting connexion with a portion of our own history:—

"A curious collection of German poems, evidently compiled from these heraldic registers, has recently been discovered in the library of Prince Sinzendorf. The reader will find an account of them and their author, Peter Suchenwirt (who lived at the close of the fourteenth century), in the fourteenth volume of the Vienna Annals of Literature.—*Jahrbücher der Literatur*, Wien, 1814 [1821]. They are noticed here for their occasional mention of English affairs. The life of Burkhard v. Ellerbach recounts the victory gained by the English at the battle of Cressy; in which this terror of Prussian and Saracen infidels was left for dead on the field, 'the blood and the grass, the green and the red, being so completely mingled in one mass,' that no one perceived him.—Friedrich v. Chreuzpeckh served in Scotland, England, and Ireland. In the latter country he joined an army of 60,000 (!) men, about to form the siege of a town called Trachtal (?); but the army broke up without an engagement. On his return from thence to England, the fleet in which he sailed fell in with a Spanish squadron, and destroyed or captured six-and-twenty of the enemy. These events occurred between the years 1332-36.—Albrecht v. Nürnberg followed Edward III into Scotland, and appears to have been engaged in the battle of Halidown-hill. But the 'errant-knight' most intimately connected with England was Hans v. Traun. He joined the banner of Edward III at the siege of Calais, during which he was engaged in cutting off some supplies sent by sea for the relief of the besieged. He does ample justice to the valour and heroic resistance of the garrison, who did not surrender till their stock of leather, rope, and similar materials—which had long been him, Weyasit), was sent into Asia. On the overthrow of Bajazet by Timur, he fell into the hands of the latter, whom he attended in all his expeditions until his death in 1405. Thus Schildberger passed from one master to another, and traversed in his wanderings Georgia, Persia, and the whole of Tartary, of which he relates many wonderful things.

their only food—was exhausted. Rats were sold at a crown each. In the year 1356 he attended the Black Prince in the campaign which preceded the battle of Poictiers; and on the morning of that eventful fight, Prince Edward honoured him with the important charge of bearing the English standard. The battle is described with considerable animation. The hostile armies advanced on foot, the archers forming the vanguard. 'This was not a time,' says the poet, 'for the interchange of chivalric civilities, for friendly greetings, and cordial love: no man asked his fellow for a violet or a rose; and many a hero, like the ostrich, was obliged to digest both iron and steel, or to overcome, in death, the sensations inflicted by the spear and the javelin. The field resounded with the clash of swords, clubs, and battle-axes, and with shouts of *Nater Dam* and *Sand Jors*.' But von Traun, mindful of the trust reposed in him, rushed forward to encounter the standard-bearer of France. 'He drove his spear through the vizor of his adversary: the enemy's banner sunk to the earth never to rise again. Von Traun planted his foot upon its staff, when the King of France was made captive, and the battle was won.' For his gallantry displayed on this day, Edward granted him a pension of a hundred marks. He is afterwards mentioned as being intrusted by Edward III with the defence of Calais during a ten weeks' siege; and, at a subsequent period, as crossing the channel, and capturing a (French?) ship, which he brought into an English port, and presented to Edward.—It is to be hoped these poems will be published.—[They were published three years afterwards, as above mentioned, but this fact is not noticed in the last edition of Warton published in 1840.]— The slight analysis of their contents given by Mr. Primisser, and on which this note is founded, is just sufficient to excite, without gratifying, curiosity."

He returned by Constantinople, Lemberg, and Cracow, to Munich, his native city, in 1427, after an absence of thirty-two years.

Schildberger was a man entirely destitute of education, and consequently was ill able to describe the wonders of the countries he passed through. By whom the German narrative of his travels was composed, we know not; probably he had a friend, to whom he dictated it from memory on his return. His work, notwithstanding many disfigurements and false accounts, is still important, more particularly for the later epoch of the Chanat of the Golden Horde, and well deserves a critical revision and explanation.

Schildberger's journal of travels appears in the following editions—

Hie vachet an d'Schildberger der vil wunders erfaren hatt in der heydenschafft vnd in d' Türkey. Without place or date. (Perhaps Ulm, 1477.) Fol. With wood-cuts.

Frankf. a. M., 1549, 4to. In somewhat different orthography.

Ein wunderbarlich history wie Schildberger aus München von den Türken in die heydenschafft geführet und wieder heimgekommen ist. Nürnberg (no date), 4to.

Eine wunderbarliche und kürtzweylige Histori wie Schildberger einer aus der Stadt München in Bayern von der Türken gefangen inn die haydenschafft gefüret und wider heym gekommen. Item, was sich für Krieg, vnnd wunderbarlicher thaten dieweyl er in die haydenschafft gewesen zugetragen gantz kürtzweylig zu lesen. Frankfort, durch Wigand Hanen Erben (about 1554), 8vo.

Magdeburg, 1606, 8vo.

Johan Schildberger's Reise in den Orient und wunderbare

Begebenheiten. Von ihm selbst beschrieben. Aus einer alten Handschrift übersetzt und herausgegeben von A. J. Penzel. München, 1814, 8vo. Modernised and without explanations.

Extracts from Schildberger's travels. By Witsen; p. 132.

Forster gives a review of these travels, th. i, p. 245-253, and Sprengel, p. 367-370.

(22.)

Josafa Barbaro. 1436.

Josafà, or properly Giosafat Barbaro, descended from a noble Venetian family, went, in 1436, as ambassador for his republic, and probably also as a merchant, to Tana, the modern Azov, which then belonged to the Genoese, and was the most celebrated market for Chinese and Indian merchandize. He tarried sixteen years in the Crimea, through which he travelled, partly by land, partly by water, and thereby gained the interior, with the view of collecting as accurate accounts as possible of the Tatars. In the last two chapters, he speaks particularly of Russia and the Tatar countries, which lie between the south and east. In 1471, he undertook a journey into Persia, in the service of his native city, to Ussum Kassan, —or, as he calls him, Assambeï,—in order to support him with military stores and advice, in the war against the Turks, so as to weaken them in their attempts against Venice. He finally returned to his native country in 1479, and first wrote eight years afterwards, in 1487, as he says himself, both his journeys, that he might be enabled to mention that

Russians had subdued Kasan and Novogorod. Barbaro died in Venice, 1494, at an advanced age.

The first of Barbaro's travels alone concerns us here. A very full and annotated extract of it will be found in Forster's " Gesch. d. geogr. Entdeck. und Schiff. im Norden," p. 203-217; as well as in Beckmann's " Liter. der älter Reisebeschreib.", th. I, p. 165-192. Here also we should especially mention the extract found under the title " Giosofat Barbaro", in Zurla's work, " Di Marco Polo e degli altri viaggiatori Veneziani piu illustri," vol. ii, p. 205-229.

Barbaro, on the whole, shows himself to have been a well-informed and careful observer; this must have drawn much attention to his work on its first appearance, and it is still valuable for its important contributions towards the history of the commerce and geography of the middle ages.

For a long time it was doubtful whether Barbaro's travels appeared by themselves, or were only to be found in Manuzio, or Ramusio's travels. The latter is given by the accurate Beckmann, as his opinion, after careful investigation; but there can be no doubt now, however, that they appeared earlier in a separate form, as Mazzuchelli mentions in his " Scrittori d'Italia" (t. II, vol. i, p. 270), an edition (Venezia, 1543, small 8vo) which Zurla himself possessed; and another still (Venezia, 1545, small 8vo.) is quoted.

Viaggio di Josaphat Barbaro, Ambasciadore di Venetia, alla Tana et in Persia. In the Raccolta di Viaggi pubblicata da Antonio Manuzio, in Venezia, 1543, 8vo; 1545, small 8vo. Apud Aldum.

Josafa Barbaro gentilhuomo Veneziano, il qual fece due Viaggi, l'uno alla Tana, et l'altro in Persia, ne' quali son descritti i nomi di molte città della Persia, molte particolarità della Tartaria, e del Cataio, con la guerra che Vssumcassan fece con Pangratio Rè di Zorzania.

Also, the Crimea travels, with the following title—

Di Messer Josafa Barbaro, Gentilhuomo Venetiano, il Viaggio della Tana. In the Raccolta di Ramusio, vol. ii, p. 91A-98; as also in a Lettera dello stesso Giosafat Barbaro scritta al R. Monsignor Piero Barocci Vescovo di Padova, nella qual si descrive l'erba del Baltracan, che usano i Tartari per lor vivere; which is wanting in Manuzio's work.

A detailed description of the Viaggio alla Tana, taken from Beckmann, but given with full acknowledgment, is found in Zurla's Marco Polo, vol. ii, p. 207-212; and a Latin extract from the journey to Persia, in J. de Laet's "Persia seu regni Persici status", ed. sec. Lugd. Bat., 1647, 24mo, p. 207-221. Barbaro has been translated into the Latin and Russian only.

The Latin version, which has the character of not being very faithfully rendered, is by Jacob Geuder von Herolzberg, and is included in Pietro Bizari's "Rerum Persicarum historia." Francof. 1601; fol.

This is also reprinted verbatim in "Georgii Hornii Ulyssea." Francof. et Lips., 1671; 12mo.

The travels, "alla Tana", were translated into Russian from the text of Ramusio by Vasiley Semenov', under the title—

Puteshestvie v' Tanu Josafata Barbaro, Venetsianskago

dvoryanina. Perevod' c' Italianskago V. S., printed with the Italian original in his Biblioteka Inostrannuikh' Pisatelei o Rossy. Part I, tom. i. St. Petersburgh, 1836; 8vo., p. vi-xvi, and 1-156.

(23.)
Nicolaus Cusanus. About 1450.

Niclas Krebs, of Cusa, a small village on the Moselle, in Trèves, was born of very poor parents in 1401. He became an ecclesiastic at an early age, and, according to the custom of his time, took the name of Cusanus from his birth-place; he raised himself through his learning and abilities to the highest dignity in the church, and died at Rome in 1464, as cardinal and governor of that city. Herberstein reckons him among the writers who have treated of Russia, and hence he must not be passed over here; there is no work of the kind, however, bearing his name, known; and even in the large collection of his works published at Basil, 1565, in 3 vols., fol., nothing is to be found respecting Russia.

Adelung suggests, however, that as Cusanus had been employed by Pope Eugene IV, to effect a union between the Greek and Roman churches, he made, on that account, a journey to Constantinople, and may on that occasion possibly have written something respecting Russia; and to such manuscript accounts of the constitution of the Greek church, or other such work, which may have been since lost, Herberstein may have made allusion. At the same time, it is possible, as Adelung himself suggests, that he only referred to the "Tabula Cusani", a map of Germany, now unknown, but of which Sebastian Münster wrote an explanatory description. From this work of Münster's, which is to be found in the "Rerum Germanicarum Scriptores" of Schardius, tom. i, it is evident that Russia was included in the map, as the work contains a short notice of that country.

Upon this subject the Editor of this translation has been favoured by Prince Lobanoff (editor of the famous "Recueil des Lettres de Marie Stuart"), with evidence confirmatory of the belief, that it is De Cusa's map alone to which Herberstein alludes. This evidence exists in the preface to a work anterior to Herberstein, viz., the German translation of Miechov's "Tractatus de duabus Sarmatiis"; a copy of which, though of extreme rarity, and unknown to Adelung, Ebert, and the other bibliographers, is in the Prince's possession. It bears the following title—

Tractat von baiden Sarmatien und andern austossenden Landen, in Asia und Europa, von sitten und gepräuchen der völcker so darinnen wonen. Ain anders vō den landen Scithia und den inwonern des selben lands, genannt Cairchassi. Vast wunderparlich zu hörën; goth. 34 feuillets in 4to. Augsburg, 1518.

The second part is a translation of G. Interiano's work.

The translation is made by Johann Mair von Eckh, as is shewn by the preface, an extract from which Prince Lobanoff has obligingly transcribed for the Editor, and is given in the note below.[1]

[1] Dem erbern unnd vesten herrn Jacoben Fugger, Rö Kay.

INTRODUCTION

A collation of the passage in italics, with what Herberstein says in his preface addressed to the Emperor Ferdinand, shews it to be highly probable that a map of Cusanus was all that was alluded to by Herberstein. This opinion, Prince Lobanoff reasonably suggests, is still further strengthened by the fact, that Herberstein, in mentioning Cusanus, Paulus Jovius, T. Fabri, and A. Bied or Wied, says, " cum *tabulas*, tum commentarios reliquerint." Now we are acquainted with the works of Paulus Jovius and of Fabri, so that the question of maps can only apply to Cusanus or to A. Weid.

(24.)

GIORGIO INTERIANO. AFTER 1450.

Giorgio Interiano, of Genoa, styled by Politian " magnus naturalium rerum investigator", went into

May. u. Radt, meinem günstigen lieben herren. Empent ich Johañ Mair von Eckh doctor, etc. Mein freuntlich willig dienst. Als ich doctor Mathis von Miechaw büchlin darinn er die völcker gegen mitternacht, zu ern dem hochwirdigen fürsten uñ herren herrn. Stanislaw Tursso Bischove zu Olmitz meinem genädigen herren, weyt und wol beschriben von euch empfangen, hab ich das mit höchster begierd überlesen. Unnd in anschung das bemelter doctor Mathis von Miechaw, in poln anhaym, und seiner beschreybung mer weder andern lateinischen oder Kriechischen schreibern, die solche lanndt nye gesehen, auch von andern Nacionen von wegen irer rauhen und groben art, mit streyt und Kriegen nit geöffnet, zu gelauben ist, *Wie wol der hochwirdig fürst und herr herr Nicolaus Cusa, der geleerten teutschen Kron, in ainem Mäpplin von disen länden vil auzaigt.* Bin ich bewegt Euwer ernnste zu gefallen solch püchlin auss dem latein in teutsch zu transferiern. Wölliches ich dann in Kurtzen tagen mit der eyl gethon und dasselbig Euwer ernnste hyemit zusende. . . .

Circassia in the fifteenth century, and on his return described the country and its inhabitants in a very simple treatise. He says in his letter to Aldus (in Ramusio, ii, 196), that many years before (*da più anni in quà*), he had seen the land of the Tscherkesses; he must consequently have visited the western Caucasus in the beginning of the second half of the fifteenth century.

His little work on the Tscherkesses, whom he calls Zychi,[1] appeared under the title—

La vita: & sito di Zichi, chiamiti ciarcassi: historia notabile. Venetiis, apud Aldum Manutium, 1502; 8vo.

A translation of this into German forms the second part of the rare work above quoted, under the article "Nicolaus Cusanus", as in the possession of Prince Lobanoff.

This Aldine edition is of extreme rarity.

It is reprinted in the collection of Ramusio, vol. ii, fol. 196.

The Marchese Girolamo Serra, in his "Storia dell' antica Liguria e di Genova" (Torino, 1834, 4to., vol. iv, page 234), calls Interiano, "un uom saggio, piacevole, amatore delle lettere, peritissimo in geografia, e ricercatore instancabile di lontani paesi, chi fù il primo a far conoscere i costumi de' Zichi e Circassi."

[1] Called by Strabo and Pliny, Zygi; by the Greeks, Ζυγοι. The word Zichu, or as some write it, Dsich, in Circassian means "a man".

(25.)

ÆNEAS SYLVIUS. 1454.

Æneas Sylvius Bartholomæus Piccolomini, who at a later period (1458) received the papal tiara under the name of Pius II, attained in 1450 the rank of cardinal, and as such was employed on various diplomatic embassies by the emperor Frederick III. In the same capacity he was once sent into Prussia, on the affairs of the Holy See, and had then an opportunity of becoming acquainted with the Poles and Lithuanians. This embassy supplied him with the means of gaining materials for his work, "De Polonia, Lithuania et Prussia sive Borussia", which is printed in the first volume of the collection, entitled, "Joan. Pistorii Polonicæ historiæ corpus, hoc est Polonicarum rerum Latini, recentiores et veteres scriptores, quotquot extant." Basil. 1582, fol. A considerable portion of the second section of this work is translated in the journal, "Sendungen der Kurländischen Gesellschaft für Literatur und Kunst" (vol. ii, p. 4), in the memoir, "Ueber einige religiöse Gebräuche der alten Letten, von Watson," in which Æneas Sylvius relates many remarkable circumstances respecting the superstitions of the ancient Lithuanians, their veneration of serpents, their fire-worship, and the oracle connected with it, their adoration of the sun, and of a great hammer by which they once delivered from captivity the signs of the zodiac, as also respecting their sacred groves, etc.

(26.)
AMBROGIO CONTARINI. 1473.

Ambrogio Contarini, descended from one of the most ancient and distinguished patrician families of the Venetian republic, was, like Giosafat Barbaro already mentioned, sent by his government as ambassador to Persia, to incite Ussumcassan to make war against Mahomet II. With a very unostentatious retinue, consisting of only four persons, he set out on the 23rd of February 1473, and proceeded by land, on account of the war, through Germany, Poland, and the Crimea, to Ispahan, where the Persian monarch then resided, and where he met with his countryman Barbaro. He returned through Georgia, Mingrelia, Derbent, Astrachan, Resen, and Moscow, at which last place he arrived on the 26th of September 1476, through the assistance and in the company of a Russian ambassador named Marco Rosso, who was likewise returning from Persia, and thence made his way back through Poland and Germany, arriving at Venice on the 21st of January.

Contarini's work contains a circumstantial journal of all that he saw from the 24th of February 1474, to the 10th of April 1477, but still more of the misfortunes that happened to himself and his attendants; owing, however, to the disturbed state of the times and unfavourable circumstances, it is not nearly so copious as that of Barbaro.

The eighth chapter of his work contains many interesting statements with regard to Russia. On the

26th of September 1476, Contarini came to Moscow, where he presented himself to the grand-prince, Ivan Vasileivich III ("il Duca Zuanne, Signor della gran Rossia bianca"), was well received, and astonished at the magnificence of the court. He describes the situation and architecture of Moscow, speaks of the cold there, of the trade in sables, ermines, fox-skins, badger-skins, lynx-skins, and those of other animals, which were brought thither from the farthest north, and makes some observations on the manners and mode of life of the Russians. Contarini quitted Moscow on the 24th of January 1477, and continuing his journey on sledges[1] through Novogorod, made his way homeward.

Copious accounts of Contarini and his travels will farther be found in—

Beckmann's Liter. d. ält. Reisebeschr., I, 193-198.
Zurla di Marco Polo, etc., vol. ii, p. 230-235.

Editions of Contarini's travels—

Questo e el viazo de misier Ambrosio contarin ambassador de la illustrissima signoria de Venesia al signor Vxuncassam Re de Persia. Impressum Venetia per Hannibalem Fosium parmensem anno 1487; 4to.

This first edition is very rare.

Itinerario del magnifico e clariss. Ambrosio Contarini,

[1] His words are:—"Li detti Sani sono quasi à modo di una casa, et con un cavallo davanti si strascinano, et sono solo per i tempi del ghiaccio, et à ciascuno conviene haver il suo. In questi sani vi si siede dentro, con quanti panni si vuole, et si governa il cavallo, et fanno grandissimo cammino, et portansi anche dentro tutte le vettovaglie, et ogn' altra cosa necessaria."

mandato (da Venetia) nel anno 1472 ad Usuncassan Re di Persia. Vineggia, 1523; 4to.

Viaggio del Ambrosio Contarini, Ambasciadore di Venetia ad Ussuncassan, Rè di Persia. In Raccolta de' Viaggi pubblicata da Antonio Manuzzi. In Venezia, 1545, 8vo.

Il Magnifico Ambrosio Contarini gentilhuomo Venetiano, che mandato ambasciadore dall' Illustrissima Signoria di Venetia ad Vssumcassan Rè di Persia, scrive il suo viaggio molto particolarmente, et descrive li siti della città, i costumi, et stati, non solo de' popoli Persiani, ma anco di molte altre provincie, per le quali passò nel suo viaggio. In Raccolta di Ramusio, vol. ii, fol., 112A-125A.

Contarini's travels are translated into Latin, French, Russian, and Polish.

Latin, by Jacob Geuder von Gerolzberg, in Bizari's Rerum Persicarum historia. Francof., 1601; fol.

A Latin extract from these travels will be found in De Laet's "Persia", p. 220.

French. Voiage de Perse, par Ambroise Contareni, Ambassadeur de la République de Venise en ce Royaume là, en l'année MCCCCLXXIII. Décrit par lui même. In Bergeron's "Recueil de divers Voyages curieux faits en Tartarie, en Perse et ailleurs," etc. Amsterdam, 1724; 4to., vol. ii.

Polish, in an extract, viz., Contarini's travels through Poland. In Skarbiec, Historii polskiej przez Karola Sienkiewieza; 4 vols. Paris, 1839; 8vo.

(27.)

NICLAUS POPPEL. 1486-1489.

Niclaus Poppel, whose birth-place is unknown, was sent by the Emperor Frederick III on two embassies to the court of Russia: the first in 1486, the second in 1489. Adelung received the information which he has been able to supply respecting this traveller from Mr. F. G. Müller, keeper of the Russian Imperial Archives, which contain partial accounts of both these embassies. It is easy, says Adelung, to perceive that Poppel, the first time as well as the second, had been furnished with a letter from his emperor to the grand-prince, but that at Moscow the validity of the first letter was doubted. The Boyars had expressed their suspicion, that Poppel might have written the letter himself, and that he had been despatched by the king of Poland to operate for the advantage of the latter with the grand-prince. Poppel thereupon proposed, that the grand-prince should send an ambassador with him to the emperor, to testify to his innocence. It would appear that some one had really been sent to Vienna, but confirmatory accounts to this effect are wanting. In any case, we may take it, that Poppel's first embassy to the grand-prince was not particularly well received; and hence it may have happened, that neither the original, nor a copy, nor a translation of the first imperial letter, is to be found among the archives.

Poppel's second embassy, says Müller, had with it a peculiarity which tended in some measure to protect him from the suspicions to which he had been exposed in the first. It had for its object, among other things, to propose that a strict alliance should be entered into between the two courts to support each other against their enemies. The imperial letter, dated from Ulm, the 26th of December 1488, is not indeed to be found; but we have the proposals of the ambassador, and what he received in answer, carefully protocoled, after he had been three times admitted to audience with the grand-prince. From these we learn that Poppel, at his own request, was allowed to hold his third audience with this prince in private, and without an interpreter. From this latter fact, we may conclude that he was of Sclavonic descent.

Poppel, at his first audience, sought above all to gain the favour of the grand-prince and his Boyars; informing them, that upon his return from his first journey, he had been asked by the emperor (whom he had met at Nurnberg) and by all the princes to give them information concerning the kingdom of Russia, of which but little was then known in Germany. He also informed them, that he had had an opportunity, and had availed himself of it, to make them acquainted with the general state of Russia, from his own observation, and had described the almost boundless extent of the countries and nations subject to its sovereign, on whose power, riches, and wisdom, he had been able to speak as an eye-witness.

His second object was to justify himself against the suspicions which the Boyars entertained, that he was not really an ambassador from the emperor, but that he assumed that name and title as an emissary from the king of Poland. "People," he says, "have believed, that I have prepared the imperial letter myself, and have desired that I should write something, that it may be compared with that letter;

while I, on the other hand, requested that an ambassador should be sent with me to the emperor. That was done,[1] and I trust that now you will place more confidence in my integrity."

Hereupon he brought forward his proposals, and begged that they might be kept secret. The first point was, if the grand-prince were not indisposed, to unite in wedlock one of his princesses to the margrave Albert of Baden, the emperor's sister's son; the emperor in that case would forward the matter, and enter into an alliance of love and friendship with the grand-prince.[2] Such an unexpected desire demanded consideration: the grand-prince sent answer to the ambassador, through the diak Feodor Kirizin, that he would explain himself thereupon through a special ambassador.

Poppel, at his second audience, expressed a wish to be allowed to see the princess who was desired in marriage for the margrave of Baden: to which he received for answer,—" that it was not the custom in Russia to let the daughter be seen before the befitting time."

Poppel now begged a third audience, at which he stated, that he had understood that an ambassador

[1] The ambassador sent by the grand-prince with Poppel was Jurj Trachaniota, or, as Müller calls him, Trachaniotton, the well-known Greek, who had arrived in Russia on the marriage of the grand-prince with the Greek princess Sophia, and was frequently employed in affairs demanding talent and subtlety.—*Adelung's note.*

[2] Müller on this observes:—" Thus at this time they sought to strengthen the power of the German empire by an alliance with Russia, notwithstanding the remoteness of these countries, a fact of which history gives many proofs."—*Adelung's note.*

had been despatched to the pope from the grand-prince, with a request that the latter might have the title of King of Russia bestowed upon him; but as it was not in the power of the pope, but of the emperor alone, to name kings, princes, and knights, he (Poppel) would interest himself with the emperor to gain him such title, since that was his wish; but that in such case the matter must be kept very secret, and that the king of Poland must know nothing about it. To this proposal, the grand-prince gave the ambassador for answer, " that he was, through God's grace, sovereign of his own countries from the beginning and by right of his ancestors, and held his station from God, and prayed to God that it might be so preserved to him and his children; and as in times past he had never desired the nomination of any other power, so neither did he then."

Poppel quitted Moscow in March 1489, and took his way home through Sweden and Denmark, in which countries also he had commissions from the emperor.

The account of his travels is probably still to be found among the imperial archives of Vienna.

See also respecting Poppel: Hormayr's "Archiv für Geographie," etc. Wien, 1819; No. 47.

(28.)

GEORG VON THURN. 1490-1492.

Georg von Thurn was sent by Maximilian, king of the Romans, as ambassador to Moscow, where he arrived on the 10th of July 1490, and was received with many proofs of honour. A few days after his arrival, he was admitted to an audience with the grand-prince, and, what until then had been very unusual, also with the grand-princess Sophia. He stated the wish of Maximilian to enter into closer alliance with the grand-prince, and at the same time to marry a daughter of the latter; and begged, in the event of this request being favourably received, to be allowed to see the princess, and to be informed what would be the amount of her dowry. With respect to religion, she should be entirely free; and it would be permitted her to have a Greek church and its priests. To this the ambassador received for answer, that it was not the custom in Russia to set out the princesses for show, and moreover, that it was unheard of among great monarchs, to fix the dowry prior to marriage; after marriage, the grand-prince would certainly endow his daughter proportionately to her rank. On the point of religion, the ambassador was desired to give a letter of assurance; but to the drawing up of this, he did not consider himself authorized.

Thurn was more fortunate than his predecessor in concluding an alliance between the grand-prince and Maximilian,—the first which had been effected between the Russian and Austrian courts. The letter which Ivan III sent to his new ally on that occasion, and which he had previously confirmed by kissing the cross, no longer exists in the original, but only in a cotemporaneous copy, preserved among the archives at Moscow.

The ambassador, as a proof of the satisfaction of

the grand-prince, received from him presents, which for that time must be regarded as extremely handsome, viz., a gold chain with a cross, an ermine mantle covered with satin worked in gold, and a pair of silver-gilt spurs.

Thurn left Moscow on the 19th of August 1490, in company with Trachaniota, already mentioned, and the diak Vasiley Kuleschin, who came with a duplicate of the document prepared by Ivan, to have it signed by Maximilian. They arrived on St. George's day, 1491, at Nuremberg, where a diet was then being held, and where the treaty of alliance was signed on the part of Maximilian. Of this official document neither the original nor a copy could be found by Müller at Moscow, but only a cotemporaneous Russian translation of it.

In November of the same year, Thurn was sent for a second time to Moscow, where he arrived on the 20th, and was admitted to an audience on the 26th. He conveyed his master's excuses for breaking off the union which he had previously wished for with a daughter of the grand-prince. He was instructed to state that a rumour had spread in Germany during his first absence, that he had been lost at sea. Maximilian had, thereupon, believed that his marriage proposals had not been mentioned; and hence, by the advice of his father and the princes of the kingdom, he had betrothed himself to the princess Anne of Brittany, through which circumstance the whole matter was at an end.

The ambassador then came to the subject of the

alliance which had been concluded between the two monarchs, and which had been confirmed by Maximilian with an oath in the presence of the Russian deputies, and now begged that the grand-prince would do the same in his presence on his side. This ceremony was performed without demur, by the kissing of the cross.

Thurn, after having thus successfully carried out all the instructions of his court, returned to Germany on the 12th of April 1492.

The narrative of this embassy is to be found among the imperial archives of Vienna.

Respecting Georg von Thurn, the reader may consult Hormayr's " Archiv für Geographie, Historie, Staats und Kriegskunst". Wien, 1819; No. 47.

(29.)

MICHAEL SNUPS. 1492.

In the year 1492 an Austrian embassy appeared at Moscow of altogether a novel character, namely, one professing to have for its object the advancement of knowledge and science. The archduke Sigismund, who took especial interest in collecting accounts of foreign countries and nations, despatched from Innspruck, where he then held his court, an able man to Moscow, and provided him with letters to the grand-prince from himself and from his nephew Maximilian, king of the Romans. This traveller was Michael Snups, whose name is only known to us through the Russian archives; he was charged to make himself acquainted with this and other countries of Europe but little known at that period, and for this purpose was required to learn the Russian language. The archduke had especially begged permission for him to travel into the interior of the kingdom, and even to venture as far as the Obi.

It was not found advisable in Moscow, however, through the general distrust of foreigners which still prevailed there, to favour such a journey, the reason being assigned that the Obi was too distant, and the difficulties of such a journey for a foreigner much too great, as even the officers who were sent to bring the tribute of those parts had always to contend with the greatest difficulties on the road. Snups now wished to return through Turkey or Poland; but this, too, was denied him, under the pretence of the great insecurity of the journey; and nothing more remained for him than to make his return by the way he had come, namely, through Livonia and Germany. The letters in reply, which the grand-prince intrusted to him for Maximilian, are dated the 5th of January 1493, and copies of them exist among the archives at Moscow.

The original of Michael Snups' narrative of his travels is probably still to be found in Innspruck or Vienna.

(30.)

JUSTUS KANTINGER. 1504.

After the battle against the Livonians, near Pleskov', on the 7th of September 1501, which proved so disastrous to the Russian army, the emperor Maximilian despatched an ambassador, named Justus Kantinger, to the grand-prince Ivan Vasileivich, to express, though somewhat tardily, his sympathy, and to offer his assistance. This, at least, was the official purport of his embassy; while at the same time he was to make himself particularly acquainted with the position of the grand-prince, and the state of affairs in Russia. The emperor's letter is dated from Augsburg, the 6th of August 1502. In another confidential letter of the 12th of August, of which Kantinger, here called the Imperial Falconer, was also the bearer, the Emperor begged to have some white falcons (kretschati) sent to him by this messenger. The grand-prince answered the first despatch in a very long and courteous letter. In a second letter he informs the emperor that he had sent him five falcons, which, for caution and on account of their great value, he had forwarded by an officer of rank, named Michaila Klepik Jeropkin.

In the following year Kantinger was sent a second time into Russia. On this occasion, however, he went, for some unknown reason, to Narva only; and from this place sent, through the medium of the governor of Ivanogorod, a letter of the emperor Maximilian's, dated at Costnitz, the 6th of March 1505, addressed to the grand-prince; and another from the emperor's son, King Philip of Castile, from Brussels, dated the 13th of October 1504, to the grand-prince and his son Vasiley Ivanovich. The principal object of these letters was the liberation of certain distinguished

Livonian prisoners of war, who, as German knights, were under the Imperial protection. These letters came to Moscow on the 16th of June, and the answer of the grand-prince reached Kantinger at Narva, on the 19th of the same month, on which day he returned for Germany. In the superscription of the letter of King Philip, the grand-prince as well as his son was addressed by the title of czar, an honour now for the first time paid to the princes of Russia by the Imperial court.

Kantinger's account of his two journeys must still, without doubt, be preserved among the Imperial archives at Vienna.

(31.)
SIGISMUND BARON VON HERBERSTEIN.
1517-26.

Next to Justus Kantinger in chronological rotation, comes the author of the " Commentarii" which we now for the first time present to the reader in an English dress. His biography, as has been already stated, has been minutely elaborated by Adelung, in an octavo volume published in St. Petersburg in 1818. Apart from the results of much learned investigation by Adelung himself, he mentions the following works as supplying him with the principal materials of his information:—

1. An autobiography of our traveller, published in Vienna, 1560, folio, under the title, " Gratæ posteritati Sigismundus Liber Baro in Herberstain

Neyperg et Guettenhag, etc., actiones suas a puero ad annum usque ætatis suæ septuagesimum quartum, brevi commentariolo notatas reliquit." In the copy of this work in the Grenville Library, are inserted original drawings of Herberstein, in the various dresses worn by him in his several embassies, accompanied by cotemporaneous engravings from the same drawings. From one of these, the etching which forms the frontispiece of the present translation has been made. The work itself is of extreme rarity.

2. An autobiography, which was only printed so recently as 1805, at Buda, by Martin George Kovachich, in his " Sammlung kleiner noch ungedruckter Stücke, in welchen gleichzeitige Schriftsteller einzelne Abschnitte der ungarischen Geschichte aufgezeichnet haben." It bears the following title, " Mein Sigmunden Freyherrn zu Herberstain, Neyperg und Guttenhag, Raittung, und Antzaigen meines Lebens und Wesens wie hernach volgt."

3. Sigmund Freyherr zu Herberstain, Neyperg, und Guttenhag, oberster Erbcamrer vnd oberster Druchsass in Kärnttn. Den Gegenwurtign vnd nach komendn Freyherrn zu Herberstain. Seines thuns dienstn vnnd Raisens mit trewer vermanung sich zu tugenden vnd gueten weesn schicken Gedruckt zu Wienn in Oestereich durch Raphaeln Hoffhalter. Folio; without date or place of publication.

4. Sigmundt Freyherr zu Herberstain, Neyperg, vnd Guttenhag, Oberster Erbcamrer vnd Oberster Erbdrucksas in Kärnthn, des Röm: Kayser Ferdi-

nanden Ratt, Camrer, vnd president der Niederösterreichischen Camer. Den viertn Khayser erlebt, den Dreyen in Kriegen, Achte jn Ratn, Polschaftn hie vertzaichnet, vnd vilen andern auch geferlichen Raysn, vier vnd viertzig jar gedient. M. D. lviij in Maio; one sheet and a half, folio, without place of publication, but probably Vienna.

5. Sigismundus Liber Baro in Herberstain Neyperg et Guetenhag, Ducatus Carinthiæ Supremus Hæreditarius et Camerarius et Dapifer: Serenissimi D. Domini Ferdinandi Rom. Hungariæ et Bohemiæ Regis, Archiducis Austriæ: Ærarii Consilii præsidens. Excellentissimo Domino Henrico Lorito Glareano Patricio Claronensi Poetæ Laureato Amico suo S. D.

"This work," says Adelung, "consisting of five folio leaves, is a strenuous attempt to vindicate the Baron von Rozzendorf, who was accused of treason; and is likewise a defence of himself from the charge brought by Poland against him, of giving the title of king to the Grand Duke of Russia. Although this appears to be the exclusive intention of the work, it contains in addition very many lights and disclosures respecting Herberstein's public life, which we have not failed to make use of."

Sigismund Baron von Herberstein was born on the 23rd of August 1486, in the castle of Wippach, granted to his father by the Emperor Frederick III, in the circle of Adelsberg, on a river of the same name in Carniola. His father was Leonhart, or Lienhart von Herberstein, a valiant warrior much in favour with the emperor, whom he attended to Rome on the occasion of his coronation; and to Naples, at the celebration of his marriage. During a second progress of the emperor into Italy he received the honour of knighthood in Rome, and in his later years became governor of Adelsberg and bailiff of Wippach. Sigismund's mother was Barbara, the daughter of Niclaus Luegger, burgrave of Linz and Lueg.

Such records of the noble family of Herberstein as are indisputable ascend to the thirteenth century. Petrus Paganus speaks of it as " familiam ultra memoriam hominum nobilem et equestris ordinis dignitate conspicuam"; and the details of the history of this distinguished family were found sufficient to fill a thick and closely printed octavo volume, published by J. A. Kumar, in three parts; Vienna, 1817. Herberstein traces the names of his ancestors up to the middle of the thirteenth century, and relates various circumstances connected with them after the year 1400. Of the early times of his family, he relates the following droll anecdote, which may be repeated here for the sake of the practical conclusion which he draws. " I have heard," says he, " from my parents, who also had it from hearsay, that once there were seven knights who lived at Herberstein, who had only one pair of breeches amongst them. I have also been told, that nine ladies of the Herberstein family were married in the same mantle. For the certainty of this, I will not answer; but it is not improbable. It only shows how the times are changed, for now-a-days no gentleman would be satisfied without seven pairs of breeches, and no lady without nine mantles."[1]

The ancient hereditary estate of this family was Herberstein, an Austrian territory with a castle, near Stubenberg, on the River Feistritz, in the circle of Grätz in Styria, which one Otto von Harperg purchased in the year 1290, and the name of which he adopted for himself and his descendants. This purchase, nevertheless, does not appear to have given rise to the family name of Herberstein. The most ancient lord of the race whom Sigismund could find bearing the name, was Hans von Herberstein, curate of Pölan about the year 1200. He mentions also a tradition, that at first they bore the name of Herulstein, from the Heruli, who waged war against Istria and Pannonia, under Odoacer, in 475.

Leonhart von Herberstein had nine children, viz., four sons, of whom Sigismund was the third, and five daughters. Herberstein himself bears witness to the

[1] For the amusement of the reader, we give here Herberstein's German in all its original quaintness. "Von meinen Eltern hab ich auch vernomen, die gleichwol nur von hörn sagen geredt, das siben Ritter zu ainer zeit da zu Herberstain gewont soltn haben darunder nur ainer hosen getragen, Gleicher masse auch vernomen, das Neun Herberstainerin auss ainem Mantel verheyrat wärn. So ist mir zu meinen tagen ainer zuckumen der gesagt hat, Er wär deren ainer von den Neun die auss ainem Mantel verhayrat sein. Das setz ich auch für khain gewishait, So es aber also war alsmüglich ist, So findt man daraus, wie sich das weltlich wesen verendert nach der zeit, Jetzo wil Kainer an (ohne) siben Par hosen auch Khaine an neün Mantln zu friden oder benugig sein, So wirt vnser jtzigs weesen auch nit ewig besteen."

mutual affection of all the brothers for each other, and states that throughout their whole life they lived in the greatest harmony; he particularly speaks with the utmost gratitude of George, the eldest, as a most excellent and distinguished man, who by his advice and example had produced the most salutary influence on the formation of his youthful character. In the early years of his life, Sigismund was very delicate, and soon became so sickly that his parents despaired of human help, and made a vow to send him to the celebrated monastery of Our Lady at Loretto. His second brother Hans, who must have been at least fifteen years older than himself, accompanied him in this journey. The brothers embarked at Lovrana, a little harbour of Liburnia, and sailed for Ancona, whence they proceeded on horseback to the end of their pilgrimage. This so-called pious expedition, we are told, had the most beneficial effects; so that Sigismund, when only eight years old, was well able, after his return, to attend the school in his native town of Wippach. His parents afterwards sent him to school at Lonsbach. Here he learned German and Windisch, or Sclavonic, which latter language subsequently proved of the greatest service to him, although his schoolfellows, on this account, called him a Windisch slave. Petrus Paganus, speaking upon this point, says that the people used to exhibit great animosity against their neighbours upon the subject of differences in language, and that Herberstein consequently was exposed to the frequent taunts of his school-fellows, because he, being a German, and sprung from a German race, spoke the Sclavonic language; and that he only overcame their unkind treatment by patient endurance.

In the year 1495, in the ninth year of his age, his father sent him to Gurk, in the circle of Klagenfurt, and placed him under the care of Wilhelm Weltzer, a relative by his mother's side, who was provost of the cathedral of that place. He often speaks with the greatest gratitude and satisfaction of his two years' residence with this relation; and describes him " as a true nobleman, who loved nobility, and brought up many noble children in learning and every other needful branch of education." He names also ten young noblemen, who were the companions of his studies and his games, and who shortly after by a remarkable accident were his companions in arms in his first campaign.

In 1497, Sigismund was sent to the public school at Vienna, under the care of Master George Ratzenperger, of whose integrity, goodness, and friendship, he frequently speaks, in his autobiography,[1] in the highest terms.

Two years after, viz. in 1499, Herberstein had the misfortune to lose his mother; shortly after which he went to the University at Vienna, where he became a student under the rector Oswald Ludwig von Weickerstorff. That he made good use of his time at Vienna under the tuition of Christoph Kalber, Paul Rockner, and also his paternal friend George Ratzenperger, is shown by the judgment of his cotemporaries, his con-

[1] Published by Kovachich; Ofen, 1805, 8vo.

stant love of his masters, and, more than all, by the subsequent events of his brilliant and laborious life. In the year 1502, when he was sixteen years old, after a most honourable and protracted examination, he was created by the rector Kaltenmarkter, bachelor of arts, or, as he himself calls it, half-master (*Halb-Meister*), a degree which brought down upon him from his frivolous companions many sneers and sarcastic appellations, such as doctor, student, scribe, etc.; " yet with all this," says the excellent Herberstein, " Latin and the arts have not been suffered to escape me, but I have loved them, persevered in, and profited by them,—thanks to God and my father, and especially my masters, who urged me on to these studies, and have remained faithful to me, and imparted them to me, whilst I remained at school." And in another place he says: " In the year 1502, I became bachelor of arts, a degree of which many are ashamed, but upon which I congratulate myself. How faithful have my masters and instructors been to me. God give them all eternal peace for their reward. Amen."

Herberstein appears soon afterwards to have left Vienna, and to have returned to his father's roof; and it was not long before an opportunity occurred by which to turn his various attainments to advantage, and at the same time not only to employ but to expand his intellect by his having committed to him the charge of very important business. His father sent him to the court of the Emperor Maximilian, that he might advance the interests of certain family concerns there; and he was also charged with similar commissions to the cities of Neustadt and Grätz. Four years were thus passed in these more private trials of his ability before we see Herberstein make his appearance in a public capacity. This period was divided between journeys, residences in the capital on the score of business, his own labours, and reading of the ancient as well as some of the modern historians. With respect to these last occupations, he himself says: "My most conscientious preceptor, Master George Ratzenperger, admonished me by no means to neglect my learning, and promised me that if I would devote at least one hour in the day to reading, it would be of great service to me. I did so, and as from time to time I studied the histories of modern writers, I remarked especially that in certain points they either from too much zeal and tendency to flattery wandered very far from the truth, or sometimes by a frivolous description detracted from the merits of good men, or attributed to others more than was just."

After this period he entered the army, and made his first campaign at the early age of twenty. It began by his accompanying his brother George to the war which Maximilian, without provocation or even the proclamation of hostilities, had commenced against Hungary, in consequence of his fear of losing his claim to the throne of that kingdom through the marriage of John Zapolski, count of Zips, with the daughter of Vladislaus, king of Hungary. This was in March 1506; but as peace was concluded that same year, Herberstein had very little opportunity of distinguishing himself. In 1508, the Venetians deprived the emperor of his possessions in Friuli, Carniola, and Istria, in which latter country Herberstein's father possessed the territory of Mährenfels; and during a short armistice, he was sent in 1509 to Venice, on a diplomatic mission to recover this estate, but he was not successful in his endeavours. During his stay in Venice, he witnessed the great fire in which the celebrated arsenal was consumed. In the same year, the lower Austrian states sent a corps to the assistance of the emperor to Friuli, under Duke Erick of Brunswick. Herberstein was in this corps, and was present in different engagements. Not long after, his eldest brother sent him, with twelve horsemen and thirty-two foot soldiers, to Mitterburg, in order to garrison the place; and he undertook this charge, because, as he says in his book, nobody else would go there. In this expedition he attacked Alben, from which place the enemy, together with the faithless inhabitants, fled at his approach. "They took refuge in a church," he says; " and when the Croats asked if they should break into it, as they should take many prisoners, I replied, that one ought not to touch the house of God. For this, God afterwards rewarded me." In the same year he was present at the siege and capture of Rasburg, where he distinguished himself so much, that on the 4th of October, he was taken into the immediate service of the emperor, or, as he himself describes it, in *Cohortem Prætorianam.* In March 1510, the Venetians again besieged Mitterburg, which was without means of defence and threatened with the rebellion of its own inhabitants. Herberstein was then in Mährenfels, and was asked by the commandant of Mitterburg to obtain assistance from the Duke of Brunswick; but as he could not pass through the country, he went himself to Mitterburg, where he found matters in a very bad state. The walls were already much injured by the enemy, and the inhabitants as well as the garrison were unwilling to obey the orders of the commandant, and deserted. The commandant urged Herberstein to take the command, but he would not accept it, and only consented to act conjointly with him. He succeeded in re-establishing order, and in compelling the enemy to withdraw. By this he gained great distinction from the duke, who was coming to assist the fortress, and on the road gained information of the delivery that had been effected. In this campaign he distinguished himself as much by prudence and order as by courage; and the states of Styria offered him in consequence the post of Paymaster of the Forces.

In the following year, viz., 1511, he lost his father, for whom he entertained a very warm affection, as is sufficiently shown by his writings, although it is but seldom that his parents are alluded to in them. He hastened to Wippach, in order to attend his father's funeral, from which place the body was afterwards brought to Grätz. Nothing specially worthy of remark appears to have occurred in the two following years of his life; it is probable that during that period he was occupied with family matters.

The year 1514 presents us with more that is worthy of notice. We now begin to find him invested with great honours, and raised to a position which shows the confidence reposed in him at so early an age as twenty-eight. It was a high distinction at such an age to be made standard-bearer,—an honour which he held as a glorious remembrance till his death, and was proud of leaving it, amongst many other glorious reminiscences, to his descendants. The fortress of Maran, in Friuli, was besieged by the Venetians, and the inhabitants suffered the most dreadful famine, upon which Maximilian ordered Herberstein and his brother George to raise troops in Styria in order to relieve the place, and to convey provisions into it. Herberstein repulsed the enemy on the 12th of July, and took the leader, Giovanni Vittoria, prisoner. The remembrance of this exploit must have been dear to Herberstein in his old age, as he has immortalized it in two wood-cuts. Immediately after the campaign, the emperor summoned him to Innspruck, where the court was then held, and knighted him, as a reward for his distinguished services, and gave him a yearly salary of three hundred florins. He also gave him rank immediately below his own officers, and not long after he took him into the Imperial Council.

Even so early as the year 1515 Herberstein was employed in important diplomatic missions to the Archbishop of Salzburg; and afterwards to Ulm, Eichstatt, and Bavaria. At the end of the year, he went to Innspruck, where the emperor then was, and received from him an expression of his satisfaction, together with an order to remain at court, as his services would shortly be again put into requisition.

With the year 1516 really begins the great diplomatic and active career of Herberstein, as he then undertook the first journey to Russia. Before starting on this, however, he was employed on a mission, the management of which was also very difficult, and required extraordinary prudence and perseverance. Christian II of Denmark had two years before married Isabella, second daughter of Philip of Spain, a princess adorned with all the good qualities of her race; but that her lot could not be a happy one, may be judged from the character and public actions of that voluptuous tyrant. She complained to Charles of Burgundy, and to her powerful grandfather, the emperor Maximilian, of the shameful neglect she suffered on account of the ill-famed Dyveke and her mother Siegbrit, for the former of whom the king was possessed with a most infatuated affection. The queen also even complained of being personally ill-treated. The two monarchs, thus appealed to by their relative, resolved to send ambassadors to Christian, in order to remonstrate with him, and to require that he should show better treatment to his wife; and this very difficult and, in any case, ungrateful office was assigned by the emperor to Herberstein. He left the court in January 1516, and after fulfilling various commissions assigned to him by the way, came to Nykoping, where the unfortunate Queen Isabella then resided. Here he found also two ambassadors from Charles of Spain, who were waiting for him. The king arrived shortly after, and without much delay granted Herberstein an audience, not however, as one would suppose, in the Royal Palace, but in a convent of the Cordeliers, at a short distance from Herberstein's hotel. This may probably have been caused by a suspicion of the purpose of Herberstein's mission, and a wish to avoid having witnesses to so disagreeable a conference. Indeed, the king on this occasion was told such things as he had never heard from any one before, for Herberstein's own words are, " I have told the king that he had acted unfairly, unjustly, and dishonestly, against the emperor and his friends. The king listened to me standing, and when I uttered these sharp words, I read them from a paper, that I might not say too much or too little." His majesty allowed him to conclude without interruption; and then the other ambassadors, who stood at each side of him, declared that what he had said conveyed the sentiments of their own masters also. The king must have been moved, or at least embarrassed, by the noble boldness of Herberstein, for he did not give his answer immediately, but said that he would reply on a future occasion. Soon after, Herberstein was admitted, together with the Spanish and Netherlands ambassadors, to an audience of the queen, on which occasion he received the honourable distinction of being permitted to read his address sitting, whereas the others were obliged to read their's in a kneeling posture. At length the king sent for Herberstein, and gave him a verbal answer for the emperor, but of too evasive and vague a character to satisfy the shrewd and resolute diplomatist. He had, therefore, the courage to tell the king, that neither the emperor nor the prince of Spain expected such an answer; nor would they believe that His Majesty would set a higher value upon a low woman than upon his own conscience, the laws of God, Christian order, his own honour, and the feelings of friendship. Herberstein demanded that at least the king's answer should be written down and sealed with the king's seal, but this Christian declined to do. All that Herberstein could obtain, after long parleying, was a short and unmeaning letter from the chancellor; but it seems that the king, although his honour was insulted, could not but appreciate the straightforwardness of the honest ambassador, for he sent him, as a present, a beautiful horse with saddle and equipments complete.

On the 10th of April he returned to Germany. He found the emperor at Tannheim, in the Tyrol, whom, after having reported the result of his mission, he was obliged to follow to Constanz.

After this, in the course of the same year he was sent several times to Zurich; and finally, at the close of the year, was sent on the most important mission upon which he had yet been engaged, namely, an embassy to Moscow, which expedition had been set on foot for a twofold purpose. It has been already mentioned, that in consequence of the marriage of the daughter of Vladislas with John Zapolski, the emperor entertained fears of his claim to the throne of Hungary being set aside, a fear which was increased by the position assumed by Sigismund, king of Poland, who had married Barbara, John Zapolski's sister. Sigismund himself likewise laid claim to some provinces in Hungary, which had not been renounced by his mother, Elizabeth of Austria, on her marriage,—the arms of which he included in his heraldic coat. The emperor, therefore, endeavoured to weaken the power of Sigismund by engaging the grand-prince of Russia in a war with that sovereign. Subsequently, however, he resorted to a different line of policy, and thought of gaining his point by bringing about marriages between his own family and that of Hungary and Poland.

One of these plans was, that Sigismund should marry Maximilian's granddaughter Bona, the daughter of John Galeozzi Sforza, Duke of Milan. With this new view, therefore, the emperor resolved upon sending an embassy to Moscow to mediate for Sigismund. Eighteen months, however, transpired, to the emperor's dissatisfaction, before the embassy started on its journey; for Christoff Rauber, bishop of Laybach, who had been appointed chief ambassador (Herberstein being only his second), made so many excuses, and, in spite of the instigations of the ambassador of Poland, who had been ordered at the same time for Moscow, and urged his speedy departure, took so long a time in preparing for his journey, that the emperor altered his plan, and charged Herberstein temporarily with the conduct of this embassy, in company with one Peter Mraxi, bailiff of Guntz. As a source of further delay, this latter also was prevented, through a journey which he was compelled to make previous to his departure, from joining Herberstein till some time after. The emperor, who had wished to finish the whole business when in Augsburg, left that place in October, and desired Herberstein to follow him. They passed through Tyrol, Switzerland, and Brisgau, to Hagenau, from which place at last Herberstein was despatched alone to Moscow on the 14th of December.

A journey to Russia at that time naturally offered many difficulties, partly real and partly imaginary. The real ones were caused by the great distance, by the severity of the climate, surpassing in coldness that of all other European countries, the danger of passing the rivers increased at this season by the floating ice, the bad state and insecurity of the high roads, more especially at this time from the cruel war which had been carried on now for many years between Poland and Russia, by the neglect with which foreigners were then generally treated in Russia, and finally by the difficulty of making themselves clearly understood. The imaginary difficulties consisted in the imperfect knowledge and strange notions which they had of the countries to be passed through, and especially of that northern country Russia, the dreadful name of which only summoned up to the imaginations of the then uninformed inhabitants of the south, the thought of encountering Scythians and barbarians, cruelty, ice, and darkness. Any journey, therefore, to Moscow, could not fail of being regarded as a very hazardous enterprise; and whoever managed to avoid it congratulated himself on escaping a great danger. How many qualities then must the man have united in himself who was to keep his dignity in a country so little known and so entirely different to all the countries of Europe in manners and customs, who could gain respect for his own person and a successful result of his mission. And all these qualities were found in a rare and happy combination in Herberstein. Possessing, as he did, a noble prepossessing countenance—a countenance shewing tranquillity and dignity—a demeanour formed by travelling, and long experience in courts and by intercourse with men of all ranks, and, together with all these very rare advantages, attainments such as could rarely be found at all in statesmen of that time, including the knowledge of the Sclavonic language,—Maximilian could not have made a better choice for a negotiation of so delicate a nature in a country like Russia, with a prince such as Vasiley Ivanovich, to whom already had been given the epithet of the "Courageous". The preference given to Herberstein in this mission was perfectly justified by the result; and although the expected effect for Poland was delayed by the deep-rooted hatred existing between the antagonist monarchs and other circumstances, his stay in Moscow was of effectual service in fastening the alliance between Maximilian and Vasiley. At Augsburg he was joined on his route by a numerous company, mostly consisting of his own attachés, and partly of ambassadors and persons of distinction returning to Moscow. These latter were Dimitrievich Sakrevski, who had been sent by Vasiley Ivanovich to the court of Maximilian, and was now on his return to Moscow, and who must, for several reasons, have been very welcome to Herberstein; and next, Chrisostomos Columnos, sent by Isabella Duchess of Milan, widow of John Sforza, to Poland, to bring about a marriage between her daughter Bona and Sigismund, there being now no obstacle to the marriage, his wife Barbara having recently died.

With this numerous company, then, Herberstein continued his journey through Bavaria. During the last days of December, and the early part of January of the next year, he was compelled by various embarrassments to stay for some weeks in Znaym in Moravia, at which place, his companion Petro Mraxi died. Herberstein was thus obliged to write to Vienna for further instructions. The emperor being absent, he was under the necessity of addressing himself to the imperial council, but received for answer, that as they were not aware of his previous instructions, they could not advise him in the present emergency. Herberstein, therefore, continued his journey alone, a resolution which the emperor afterwards approved of. Others, it is true, were ordered to follow him, but some excuse or another was always brought forward to delay or prevent their departure. He first went to Poland to Wilna, where Sigismund then was, and was admitted to an audience. From Wilna he could not take the shortest and ordinary route by Smolensko, on account of the insecurity which was caused by the war, but was obliged to take a circuitous route and make a passage over many small rivers. Between Wilna and Drissa, he lost the company of the Milanese ambassador, who could not endure the severity of the climate. Near Drissa, he was exposed to a formidable trial of courage, for the passage over the Dwina was on a small strip of ice, and he was informed that not long before six hundred Russians had tried to cross on the ice, and were all drowned. Here he was again joined by the Russian ambassador. At Opochka he was obliged to make a circuit, because it was besieged by Sigismund, although that monarch was at the same time sending messengers of peace to Moscow. He reached Novogorod on Palm Sunday, the 4th of April, and was received with every courtesy by the governor, who expressed his wish to render the stay which he hoped he would make as agreeable as possible, but his real object was of course to gain time, it being the custom immediately to write to Moscow to announce the arrival of an ambassador and obtain permission for the continuance of his journey. Herberstein was anxious to proceed, but was obliged to stay a week in that city, which was even then a place of great note. The German merchants of Novogorod were so impressed with the importance of Herberstein's journey, and regarded him as so remarkable a person, that they begged him to present them with the sledge in which he had travelled from Cracow, and suspended it in their church for a memorial. He left his own servants and horses at Novogorod, and continued his journey with post horses to Vishni Volotchok, where he kept the feast of Easter. Thence he travelled by the river Tverza to Tver. The travellers were anxious to make their passage in a larger vessel, but could not proceed for the floating ice, which caused them great trouble in reaching the shore. On landing, they had to travel for a short time on foot, but at length found some wretched horses at a peasant's house. In the convent of St. Ilia he found a man named Michaila Schaffroff, who came to meet him with a present from the grand-prince to him and to his nephew, of two horses apiece. From this point the grand-prince undertook the entire providing of the company. Shortly before reaching Moscow, an interpreter named Gregory Istumen announced to him the arrival of a noble courtier, sent by the grand-prince to meet him, named Timofei Constantinovich Chaldeneff, and begged Herberstein to descend from his horse in order to listen standing to the greeting which was to be offered him in the name of the grand-prince. Herberstein first excused himself on the score of fatigue, and then only agreed to alight on the condition that the other should do the same at the same moment, and when, after long parleying, this was agreed to, Herberstein contrived to descend very slowly, so that he should not touch the ground before the other.

On the 18th of April he arrived at Moscow with a suite of fifteen noblemen and thirty grooms belonging to the household of the grand-prince. He was conducted to the house of Prince Peter Repolovski, which the grand-prince had appointed for his residence, and which had been prepared very hastily with all necessary furniture and conveniences. An officer, named Ostan, called in Russian podietchi, which means under-secretary, and who was charged with his daily provisions, was allotted to him at the same time. His daily provisions were a large piece of beef, a piece of bacon, a live sheep, one live and one dead hare, six live fowls, vegetables, oats, and once a week, as much salt, pepper, and saffron, as he required; also fish, especially large dried sturgeon; together with a bottle of brandy, three different sorts of mead, and two sorts of beer. According to the season the fish were delivered frozen, but on one occasion when Herberstein sent to get live fish with his own money, it was considered an affront, and from that time he was supplied with live fish.

Herberstein himself says that they placed persons in the house who were considered noble, and whose office it was to keep close watch that nobody should come or go without their knowledge. The general cause of this precaution was to be ascribed to the spirit of the times, but Herberstein himself had partly caused it by an inadvertence which he lays to his own charge. He had been very anxious to gain all the information he could respecting Moscow; he began to do this, as he himself acknowledges, too early, and even on the day of his arrival he made various inquiries of his interpreter, and told him that such information would be very interesting to his countrymen. At the same time he offered to give him information of other countries, and to explain to him the maps which he had brought with him, by which of course he caused suspicion, and was observed so closely that nobody was allowed to visit him unless two or more of his watchful attendants were permitted to be present, and to hear what was said. Afterwards he was more cautious, and was obliged to adopt a very circuitous process when he wanted to gain any information. On the 20th of April he was informed that the grand-prince wished to see him on the following day. Early in the morning several noblemen on horseback were sent to his house to escort him. The nearer he came to the Kremlin, the more the procession increased. All the shops were closed, and the crowding of the curious at such a rare sight was so great that force was necessary to make a passage through them. When they came near the steps of the palace, the grooms leading Herberstein's horse would not allow him to ride near it, but he spurred the horse as near as possible to the steps, in his desire to claim a peculiar honour for his master. Here he was received by the councillors of the grand-prince, who offered him their hands, and saluted him. On the stairs a greater number of courtiers joined the procession. In the ante-room many well-dressed noblemen were sitting and standing, of whom however none spoke to him, or took the least notice of him. In the first state-room were several nobles dressed in silk and brocade. In the second, were the young princes, with other high people, who wore caps richly adorned with pearls and jewels. From this room he was led by the officers into the reception room of the grand-prince, who was sitting on a somewhat raised chair, and had a footstool under his feet. On each side of him sat one of his brothers, and next to the one at his right hand his brother-in-law, Czar Peter, as Herberstein calls him, who was brother of the Tartar Khan, and had been baptized. The whole room was full of princes and nobles, who all arose at Herberstein's entrance. When he had respectfully approached the grand-prince, the latter addressed him first, and told him to stand before him next to a little low bench covered with carpet, which he did, and spoke a few words by way of introductory compliment. When he mentioned the name of the emperor Maximilian, the grand-prince rose from his seat, stood next to the little bench, and asked, " How is our brother Maximilian, elected Roman emperor and high and noble king?" and when the answer was given that Herberstein, at the time of his departure, had left him quite well, he sat down again, and listened to the rest of the speech. After Herberstein had delivered his credentials, he had to give his hand to the grand-prince, who asked him, " Hast thou travelled well?" To which Herberstein had been instructed to answer, " Through the mercy of God and your grace, quite well. God give your grace good health." The grand-prince then bade him sit down, called the interpreter, and whispered to him. The interpreter then approached Herberstein, and told him in a low tone that he might now say what he had to say. Upon this Herberstein rose, and explained in a long speech the object of his mission, of which however the interpreter never would translate more than two or three words at once. Herberstein was at the conclusion of his speech desired again to sit down, when the grand-prince himself invited him to dinner, as it was customary that foreign ambassadors should dine with the grand-prince on the day of their presentation, and on the day of their taking leave.

A few days after the presentation of Herberstein, the negotiations concerning the peace with Poland began, but before the Boyars, whom the grand-prince had appointed for that purpose, would enter into any discussion, they demanded, in the name of their master, that the king of Poland should make his defence for having besieged Opochka, an occurrence which had only recently taken place; and, at the same time required, that if peace were really his desire, he should himself send ambassadors to Moscow. Herberstein thought he might modify this demand by proposing that both parties should send their mediators to Riga, or some other place on the Lithuanian frontier, but the grand-prince insisted on having the Polish ambassadors sent to Moscow. Herberstein, therefore, on the 27th of April, despatched his nephew, John von Thurn, to Wilna, with a letter to the king of Poland, requesting him, in the name of Maximilian, to yield to the wish of the grand-prince, and to send ambassadors to his court. He himself endeavoured zealously to clear away all the difficulties caused by the mistrust against Sigismund, and he succeeded in his other conversations with the grand-prince in obtaining his favour and confidence in a very high degree. It was not without great trouble that Herberstein could prevail upon Sigismund to send ambassadors. At length, however, they arrived; but no sooner had he had an audience and commenced negotiations with them, than the grand-prince received intelligence that Sigismund had already sent a new army into Russia, a circumstance which not only made him suspect the ambassadors, but even Herberstein himself. The latter, nevertheless, was soon able to clear his own character; but when the Polish delegates declared that their king insisted on the restoration of Smolensko, then, in spite of Herberstein's indefatigable exertions, all hopes of a peaceable termination vanished. The grand-prince, however, gave perfect credit to his intentions and his zeal; and in the Russian archives we find, amongst other distinctions given to him, that whenever he was invited to court together with the Poles, the grand-prince always gave him his hand, an honour never bestowed on the other delegates.

At length, on the 15th of November, Herberstein sent in his last memorial, to which he received on the following day a decisive answer, destroying all hopes of a friendly arrangement with Sigismund, and of so definite a character as to cause the Polish delegates to leave Moscow on the 18th of November. Meanwhile Herberstein was treated constantly with regard and respect, and invited to different festivities and amusements of the court; amongst others, he witnessed a coursing match, of which he gives a detailed description; he mentions also a hawking match, in which he makes particular allusion to the beautiful Tartar hounds that were used in the sport. Besides the negotiations for the peace of Poland, Herberstein had received several other communications from the emperor, one about the delivery of the Knes Michaila Lwowich Glinsky from prison, but in this particular he was not successful. As Herberstein at last saw that, in consequence of the obstinate continuation of hostilities by Sigismund, nothing was to be done for the principal purpose of his journey, he asked for his dismissal, which he received at a solemn audience, on the 20th of November, and left Moscow, after a stay of eight months, on the following day.

In his writings, he gives fewer details of this first journey to Russia than of the second. His remarks relate principally to the names of provinces and different tribes of the Russian empire, more especially on the parts of the ocean bordering it, and on the rivers passing through it. At his departure, he received from the grand-prince costly sables, ermines, and Russian hunting dogs, and several rare specimens of produce of the country. He had also made for him a comfortable travelling sledge, with fur accoutrements, and gave him an uncommonly large horse from his own stables, with ample provisions for his journey, and had him conducted to the frontier with a number of his own servants and soldiers, altogether about two hundred horsemen. At the same time a

Russian ambassador, named Vladomir Smenovich Plemerikov, and an interpreter, called Ustoma the Little, accompanied him to Vienna, in order to explain at the imperial court the reasons why the peace with Poland could not be established. Herberstein at this time was able to take the shorter road by Smolensko, for which the grand-prince himself gave him a safe conduct, though part of his men and his horses had been left in Novogorod. He travelled by Smolensko, Wilna, Bulsk, and arrived in Cracow the 25th January 1518, where he was well received by the king, and, after some adventures, arrived at Vienna on the 25th February. Here he stopped a few days to refresh himself, and then went to Innspruck to the emperor, who was very well satisfied, not only with the manner in which he had fulfilled his commissions, but also with the account given to him of the state of Russia, and the manners and customs of its inhabitants, and would sometimes listen to his narrative in the evening, long after his usual hour, till sleep overcame him. As a proof of the emperor's satisfaction with his mission, Herberstein was shortly afterwards presented with the bailiwick of Clamm. After a stay of four weeks, Maximilian sent Herberstein back to Vienna, together with the Russian delegates, and the two new ambassadors destined for Moscow, Francesco da Collo and Antonio de' Conti, who were glad of the occasion to get information from him, and to turn his experience to their own account.

Before Herberstein's departure from Innspruck, he

had already received from the emperor a new commission, which was to take him to Hungary, it being again reported that the count John of Zips was to be appointed regent during the king's minority. Maximilian hastened to prevent this innovation as dangerous to his own claims, and being himself the tutor of the young king, he appointed an extraordinary embassy to Hungary, of which Herberstein was a member. The ambassadors met in Vienna, and without delay hastened to Buda, where just at that time the diet was sitting.[1] The king of Poland being also a guardian of the young king, sent Andreas Tanznitski and the Provost Carnorovski. From the pope likewise a delegate was sent, brother Nicolas, of the noble family of Schönberg, a Dominican, who had possessed the unlimited confidence of Leo the Tenth even when he was a cardinal. At the commencement of the negotiations, this cunning priest showed himself so much in the interest of the emperor, that Herberstein himself says, " I thought he was a godsend."

[1] Hungarian invention of coaches.—Herberstein, in his autobiography, published by Kovachich, 1805, when alluding to his journey to Hungary, speaks of *coaches* under the name of *cotschien* or *kotzschi wägnen*, and adds : " They are so called after a village ten miles distant from Buda (*Kotsee, Kotsch,* now *Kitser*); they are drawn by three horses, which run abreast of each other, and at those times when there is little or no ice on the ground. They carry four persons along with the driver, and it is indeed a very agreeable conveyance—so that any one can convey his bed, clothes, eatables and drinkables, and other conveniences, provided the load be not a heavy one." See also upon this subject, *Beckmann's Hist. of Inventions,* where Herberstein's work on Russia is quoted, but not the above passage, which was not then published.

But he soon shewed his real intentions, for by his craftiness and underhand movements, he contrived, with the assistance of the bishops of Hungary, to carry his point that the pope should be allowed to appoint a nuncio [hauptmann] in Hungary, who should be dependent solely upon himself. He had also the effrontery to state before Herberstein that he himself had given his acquiescence to this arrangement. But as Herberstein had the firmness to declare this statement to be untrue, the wily ambassador did not gain his object, and mainly through Herberstein's adroitness, the adoption of a nuncio was contravened. He was very active all the time he was in Buda, and proved himself a very able diplomatist. He left that city for Augsburg, where Maximilian was holding his last diet before his death, a diet especially celebrated for the presence of Martin Luther, who had been summoned thither by the pope's nuncio, cardinal Cajetan, on the question of the famous ninety-five propositions.

In October 1518, the estates of Styria appointed Herberstein to be their councillor at the imperial court, and the emperor confirmed his appointment. Maximilian died on the 12th of January 1519, and Herberstein was one of the bearers of the imperial pall at the funeral. Maximilian had ordered that all the affairs of the government should remain unaltered until the arrival of his successor, and therefore had appointed a special regency; but several provinces, and more especially Lower Austria, took advantage of the interregnum for introducing alterations in their constitution. In Vienna a committee was formed, consisting of the nobility, university, and citizens, who upset the regency, and got possession of the arsenal and the treasury. At last they agreed to hold a meeting in Pruch an der Muhr, at which Herberstein also was present, and there they came to the conclusion that the provinces of Austria, Styria, Carinthia, Carniola, and Austria ob der Enns, should send embassies to king Charles, to lay their complaints before him, and to invite him to a speedy assumption of the reins of government. Styria appointed Herberstein as their ambassador. The ambassadors met at Villach, and went to Spain by way of Italy, passing through Treviso, Venice, Rome, and Naples. At Naples, Herberstein took ship for Barcelona, but was wrecked at Sardinia. A similar accident happened off Minorca, but at length, after many adventures (among which may be mentioned, that the ship in which he was took fire twice, because, says Herberstein, the German cooks could not manage with small fires), he reached Barcelona. At Barcelona an epidemic was prevailing, so that the emperor had shortly before left the place for Molino del Rey, where the first audience was given.

After a short stay in Spain, during which the new emperor seems to have become much attached to Herberstein, they had their farewell audience on the 17th of December 1519. They returned by the south of France, by Piedmont, Milan, Peschiera, Verona, and Vicenza, to Villach.

Soon after the coronation at Aix-la-Chapelle, the

emperor appointed the 6th of January of the next year, 1521, for the celebrated diet of Worms, the principal object of which was the re-establishment of peace in Germany, but at the same time the emperor was to decide upon several private affairs. Herberstein, therefore, was ordered to appear there on the 24th of February, in order that an interchange of territories, which had already been sanctioned by Maximilian, should be finally settled. This consisted in a transfer of the castle and town of Mährenfels, which belonged to the family of Herberstein, in exchange for the territory of Neyperg in Styria. During the term of his stay, he was appointed to a seat on the imperial council. He mentions in his diaries Martin Luther, who then came to Worms; and speaks of the astonishing crowd of men of all classes that came to see him.

Shortly before his departure from Worms, he saw the archduke Ferdinand, to whose share all the Austrian provinces had fallen, and was received very kindly by him. He returned from Worms to Linz, where he stopped till the arrival of Ferdinand, who came to Linz for his marriage with Mary, daughter of Vladislaus of Hungary. Before Ferdinand returned to the Netherlands, he requested Herberstein to accompany him. Herberstein was then about to marry Helena von Saurau, widow of Graswein zu Weyer, consequently he was obliged to hasten his betrothal, which took place on the 7th of October, and left on the 18th for Brussels, where he arrived on St. Andrew's day, for the celebration of the chapter of the Golden Fleece, which Charles the Fifth celebrated with great pomp. The emperor on that occasion gave him in reward for his services the uncommon distinction of allowing him to add to his own arms those of the archduke of Austria, and of the king of Castile, and to bear as his crest the portraits of the Roman emperor, of the king of Spain, and the czar of Russia. From the Netherlands Herberstein went to Nuremberg, where at the imperial diet he had to represent the archduke Ferdinand. Subsequent to this he was employed upon various commissions: first at Stuttgard, twice to Prague, then to Nördlingen, where the Swabian diet was held, then twice to Hungary, where he succeeded in bringing about an amicable relation between the archduke Ferdinand and king Louis of Hungary.

It was not till this year that Herberstein's marriage with Helena von Saurau, which had been arranged in 1521, could be solemnized. In his Latin autobiography, he mentions his marriage in these few words:—" Hoc anno uxorem duxi"; and, as has been mentioned above, he never speaks about his wife's family, nor of his wife, nor had he any children. But she survived him by nine years, and died in 1575.

Herberstein's second journey to Poland and Russia took place in 1526. The more immediate purpose of this new mission was to return the civilities of Vasiley Ivanovich, who, on receiving the news of Charles the Fifth's election as emperor of the Romans, had sent ambassadors to Spain, expressing his wish for a continuation of the amicable relations between the two countries, and a renewal of the league concluded with Maximilian against the Poles. Charles and Ferdinand, however, were still influenced by the same motives as had caused the first mission of Herberstein, viz., to bring about a durable peace between the grand-prince and the king of Poland. Sigismund, on the other hand, seemed to wish to trust the matter solely to the success of his arms, and possessed too much pride to ask for peace so far as he was concerned. Count Nugaroli, therefore, was sent on behalf of Charles the Fifth, and Herberstein on behalf of the archduke Ferdinand, to Hungary, in order that the king of Poland might be persuaded through the mediation of the king of Hungary; and in this they were successful.

Herberstein, after his return to Vienna, gave an account of the success of his mission to the archduke Ferdinand, then at Augsburg, and received from him a letter of praise, together with his credentials for the embassy to Russia; and, at the same time, Ferdinand desired him to write an account of all the things he might observe in this journey, as he had done before. Charles the Fifth, likewise, who had been obliged by the disturbances in Spain to return to Toledo the year before, expressed his approbation of the choice of Herberstein in a letter to his brother, as well as of the instructions given to him, at the same time bestowing the utmost praise upon Herberstein with respect to his former embassy. A copy of this letter was sent by the archduke to Herberstein, who already had departed on his journey; and, at the same time, unlimited power was given to the ambassadors for all cases in which the instructions received should appear insufficient. They left Vienna on the 12th of January 1526. Besides the principal personages, there were also in the embassy Gunther and Christoph von Herberstein, two distinguished sons of Herberstein's second brother, George. They took the route through Moravia and Silesia to Poland. They had not advanced far when an order from the archduke Ferdinand, dated Augsburg, February 1st, was sent after them, in which both ambassadors were expressly desired to pay the utmost attention to the religion, ceremonies, and ecclesiastical rules of the Church of Russia, for which purpose they had to use as a guide a little book recently published by Johann Fabri, the materials of which had been collected by the author from the above-mentioned Russian ambassadors to Spain during their stay at the court of Ferdinand in Tübingen. It was very favourable for Herberstein's journey that he could join these ambassadors, who were returning to their country by the way of Vienna, and travel to Moscow in their company. The king of Poland imagined that he had good reason to mistrust the intentions of Austria, and from the beginning of this new embassy he ascribed another purpose to it than that which was really correct; and in this suspicion he was corroborated by the circumstance that the ambassadors travelled in the company of the returning Russian delegates. He was therefore quite convinced, as Herberstein afterwards learned from himself, that the emperor was forming a new league with the crown-prince against him. He therefore appeared at the first not to take any notice of the embassy; and contrary to the law of nations, the ambassadors were not received, or provided for, either at the frontier of Poland, or during their travels through that country. The king was then attending the diet at Pedrikov', to which place the ambassadors directed their course, and at some distance they sent messengers to the court to give notice of their arrival, but an answer was sent back to them that the diet was already at an end, and that the king was about to go to Cracow, where they would be received. Upon their arrival in the capital, they were much astonished that there was nobody to welcome them, and that there was not the least preparation made for their reception. Moreover, they had reason to apprehend from different circumstances that the continuation of their journey through Poland would be impeded. Six days after their arrival, however, they obtained an audience of the king, in which they informed him that they were sent to Moscow to negotiate peace between him and the grand-prince, and begged his assistance in effecting so desirable an object, by making some concessions himself. Sigismund, however, received this communication very ungraciously, and asked the ambassadors indignantly, who had desired their masters to trouble themselves about him? that he knew well enough how to bring his enemies to their senses, and wanted no mediator. " What have your masters to do with the Muscovite," said he; "is he their neighbour, or even friend, that they trouble themselves so much about him?" Herberstein then explained to him quietly and with dignity the purpose of their journey, and proved that their travelling in company with the Russian ambassadors was only by accident, and that their sovereigns could not decline to receive an embassy sent from so great a distance purely for the purpose of asking their friendship; that, moreover, their intention was to act according to the precepts of religion in trying to make peace between two Christian sovereigns. If, however, the king should not feel inclined to have these negotiations carried on through the German ambassadors, they were ready to return home, and to give an account to their respective sovereigns of the king's wish, and to wait for the answer. They even would go so far as to show the king their instructions, although this was quite contrary to all custom. This open and noble speech was effectual: Sigismund became more friendly, gave up his mistrust, and finally showed himself ready to enter into a negotiation for the peace which was to be interceded for at Moscow. He endeavoured to facilitate the continuation of their journey, and sent fifty florins to each of them to pay their bill at the hotel, as properly and according to custom he ought to have provided for them from their first arrival. Herberstein thought this occasion favourable for producing the bond which he had received eight years before from the duchess of Milan for the same, to be paid to him in case he succeeded in bringing about the marriage of her daughter Bona with the king of Poland. He therefore delivered this paper to the king, begging for his assistance, and had the pleasure to find the king quite willing to take upon himself the payment of this debt. Herberstein says, in his own words, "He sent me word that when I returned he would give me a favourable answer, and afterwards sent me a thousand florins in good Hungarian gold, like an honest king."

On the 14th. of February, Herberstein and his party left Cracow; and were now able to continue their journey on sledges, which was very convenient for their luggage. They proceeded by way of Lublin to Brest, through a dreadful and very dangerous snow-drift, which compelled them to pass the whole night on the ground under their sledges, which they turned upside down for a screen. Thence to Borisov on the Beresina, which Herberstein supposed to be the Borysthenes of the ancients, drawing his conclusions from Ptolemy and the similarity of the name. From Beresina they did not take the nearest way by Wilna, in consequence of the wildness of the road, but took the way by Mohilev and Dobrovna to Smolensko.

Upon Herberstein's arrival at the Russian frontier, before reaching Smolensko, the providor who had been sent from Moscow, instead of treating him hospitably by providing him with provisions and a roof, allowed him to be two nights under the open air—one on the snow, and another during a fall of rain. Nor would he even permit him to buy food with his own money, saying, that he ought to be satisfied with the provisions with which he supplied him; until Herberstein used a different tone, and threatened to report his conduct to the grand-prince.

The latter part of the journey to Moscow was very dangerous, on account of the great inundations. Most of the bridges were so much damaged, that it was only with the greatest trouble they could get the horses over them. Half-a-mile before reaching Moscow, they were received with great honour by some noblemen, who came on the part of the grand-prince.

The description given by Herberstein of his reception at Moscow, and of the preparations for his first audience, is so similar to that given in the account of his visit in 1517, that it is needless to repeat it here. The audience is thus described:—" When we entered the room," says he, " where the prince was sitting, directly we made our first obeisance, all the old princes and noblemen sitting around stood up, and only the grand-duke and his brothers remained sitting. Then one of the chief councillors, equal in rank to a marshal, approached the grand-duke, and said: " Great master and king of all the Russians, Count Leonard strikes his forehead before thee for thy great favour." Then, " Sigismund," etc., " strikes his forehead before thee." The seat of the grand-duke as well as his footstool were one palm higher than the rest. He sat all the time uncovered; over him, on the wall, was a picture of an angel or saint. On his right-hand lay his cap, and on his left his staff or possoch, and next to it two ewers and a washhand basin, that he might, after the departure of the foreigners, wash his hands from the pollution of having touched those of an ambassador of another creed. It is likewise the custom for ambassadors coming from Lithuania, Sweden, Livonia, etc., to offer presents to the grand-duke, which are delivered publicly at their first audience; and, indeed, it is customary not only for the ambassadors themselves, but also for the friends who accompany them, to bring presents. It is usual, therefore, after the delivery of the address, for one of the chief councillors to say to the prince:—Great Master, N. N. strikes his forehead to thee, and gives thee pominki—so they call the presents—which he mentions by name; after which, a secretary writes down the names of the donors, and the description of the presents. When we had delivered our address, those who stood behind us amongst our suite called out 'pominki', in order to remind us to deliver the presents, to which our attendants answered, that this custom was no longer in use at the court of Austria. It was true, that this had been the custom also amongst us in former times; but as it was generally expected that presents of as much value were to be given in return, in consequence of which they became more and more extravagant, the custom was at last abolished."

The first dinner is described at length by Herberstein, from which we only quote the following details as peculiarly worthy notice:—Brandy was served round before the eating commenced. The principal dish consisted of swans, which was served round with sour milk, pickled gerkins, and plums. The principal drinks were malmsey, Greek wines, and mead. The grand-prince first called for drink, tasted the wine, and summoned the Count Nugaroli to his table, and then handing him the goblet, said, "Leonhard, thou art sent from a great master to a great master on great affairs, and hast travelled a long distance—it is well for thee to have received marks of my favour, and to have beheld the lustre of my eyes. Drink, therefore, drain your glass, and eat your fill, that thou mayst return in health to thy master." These words he addressed also to Herberstein, of whom he inquired in a familiar way, whether he had ever shaved off his beard; and when Herberstein, without the aid of an interpreter, replied in the affirmative, the grand-duke remarked, that he also had once done the same, and this was on the occasion of his marriage. Not only the tables at which the company sat, but also certain tables of state ranged along the middle of the room, were covered with golden plate. The servers and other court attendants wore on this festive occasion a dress called *therlik*, which was like a herald's coat, covered with pearls and precious stones.

On taking leave of the grand-prince after dinner, the noblemen accompanied Herberstein to his own private residence, and here began again to drink bravely. The gentlemen from the court said it was the order of the grand-prince that they should remain with the ambassadors and make them merry; for which purpose a cart with silver vessels, and two smaller carriages with drink, were sent from the palace, accompanied by the secretaries and other honest people, "for the very purpose," as Herberstein quaintly describes it, "of making the ambassadors full". As it was considered an honour to pledge one's guests, they omitted no sort of persuasion to drink, and when all was in vain, one got up and proposed the health of the grand-duke, which, of course, admitted of no refusal; and after an interval of continued pressing to drink, the health of the emperor of Germany was proposed; afterwards the health of all those present, foreigners as well as residents, in which cases also there was no excuse. "Such drinking," says Herberstein, "is done with great grace; the person who proposes the toast, stands in the middle of the room and pronounces the sentiment,—such as fortune, or victory, or health, or what not, with the wish, that not so much blood may remain in his enemies as he means to leave in his goblet. Having said this with uncovered head, and finished the draught, he turns the goblet upside down over his head.[1] Both on this and on my former visit, not wishing to drink so much, I had no alternative but to assume the appearance of being drunk, or to say that I was too sleepy to drink any more."[2]

[1] This reminds one of the German *nagel probe*, or "nail test", in which the goblet was shewn to be empty by there not remaining sufficient in it, when turned upside down, to wet the thumb-nail.

[2] With respect to the drinking habits of the Russians, the editor has thought it would not be unacceptable to the reader to add, by way of appendix to this introduction, the curious and rare metrical epistles of George Turberville, described by Ant. à Wood (in his *Athenæ Oxonienses*, i, 627), as "much admired for his excellencies in

At the outset Herberstein met with no small difficulty with regard to carrying out the object of his embassy, in consequence of the bitter feeling which existed between the two courts of Russia and Poland, and the probable prospect of advantage to the grandprince from a continuance of the war. In spite of this, however, Herberstein's endeavours were not without good results; and he had the gratification, after his first report to the archduke Ferdinand, to receive a letter, in which he showed his great satisfaction at what he had accomplished. The grandprince, nevertheless, demanded, as he had done in Herberstein's former embassy, that the king of Poland should, as a proof of his own wish to establish peace,

the art of poetry. Being esteemed a person fit for business, as having a good and ready command of his pen, he was entertained by Thos. Randolph, Esq., to be his secretary, when he received commission from Queen Elizabeth to go ambassador to the Emperor of Russia. After his arrival at that place, he did, at spare hours, exercise his muse, and wrote, *Poems describing the Places and Manners of the Country and People of Russia*"; an. 1568 (1569).

The three poetical epistles, in the last of which he alludes to Herberstein, are addressed to the author's friends, "*Edward Dancie, Spencer,* and *Parker.*" Ant. à. Wood, in his life of Turberville, refers to the second name as *Edm.* Spencer, meaning, of course, the poet; but there is no mention of *Edmund* in Turberville or Hakluyt. He is merely called *Spencer*, and certainly was not the celebrated author of the *Fairy Queen*, who was then only about fifteen years of age. The same error has been made by the editor of the reprint of Turberville's *Tragical Tales;* 4to., Edinb., 1837. Of the two other persons, the editor can find no account. These letters on Russia are likewise included among the *Epitaphs* and *Sonnets* attached to the *Tragical Tales*, the original edition of which work (printed in 1587) is exceedingly rare. A reprint of this, limited to fifty copies, 4to., appeared at Edinburgh in 1837. A copy is in the Grenville Library.

himself send ambassadors to Moscow, and the imperial legates accordingly sent to Sigismund, who was at that time staying at Dantzig, to request his compliance with this demand. The king received the proposal without objection, and sent two noblemen as negociators; a delegate was, at the same time, sent from the pope, likewise to plead for peace between the two sovereigns; and by these means, after many difficulties, and a considerable lapse of time, an armistice for five years was finally agreed upon.

During Herberstein's abode in Moscow, he had an opportunity of witnessing several of the festivities and recreations of the court,—especially some hunting scenes, of which he gives a particular description: such as hunting the hare, bear-baiting, and hawking. In speaking of a hare-hunt, he says that an immense number of hares were preserved in narrow enclosures, and the entire circuit spread round with nets. The huntsmen in various dresses, each leading two dogs in a leash, made their way, with loud shouts, through the enclosure to rouse the game. The grand-prince hunted with particularly fine dogs, called *kurtzen* (probably the beautiful long-haired Siberian greyhound). His hunting-dress consisted of a white cap, with a border covered all round with precious stones, and adorned in front with feathers of gold, which waved with every motion of his head. His garment was a *therlik*, "similar to a herald's coat", embroidered with gold; a couple of knives and a dagger hung from his girdle, and at his back, beneath the girdle, was a weapon called *kestene*, which was a staff of wood two spans long, with a thong of the same length attached to it, at the end of which was a large angular piece of metal ornamented with gold. The train consisted of nearly three hundred horsemen. The grand-prince called the strangers frequently to him, and invited them to follow his example, and also to lead dogs, as he did, to the chase. This encouragement was necessary, remarks Herberstein, because with them dogs, being regarded as unclean beasts, are not usually to be handled by honourable persons. The produce of this hunt was three hundred hares.

On the morning of their leave-taking, the ambassadors received very costly dresses from the grand-prince, in which they were to appear at their last audience. After the dinner which followed this audience, they were each presented by the grand-prince with eighty rubles, three hundred ermine, and fifteen hundred miniver skins. When they had finally taken leave, and returned to their residence, the grand-prince again sent to them, to ask which way they intended to return. Their answer was, by Wilna and Cracow to Vienna; to which the secretaries replied, that the grand-prince had just received information from the frontier of the taking of Buda by the Turks, which news he communicated to them for their own guidance.

One circumstance ought to be mentioned here particularly as having caused an injurious impression against Herberstein in Poland, viz., the pride and jealous rivalry of the Poles, who would not allow to the sovereign of their hostile neighbours the title of czar, much less that of emperor, although already under Vasiley Ivanovich it was the general custom to translate the title of czar into Latin by the word *imperator*. Herberstein also was accused at the Polish court, on his second return from Russia, with having in his address given to the grand-prince the title of king; but this he denied, declaring that he had used no other title than Magnus Dux. On his way from Smolensko to Wilna, he learnt from a Lithuanian providor the news of the battle of Mohacz, and the death of King Louis of Hungary, which news affected essentially the interests of Austria, and had a very important bearing upon the object of Herberstein's embassy to Poland. He describes the journey from Wilna to Grodno as so intensely cold, that his nose was frozen. He only saved it by very quick and long rubbing with snow, which remedy was recommended him by his Polish guide; but some of his suite had their hands and feet frozen, and others fell sick under the cold, so as to detain the embassy.

He arrived at Cracow on the 12th of January 1527, where the king then was. His reception was very different to what it had been on the former occasion, for the king now had satisfactory reason to be convinced that the intentions of the emperor and the archduke were sincere and faithful, and expressed to both the ambassadors his satisfaction at the peace concluded in his favour. Here again Herberstein had an opportunity of showing his ability as a statesman and his fidelity to his sovereign; for having received the report of the death of the king of Hungary, and being certain that the archduke Ferdinand, who was newly elected king of Bohemia, would also be entitled to the crown of Hungary, he took advantage of his knowledge of these circumstances to bespeak all the consequent alterations in the relations between his master and the king of Poland, so that when the archduke's ambassador Johann Mraxi arrived, everything was already prepared and settled; and as Mraxi was taken ill immediately after his arrival in Cracow, Herberstein took the management of the whole affair which Mraxi had been commissioned to carry out.

The ambassadors then travelled by way of Silesia to Prague, where they found the archduke Ferdinand, who, by the free election of the States, was declared king of Bohemia upon the death of Louis, and were in time to be present at the celebration of his coronation. The Russian ambassadors arrived soon after, and Herberstein was sent to receive them, and to escort them through the town of Prague as a guide to show them the curiosities. The beautiful situation and the great size of Prague surprised one of the ambassadors so much that he exclaimed, "This is not a city, it is a kingdom; and a great thing it is to acquire such a kingdom without bloodshed!"

When Herberstein reported the result of his mission to the archduke, and mentioned his negotiations in Poland, Ferdinand considered it necessary immediately to send another ambassador thither, and proposed to Herberstein to undertake the journey. The answer of this indefatigable servant of his royal master was, that although he was very ill, he would immediately set out on his journey if the king considered it necessary; nay, if he could not go on horseback, he would ride in a carriage; or, if he could not ride in a carriage, he would be borne by men, but he would never neglect the cause of his majesty for the sake of his own health; but in his opinion the journey was not at all necessary, as he had already settled all the negotiations with the king of Poland with respect to the recent change in the position of affairs. He even showed reasons why an embassy should not be sent, which reasons Ferdinand finally agreed to, and the idea was given up.

Herberstein now begged permission to retire to his own estate for some time that he might recover his health, which permission was granted to him after the Russian embassy had left. Before his departure, however, Ferdinand honoured him with the public expression of a threefold thanksgiving: firstly, for the settlement of the affairs of the peace embassy in Moscow; secondly, for the attention paid to the interests of his masters in Poland; and, thirdly, for the offer of undertaking a new journey in spite of his bad health. From Prague he went to Vienna, where he lay ill for four weeks.

After the death of Louis, John Zapolski put himself at the head of an army of forty thousand men, and succeeded in obtaining possession of the throne of Hungary; so that Ferdinand, who had already been crowned in Prague, and taken possession of Moravia and Silesia, was obliged to enter Hungary with a powerful army, in order to enforce his claims upon that country. He became master of Buda, and shortly after of the greater part of the kingdom, and was at length crowned king of Hungary at Gran, on the 13th of November 1527. As it was to be feared that the pretender to the crown of Hungary would succeed in gaining the assistance of his brother-in-law Sigismund, Ferdinand thought it necessary to send an embassy to Poland, of which embassy Herberstein had the essential management, and had the special honour of being entrusted with separate private instructions. This gave rise to so many private interviews with the king, that it caused the envy of his colleagues, and they even went so far as to complain to the king on the subject. His majesty himself explained the cause of the preference given to Herberstein, saying that it was because he had been to Poland many times before, and was so much initiated in Polish affairs, that he himself was unwilling that every body should know all that Herberstein was already acquainted with. In returning from Poland he had a narrow escape, as Nicolas von Tschaplitz, an old enemy of his, laid wait for him, with the view of wreaking his vengeance on him, and he only saved his life by having accidentally chosen another road for returning. After his return to Vienna, he was taken ill of the Hungarian sickness, which soon increased so much, that there was great fear for his life, and the recovery was slow, and required several months of quiet life to restore his strength. Meanwhile, the Turkish Sultan Suliman, having become an ally of John Zapolski, had sent back with insolence the ambassadors that Ferdinand had sent to demand the restoration of Belgrade, and in a new invasion on Hungary had made such progress, that his advances became more and more alarming for the house of Austria. After having plundered and burnt Buda, and again proclaimed John Zapolski king, he advanced at the head of an immense army, now become habituated to victory and plunder, towards the states of Austria. It consequently became more and more necessary for Ferdinand to avail himself of the friendship of Sigismund of Poland. Herberstein was employed upon this errand. In short, during the remainder of Herberstein's life, the Hungarian question underwent so many fluctuations, that it would be tedious to the reader to lead him even cursorily through their details.

From the year 1527 to the year 1533, Ferdinand was kept in suspense as to his claim to the throne of Hungary, a suspense occasioned mainly by the interference of the sultan Solyman, whose invasion of Hungary met with fluctuating success; and during this period Herberstein was engaged in the most harassing political expeditions from Ferdinand, both to the court of Poland and the various congresses which were held in different places from time to time in Hungary. From 1533 to 1541, with the exception of the year 1535, he was repeatedly employed in diplomatic missions to Bohemia and various parts of Germany, as well as to Hungary and Poland, and so unremitting was the labour of this portion of his life, that during the intervals of these embassies he had to perform the duties of the various honourable offices which he held at home, amongst which may be mentioned that he was president of several diets, a member of the war department, and a councillor of the ministry of war. In 1537 he was rewarded by the dignity of freyherr or baron, which he had asked for in the year 1531, and had been then provisionally granted, but was not solemnly confirmed until the year 1537.

The remainder of the life of Herberstein was spent in similar political labours, among which should be specially mentioned an embassy to the camp of Sultan Suliman II, in 1541, while that monarch was engaged in active defence of his ally, John Zapolski, the rival of Ferdinand.

So late as the year 1560, when he was in his seventy-fourth year, we find his still arduous labours in the cause of the state thus alluded to by Petrus Paganus:—" *Cujus opera* iam ætate confecti et emeriti Cæsar Ferdinandus *adhuc indies in arduis negotiis vtitur*, quique annum agens LXXIIII Austriacis prouentibus adhuc Præsidens incumbit, vt non sibi, sed domui Austriæ, cui se ad extremum vitæ articulum deuouit, natus esse videatur."

He died at Vienna on the 28th of March 1566, being then in his eightieth year. The archduke Charles of Styria caused the following inscription to be placed on his tomb, which we quote on account of the quaint verses with which it concludes:—" Den 28 Martii im 1566 Jahr starb der wohlgebohrne Herr Herr Sigismund Freyherr zu Herberstain, Neyperg vndt Guetenhag, Obrist Erbcamrer vndt Obrist Erbtruchsäss in Khärnten, Romisch Kays. Mjt. Rat vndt President der N. Oe. Cammer.

> "Von Herberstain Herr Sigmund
> Hier liegt, welchs Lob zu aller Stund
> Wurd seyn bey Kaysern wohlbekannt,
> Auch bey aller Leuten in ihren Lannt.
> Dann er bey 4 Kaysern hat
> Gelebt als getreur Diener und Rat,
> Ums Vatterlandt sich wohl verschuldt,
> Davon er bracht hat Ehr vnd Huldt."

We now proceed to the bibliography of the "Rerum Moscoviticarum Commentarii". The first edition was published at Vienna in 1549, under the following title:

Rerum Moscoviticarum Comentarii. In hijs Comentariis sparsim contenta habebis, candide lector, Russie et que nunc eius Metropolis est, Moscouie breuissimam descriptionem. De religione quoq̨ varia inserta sunt: et que nostra cum religione non conueniunt. Corographiam deniq̨ totius imperii Moscici: et vicinorum quorundam mentionem. Quis deniq̨ modus excipiendi et tractandi oratores: disseritur. Itineraria quoq̨ duo in Moscouiam sunt adiuncta. Vindobonæ, (1549), folio.

A copy of this exceedingly rare first edition is in the Grenville collection, British Museum. It is without imprint or colophon; but the dedication to King Ferdinand is dated from Vienna ("Vienne Austriæ"), March 1, 1549. That this was the year in which the book was printed likewise clearly appears from Herberstein's own statement in his autobiography published at Vienna in 1560, entitled, "Gratæ posteritati Sig. lib. B. in Herberstain actiones suas reliquit," etc.; where he says: " MDXLIX. Historiam Moscoviæ stilo simplici congessi eandemque typis excudi curavi." On the reverse of the title-page are the arms of Herberstein. The dedication is followed on fol. iii and iv by some Latin panegyric verses addressed to the author by various writers; the text commencing on fol. v. The work is divided into three sections: I. Itinera in Moscoviam; fol. v-xii, reg. B-C. II. Moscovia; fol. i-ix, reg. A-E. III. Chorographia; fol. i-xxxvii, reg. A-G. The rarity of this book is such, that Denis, who wrote on the early history of printing at Vienna, was not able to see a copy, and describes it only from Gesner's " Bibliotheca", whose description, in fact, applied to the second edition of 1551.

Two years later an improved edition appeared at Basle, at the instance of Wolfgang Lazius. The title is the same as that of the first, except that we find this addition to it: " Accessit etiam locuples rerum et verborum in his memorabilium Index. Basileæ, per Joannem Oporinum": s. a. (1551), fol., 175 pages, and 3 leaves of index; and also the work of Paulus Jovius, " De Legatione Moscoviticarum."

In a letter addressed to the publisher, printed on the reverse of the title-page, Lazius says of the first edition: " Fuere quidem obiter hi (commentarii) apud nos excusi—sed adeo corrupte, adeoque absurdis typis, uti vides, ut ni tua industria accedat, opus mehercule memorabile iniuriam patiatur"; and, in a postscript, he says: " De prærogativa uti tu statues res certa erit; eo enim loco is vir est. Sed cupit insignia sua sub finem, et chorographiam a frontispicio operis collocari, quæ tu sumptu tuo curabis sculpi." The copy in the British Museum has the large map of " Moscovia" dated 1549, followed on the next page by a portrait of the grand-prince seated, with the following lines placed above it:

> " Russorum Rex et Dominus sum jure paterni
> Sanguinis, imperii titulos a nemine, quavis
> Mercatus prece, vel precio, nec legibus ullis
> Subditus alterius, sed Christo credulus uni
> Emendicatos aliis aspernor honores."

The colophon runs thus: "Basileæ, ex officina Joannis Oporini, 1551. Mense Julio." On the verso of the last leaf are the arms of Herberstein.

Five years after, another edition was required, which received the author's additions and improvements. The title is like the preceding, with the following addition: " Ad hæc, non solum nouæ aliquot tabulæ, sed multa etiam alia nunc demum ab ipso autore adiecta sunt: quæ, si cui cum prima editione conferre libeat, facile deprehendet. Cum Caes. et Regiæ Maiest. gratia et privilegio ad decennium. Basileæ. Per Joannem Oporinum": s. a. (1556), fol., 205 pages, and 16 pages of Index. After the title-page comes Oporinus's dedication to Daniel Mauchius, who was in Moscow at the time of Herberstein's second residence in Russia. It is subscribed, "Calendis Julii 1556," and in it he says that he sends him at last " toties efflagitatam, tantoque jam tempore expectatam Moscoviam"; and in an edition, certainly " longe aliam quam priore editione in publicum prodierat: plurimis nempe non solum Chorographiis atque aliis Tabulis, sed et rerum scitu dignissimarum descriptionibus passim de novo insertis locupletatam."

Rerum Moscoviticarum Commentarii. Sigismundo Libero[1] authore. Russiæ breuissima descriptio, et de religione eorum varia inserta sunt. Chorographia totius Imperii Moscici, et vicinorum quorundam mentio. Antuerpiæ in ædibus Joannis Streelsii, 1557. In octavo, 198 leaves.

This edition appears to be a reprint made without Herberstein's sanction, as the imperial protective privilege does not appear on the title-page.

Antuerpiæ, 1557, fol. This edition is only quoted in the Hamburg "Bibliotheca Historica," where, on page 267, it says: The "Antwerp edition of a°. 1557, in fol., is indisputably the best."

Francofurti, 1560, fol. This impression, Denis only mentions in his work, "Wien's Buchdruckergeschichte bis MDLX" (Wien, 1782, 4to.), where he says: "A°. 1560, the Oporin edition was reprinted at Frankfort by Wechel's heirs."

[1] Herberstein's correct designation was, Siegmund Freyherr zu Herberstein, Neyperg, etc., which, literally translated, becomes, "Sigismundus Liber Baro in Herberstein", both of which forms of title he himself uses. But as the title of "Freyherr", *Free* Baron, is peculiar to Germany, its Latin rendering of "Liber Baro" has led many into the mistake, that "Liber" was the family name, and "Baro" the title. Hence the blunder in the above title. In the Italian translation of his works, he is called "Sigismundo Libero et Barone in Herbesten". Some have shortened his name into "Sigismundus Baro et Herr Siegmund"; and in the Russian archives and annals, according to Adelung, he is called Siegmund Herbenster, Shidimant and Schichdimont Herbenstene, Shiginon Hirbresten, Hermonster, etc., etc.

Basileæ, 1567, fol. This edition, Adelung says, is only to be found in the superficial and untrustworthy Burch. Ad. Sellius in his Schediasma Literarium de scriptoribus qui Historiam Rossicam scriptis illustrarunt." Revaliæ, 1736, 8vo., p. 19.[1]

Basileæ, 1571, fol., ex officina Oporiniana; 327 pages. A more correct impression of the edition of 1556, with several additions, which are thus announced on the title-page: " His nunc primum accedunt, Scriptum recens de Græcorum fide, quos in omnibus Moscorum natio sequitur: et Commentarius de bellis Moscorum aduersus finitimos, Polonos, Lituanos, Suedos, Liuonios et alios gestis, ad annum usque LXXI, scriptus ab Joanne Leuuenclaio."

Basileæ, 1573, fol. This edition likewise is only mentioned by Sellius, in his "Schediasma Literarium", and is consequently not to be trusted.

Basileæ, 1574, fol. This edition Meusel mentions in his "Literatur der Statistik", but it is not found quoted anywhere else.

An exact reprint of the Basil edition of 1556, is found in the well-known collection—

Rerum Moscoviticarum Auctores varii: vnvm in corpvs nvnc primvm congesti. Quibus et Gentis Historia continetur: et Regionvm accvrata descriptio. Francofurti apud haeredes Andreae Wecheli, Claudium Marnium et Joan. Aubrium, 1600, fol., p. 1-117.[2]

---

[1] It is he who says that Herberstein was in Russia in 1497 and 1523.

[2] This edition contains some points of advantage over those which preceded it, as containing nine documents, then printed for the first time, having reference to Herberstein's travels in Poland and

TRANSLATIONS.

Italian. An Italian translation of Herberstein's work appeared at Venice a year after the publication of the original, and with his own permission, as he himself says.[1] The title is—

Comentari della Moscovia et parimente della Russia, et delle altre cose belle e notabili, composti già latinamente per il signor Sigismondo libero Barone in herberstain, Neiperg et Guetnhag, tradotti nouamente di latino in lingua nostra uuolgare Italiana. Simelmente vi si tratta della religione delli Moscouiti, et in che parte quella sia differente dalla n'ra benche si chiamino chr'iani. Item una discrittione particolare di tutto l'imperio Moscouitico, toccando ancora di alcuni luoghi vicini, come sono de Tartari, Lituuani, Poloni, et altri molti riti et ordini di que' popoli. In Venetia per Gioan Battista Pedrezzano. Cum priuilegio del Illustriss. Senato Venetiano, Per anni X. MDL. 90 leaves, in quarto.[2]

Respecting this translation, Adelung states that "it is very rare; the author of it is not known; but in a manuscript note he found it ascribed to F. Corvinus, without, however, having been able to find

Russia. These are letters of Maximilian, Charles V, Ferdinand, Ludwig II. of Hungary, and Sigismund of Poland, which the editors, Claude Marne and Jean Aubri, appear to have obtained from the family archives, through the Baron Felicianus von Herberstein, whose personal acquaintance they boast of in a dedication to Marquard Freher.

[1] In the preface to his German "Moscovia", Herberstein says: "I wrote the whole in Latin, and so printed it, and lately it has been printed in the Italian tongue."

[2] Buhle "de antiquis delineat. geograph. Russiæ," p. 7, regards this Italian translation as the earliest edition of Herberstein's work, as he was not aware of the Latin original of 1549.

this statement confirmed by any authority." It was again printed in the "Raccolta di Navigazioni e Viaggi di Ramusio". Venezia, 1583, fol., t. ii, p. 137, etc.; and this reprint is sometimes erroneously mentioned as a distinct translation, or as a new edition of the impression of 1550.

German. Moscouia der Hauptstadt in Reissen, durch Herrn Sigmunden Freyherrn zu Herberstain, Neyperg und Guetenhag, Obristen Erbcamrer, vnd öbristen Erbtruckhsessen in Kärntn, Römischer zu Hungern und Behaim Khii. May. etc. Rat, Camrer vnd Presidenten der Niederösterreichischen Camer zusamen getragen. Sambt des Moscouiter gepiet, vnd seiner anrainer[1] beschreibung und anzaigung, in weu (*sic*)[2] sy glaubens halb, mit vns nit gleichhellig. Wie die Potschaften oder Gesandten durch sy emphangen vnd gehalten werden, sambt zwayen vnderschidlichen Raisen in die Mosqua. Mit Röm. Khii. May. gnad vnd Priuilegien getruckt zu Wienn in Osterreich durch Michael Zimmermann in S. Anna Hoff, 1557. Small folio, 24 double sheets, without pagination; reg. A—Zij.

This translation was made from the Basle edition of 1556, and seen through the press by Herberstein himself. It is also very rare. A circumstantial account of this translation, and of its relation to the original, will be found in *Siegm. Freih. v. Herberstein, etc., von Friedr. Adelung*, p. 343-353.

Moscoviter wunderbare Historien: In welcher desz treffenlichen Grossen land Reüssen, sampt der hauptstatt Moscauw vnd anderer nammhafftigen vmligenden Fürstenthumb vnd stetten gelegenheit, Religion, vnd seltzame gebreüch: Auch desz erschrockenlichen Groszfürsten zu Moscauw här-

---

[1] Frontier countries.   [2] Worin.

kommen, mannliche thaten, gewalt, vnd lands ordnung, auff das fleyszigest ordenlichen begriffen: so alles bisz här bey vns in Teütscher nation vnbekandt gewesen. Erstlich durch den wolgebornen herren Sigmunden Freyherren zu Herberstein, Neyperg, vnd Guttenhag, etc., welcher zu etlichen malen Röm. Kay. vnd Künig. May. in selbigen landen Legat gewesen, fleyszig zu latein beschriben: Ietz zu malen aber, zu ehren vnd wolgefallen dem wolgebornen herren Johans Grauen zu Nassaw etc. durch Heinrich Pantaleon, der Freyen Künsten vnd Artzney doctorn zu Basel, auff das treüwlichest verteütschet vnd in truck verfertiget: Alles gantz wunderbar, nutzlich, vnd kurtzweylig zu lesen. Mit sampt H. Pauli Jouij Moscouitischer Landen, und H. Georgen Wernhern Ungarischer wunderbaren wasseren beschreibung, auch etlichen schönen Figuren und Landstaflen, darzu einem vollkommenen Register bezieret. Basel, anno 1563. 215 pages, folio.

At the end stands, "Getruckt zu Basel bey Niclauss Brillinger vnnd Marx Russinger, 1563." It is curious, that in this translation no allusion is made to that published by the author himself six years previously; indeed, as the title-page sets forth, that this work had been hitherto unknown in Germany, we should infer that Dr. Pantaleon was ignorant of Herberstein's translation.

A reprint of this translation by Pantaleon, appeared at Basle, 1567, fol. Upon the title-page, after the words, "Pauli Jovii Moscovitischer Landen", is added—

Vnd h. Heinrich Pantaleon Littauwischen, Polnischen, Schwedischen, Leyfflendischen, Nordwegischen, Ungarischen, Türckischen, vnd Tartarischen völkeren, so zu ringharum an die Moscouiter stossend. Alles gantz wunderbar, nutzlich und kurtzweylig zu lesen. 246 pages, and five pages of index. The Beschreibung von Litthauen, etc., mentioned in the title begins at page 192.

Prag, 1567. A copy of this edition is in the Royal Library of Dresden. It corresponds in every respect with the foregoing.

Die Moscovitische Chronica, d. i. Beschreibung des Grossfürsten in der Moscau sammt dessen Ländern, etc. erstlich von Paul Jovio und Sigm. Herberstein in Latein, hernach von Pantaleon ins Teutsche übersetzt. Frankfurt, A.M. 1576, folio.

Frankfurt, A.M., 1579, folio. A repetition of the edition just mentioned.

Frankfurt, A.M., 1589, folio. This impression is mentioned by G. C. Gebauer (Progr. de Vita, Fatis et Scriptis Sigismundi L. B. ab Herberstein), who gives the title as follows—

Die Moscouitische Chronica edita et Georgio a Munster Consiliario Herbipolensi Præfectoque Arnsteinensi inscripta; prioribus merito postponenda cum priorem Pantaleonis, vt reor, editionem secutus, eiusdem de populis Moscouiæ vicinis commentarios non addiderit, et insertis more suo dudum sculptis nihilque ad rem facientibus figuris, Czari Basilii effigiem, Tabulas Geographicas, Chorographicamque, Vri Bisontisque imagines, et reliqua in vtraque Pantaleonis editione seruata ornamenta omiserit.

Wien, 1618, folio. This edition is quoted by G. H. Stuck, in his "Verzeichniss ält. u. neuern Land- und Reisebeschr." I, p. 142. It appears to be a reprint of the first Vienna edition of 1557.

St. Petersburg, 1795, folio. This edition of the

translation by Pantaleon was printed by order of Catharine II.

Bohemian. Zymunda swobodncho Pána z Herbersteina Cesta do knjzetstwj Moskewského.

This is an extract from Herberstein's work, referring only to his journey to Russia. It is printed in the work—

(Frant. Faustyn Prochazka). Weytah z Kronyky Mozkewské někdu Latině ad Alexandra Gwagnyna sepsané, potom w Cesky gazyk prelozené od Matausse z Wysokého Meyta. Pridana gest Zygmunda z Herbersteina dwogi cesta do Moskwy. (W. Praze) 1786; 8vo., pp. 144-175.

EXTRACTS.

Descriptio Lithuaniæ, ex Moschovia Sigismundi Liberi Baronis ab Herberstein.

Printed from the Basle edition of 1557, in—

(*a*) Polonicæ historicæ Corpus; hoc est Polonicarum rerum Latini scriptores recentiores et veteres, quotquot extant uno volumine comprehensi omnes, ex bibliotheca Jo. Pistorii. Basileæ (1582); fol., tom. i, pp. 151-157.

(*b*) Alex. Guagnini Res Polonicæ. Francofurti, 1584; 8vo., tom. iii, p. 550.

(*c*) Historiæ Polonicæ et magni Ducatus Lithuaniæ scriptorum collectio magna ed. Laur. Mitzler de Kolof. Varsaviæ, 1761; fol., tom. i, cap. 7.

Fragmentum de bello Poloni et Moschi.

This is an extract from the "Commentaries", in the Basle edition of 1557, and is printed in the "Polonicæ historiæ corpus", t. iii, p. 13-15.

Eight chapters from Herberstein's "Commentaries" are printed in the Elzevir edition of the work, "Russia sive Moscovia." Lugd. Bat. 1630, 16mo., p. 79-100.

It only remains for the editor to express his great obligations to his friend William Brenchley Rye, Esq. of the British Museum, both for his obliging contribution of the etching of the grand-prince, which forms the frontispiece of the second volume, and also for most valuable assistance in this introduction, and more especially in the bibliography, which forms so considerable a portion of it.

CERTAINE LETTERS IN VERSE,

WRITTEN BY MASTER GEORGE TURBERUILE,

OUT OF MOSCOUIA,

Which went as Secretaire thither with Master Tho. Randolph, her Maisties Embassadour to the Emperour, 1568, to certaine friends of his in London, describing the manners of the countrey and people.

(Referred to at p. cxxvii of the Introduction.)

TO HIS ESPECIALL FRIEND, MASTER EDWARD DANCIE.

My Dancie deere, when I recount within my brest,
My London friends, and wonted mates, and thee above the rest:
I feele a thousand fittes of deepe and deadly woe,
To thinke that I from land to sea, from bliss to bale did goe.
I left my native soyle, full like a retchlesse man,
And unacquainted of the coast, among the Russies ran:
A people passing rude, to vices vile inclinde.
Folke fitting to be of Bacchus' trayne, so quaffing is their kinde,
Drinke is their whole desire, the pot is all their pride,
The sobrest head doeth once a day stand needfull of a guide.
If he to banquet bid his friends, he will not shrinke
On them at dinner to bestowe a douzen kindes of drinke:
Such licour as they have, and as the countrey gives,
But chiefly two, one called Kuas, whereby the Mousike lives,
Small ware and waterlike, but somewhat tarte in taste,
The rest is Meade of honie made, wherewith their lippes they haste.
And if he goe unto his neighbour as a guest,
He cares for litle meate, if so his drinke be of the best;
No wonder though they use such vile and beastly trade,
Sith with the hatchet and the hand their chiefest gods be made;
Their idoles haue their heartes—on God they never call,
Unlesse it be (Nichola Bough[1]) that hangs against the wall.

[1] Nicholas of Bari.

The house that hath no god or paynted saint within,
Is not to be resorted too—that roofe is full of sinne.
Besides their priuate gods, in open places stand [hand;
Their crosses, unto which they crooch, and bless themselves with
Devoutly downe they ducke with forehead to the ground,
Was neuer more deceit in ragges and greasie garments found.
Almost the meanest man in all the countrie rides;
The woman eke, against our use, her trotting horse bestrides:
In sundry colours they, both men and women goe,
In buskins all, that money haue on buskins to bestoe.
Eche woman hanging hath a ring within her eare,
Which all of aunctient vse, and some of very pride doe weare;
Their gate is very brave, their countenance wise and sadde,
And yet they follow fleshly lustes, their trade of living badde.
It is no shame at all accounted, to defile
Anothers bedde, they make no care their follies to concile;
Is not the meanest man in all the land but hee,
To buy her paynted colours, doth allow his wife a fee,
Wherewith she deckes herselfe, and dyes her tawnie skinne,
She prankes and paints her smoakie face, both browe, lippe, cheeke, and chinne.
Yea those that honest are, if any such there be
Within the land, doe use the like; a man may plainely see
Upon some womens cheekes the paynting how it lies,
In plaister sort for that too thick, her face the harlot dies.
But such as skilfull are, and cunning dames indeed,
By daily practise doe it well, yea sure they doe exceede;
They lay their colours so, as he that is full wise,
May easly be deceiv'd therein, if he doe trust his eyes.
I not a little muse, what madnes makes them paint
Their faces, waying how they keepe the stoove by meere constraint;
For seldome when, vnlesse on church or marriage day,
A man shall see the dames abroade that are of best aray;
The Russie meanes to reape the profit of her pryde,
And so he mewes her to be sure she lye by no mans side.
Thus much, friend Dancie, I did meane to write to thee,
To let thee weete in Russia land what men and women bee.
Hereafter I perhaps of other things will write
To thee, and other of my friendes, which I shall see with sight;
And other stuffe besides, which true report shall tell,
Meanewhile I ende my louing lines, and bid thee now farewell.

TO SPENCER.

If I should now forget, or not remember thee,
Thou, Spencer, mightest a foule rebuke and shame impute to mee;
For I to open shew did loue thee passing well,
And thou wert he at parture whom I loathed to bid farewell;
And as I went thy friend, so I continue still,
No better proofe thou canst then this desire of true good will.
I doe remember well when needes I should away,
And that the poste would licence us no longer time to stay;
Thou wrongst me by the fist, and holding fast my hand,
Didst crave of me to send thee newes, and how I liked the land.
It is a sandy soile, no very fruitfull vaine,
More waste and woodie grounds there are then closes fit for graine:
Yet graine there growing is, which they untimely take,
And cut or eare the corne be ripe; they mowe it on a stake;
And laying sheafe by sheafe, their haruest so they drie;
They make the greater haste for feare the frost the corne destroy.
For in the winter time, so glarie is the ground,
As neither grass nor other graine in pastures may be found:
In coms the cattel then, the sheepe, the colt, the cowe,
Fast by his bed the mowsike then a lodging doth allowe,
Whom he with fodder feedes, and holds as deere as life,
And thus they weare the winter with the mowsike and his wife.
Seuen months the winter dures, the glare it is so great,
As it is May before he turne his ground to sowe his wheate;
The bodies eke that die, unburied lie they then,
Laid up in coffins made of firre, as well the poorest men,
As those of greater state; the cause is lightly found,
For that in winter time they cannot come to breake the ground;
And wood so plenteous is, quite throughout all the land,
As rich and poor, at time of death, assur'd of coffins stand.
Perhaps thou musest much, how this may stand with reason,
That bodies dead can uncorrupt abide so long a season;
Take this for certaine trothe, as soon as heate is gone,
The force of colde the bodie binds as hard as any stone,
Without offence at all to any living thing:
And so they lye in perfect state till next returne of springe.
Their beasts be like to ours, as farre as I can see, [be;
For shape and shewe, but somewhat lesse of bulke and bone they

Of watrish taste, the flesh not firme like English beefe,
And yet it serues them very well, and is a good releefe.
Their sheepe are very small, sharpe singled, handfull long,
Great store of fowle on sea and land, the moorish reedes amonge,
The greatnes of the store doth make the prices lesse;
Besides in all the land they knowe not how good meate to dresse.
They use neither broach nor spit, but when the stooue they heate,
They put their victuals in a pan, and so they bake their meate;
No pewter to be had, no dishes but of wood,
No use of trenchers; cups cut out of byrche are very good.
They use but wooden spoones, which hanging in a case,
Eache mowsike at his girdle ties, and thinkes it no disgrace;
With whitles two or three, the betterman the moe,
The cheefest Russies in the land with spoone and kniues doe goe.
Their houses are not huge of building, but they say
They plant them in the loftiest ground to shift the snowe away;
Which in the winter time, each where full thicke they lie,
Which makes them have the more desire to set their houses high;
No stonework is in use, their roofes of rafters be,
One linked in another fast, their walls are all of tree;
Of masts both long and large, with mosse put in betweene,
To keepe the force of weather out, I neur earst haue seene;
A grosse deuise so good, and on the roofe they lay,
The burthen barke, to rid the raine, and sudden showers away.
In euery roome a stoue, to serue the winter turne,
Of wood they haue sufficient store as much as they can burne;
They have no English glasse, of slices of a rocke,
Hight Sluda, they their windowes make, that English glass doth mocke.
They cut it very thinne, and sowe it with a thred,
In pretie order like to panes, to serue their present neede;
No other glasse good faith, doth giue a better light,
And sure the rocke is nothing rich, the cost is very slight.
The chiefest place is that, where hangs the god by it,
The owner of the house himself doth neuer sit,
Unlesse his better come, to whom he yeelds the seat;
The stranger bending to the god, the ground with brow must beat,
And in that very place which they most sacred deeme,
The stranger lyes; a token that his guest he doth esteeme.
Where he is woont to have a beares skinne for his bed,
And must in stead of pillow clap his saddle to his head.

In Russia other shift there is not to be had,
For where the bedding is not good the boalsters are but bad;
I mused very much what made them so to lie,
Sith in theyr countrey downe is rife, and feathers out of crie;
Vnlesse it be because the countrey is so hard,
They feare by nicenesse of a bed theyr bodyes would be mard.
I wisht thee oft with us, saue that I stood in feare,
Thou wouldst haue loathed to haue layd thy limmes upon a beare,
As I and Stafford did, that was my mate in bed;   [sped.
And yet (we thank the God of heauen) we both right well haue
Loe thus I make an end; none other newes to thee,
But that the countrey is too colde, the people beastly bee.
I write not all I know; I touch but heere and there;
For if I should, my pen would pinch, and eke offend I feare:
Who so shall read this verse, coniecture of the rest,
And thinke by reason of our trade that I do thinke the best.
But if no traffike were, then could I boldly pen
The hardnesse of the soile, and eke the maners of the men;
They say the lions paw giues iudgement of the beast,
And so may you deeme of the great by reading of the least.

TO PARKER.

My Parker, pen and inke were made to write,
And idle heads that little do haue leisure to indite;
Wherefore, respecting these, and thine assured loue,
If I would write no newes to thee, thou might'st my pen reproue.
And sithence fortune thus hath shou'd my shippe on shore,
And made me seeke another realme vnseene of me before;
The maners of the men I purpose to declare,
And other priuate points besides, which strange and geazon are.
The Russie men are round of bodies, fully faste,
The greatest part with bellies bigge that ouerhang the waste,
Flat headed for the most, with faces nothing faire,
But browne, by reason of the stoue, and closenesse of the aire;
It is theyr common vse to shaue or els to sheare
Theyr heads, for none in all the land long lolling locks doth weare,
Vnlesse perhaps he haue his souereigne prince displeas'd,
For then he neur cuts his haire vntill he be appeas'd.
A certaine signe to know who in displeasure be,
For every man that views his head will say, Loe this is he.

x

And during all the time he lets his locks to grow,
Dares no man for his life to him a face of friendship show.
Theyr garments be not gay, nor handsome to the eye,
A cap aloft theyr heads they haue that standeth very hye,
Which colpacke they do terme. They weare no ruffes at all;
The best haue collers set with pearle, which they rubasca call;
Theyr shirts in Russie long, they worke them downe before,
And on the sleuees with coulered silks two inches good and more.
Aloft theyr shirts they weare, a garment iacket wise,
Hight onoriadka, and about his burlie waste he tyes
His portkies, which in stead of better breeches bee:
Of linnen cloth that garment is, no codpiece is to see.
A payre of yarnen stocks to keep the colde away,
Within his boots the Russie weares, the heeles they underlay
With clouting clamps of steele sharp-pointed at the toes,
And ouer all a suba furd, and thus the Russies goes.
Well butned is the sube according to his state,
Some silke, of silver other some, but those of poorest rate
Do weare no subes at all, but grosser gownes to sight,
That reacheth downe beneath the calfe, and that armacha hight:
These are the Russies robes. The richest vse to ride
From place to place, his seruant runnes, and followes by his side;
The Cassacke beares his felt to force away the raine:
Their bridles are not very braue, their saddles are but plaine,
No bits, but snaffles all, of birch their saddles bee,
Much fashioned like the Scotish seats, broad flacks to keepe the
    knee
From sweating of the horse, the pannels larger farre,
And broader be then ours, they use short stirrups for the warre;
For when the Russie is pursued by cruell foe,
He rides away, and suddenly betakes him to his boe,
And bends me but about in saddle as he sits,
And therewithall amids his race his following foe he hits.
Theyr bowes are very short, like Turkie bowes outright,
Of sinowes made with birchen barke, in cunning maner dight;
Small arrowes, cruel heads, that fell and forked bee,
Which being shot from out those bowes, a cruell way will flee:
They seldome vse to shoo their horse, vnlesse they ride
In post vpon the frozen fluds, then cause they shall not slide
He sets a slender calke, and so he rides his way.
The horses of the countrey go good fourscore versts a day,

And all without the spurre, once prick them and they skippe,
But go not forward on their way, the Russie has his whippe
To rappe him on the ribbes, for though all booted bee,
Yet shall ye not a payre of spurres in all the countrey see.
The common game is chesse, almost the simplest will
Both giue a checke and eke a mate; by practise comes theyr skill.
Againe the dice as fast, the poorest rogues of al
Will sit them downe in open field, and there to gaming fall;
Their dice are very small, in fashion like to those
Which we do vse; he takes them up, and ouer his thumb he throwes,
Not shaking them a whit, the cast suspiciouslie,
And yet I deeme them void of art that dicing most applie.
At play when siluer lacks, goes saddle, horse, and all,   [small;
And each thing else worth siluer walkes, although the price be
Because thou louest to play, friend Parker, other while,
I wish thee there the weary day with dicing to beguile.
But thou weart better fare at home, I wist it well,
And wouldest be loathe among such lowts so long a time to dwell;
Then iudge of vs, thy friends, what kinde of life we had,
That neere the frozen pole to waste our weary dayes wer glad;
In such a sauage soile, where lawes do beare no sway,
But all is at the king his will, to saue or els to slay;
And that sans cause, God wot, if so his mind be such:
But what meane I with kings to deale, we ought no saints to touch.
Conceiue the rest yourselfe, and deeme what liues they lead,
Where lust is law, and subiects liue continually in dread;
And where the best estates have none assurance good,
Of lands, of liues, nor nothing falles vnto the next of blood:
But all of custome doth vnto the prince redowne,
And all the whole revenue comes vnto the king his crowne.
Good faith I see thee muse at what I tell thee now,
But true it is, no choice, but all at princes pleasure bow.
So Tarquine ruled Rome, as thou remembrest well,
And what his fortune was at last, I know thy selfe canst tell;
Where will in common weale doth beare the onely sway,
And lust is law, the prince and realme must needs in time decay;
The strangenesse of the place is such for sundry things I see,
As if I would, I can not write, ech priuate point to thee.
The colde is rare, the people rude, the prince so full of pride,
The realme so stored with monks and nunnes, and priests on
    euery side:

The maners are so Turkie like, the men so full of guile,
The women wanton, temples stuft with idols that defile
The seats that sacred ought to be, the customes are so quaint,
As if I would describe the whole, I feare my penne would faint.
In summe, I say, I never saw a prince that so did raigne,
Nor people so beset with saints, yet all but vile and vaine:
Wilde Irish are as ciul as the Russies in theyr kinde,
Hard choice which is the best of both, ech bloudy, rude and blinde.
If thou be wise, as wise thou art, and wilt be rulde by me,
Liue still at home, and couet not those barbarous coasts to see;
No good befalles a man that seekes, and findes no better place,
No ciul customes to be learned, where God bestowes no grace.
And truelie ill they do deserue to be belou'd of God,
That neither loue nor stand in awe of his assured rod:
Which though be long, yet plagues at last the vile and beastly sort,
Of sinful wights, that all in vice do place theyr chiefest sport.
Adieu, friend Parker, if thou list to know the Russies well,
To Sigismundus booke repayre, who all the trueth can tell,
For he long earst in message went unto that sauage king,
Sent by the Pole, and true report in ech respect did bring.
To him I recommend myself, to ease my penne of paine,
And now at last do wish thee well, and bid farewell againe.

RERVM MOSCO-VITICARVM CO-MENTARII.

In hiis comentariis sparsim contenta habebis, candide Lector,

Russie & que nunc ejus Metropolis est, Moscovie, brevissimam descriptionem,

De Religione quoque varia inserta sunt: Et que nostra cum Religione non conveniunt.

Corographiam deniqve totius imperii Moscici: Et vicinorum quorundam mentionem.

Quis denique modus excipiendi et tractandi oratores disseritur.

Itineraria quoque duo, in Moscoviam sunt adiuncta.

DEDICATION.

To the Most Serene Prince and Lord, the Lord Ferdinand, King of the Romans, Hungary, and Bohemia, Infant of Spain, Archduke of Austria, Duke of Burgundy and Wirtemberg, and Duke, Marquis, Count, and Lord of many provinces, my most gracious master:

IN ancient days, when the Romans sent ambassadors to any distant and unknown country, they are said to have charged them as a duty to commit carefully to writing a description of the manners, institutes, and entire mode of living of the people with whom their embassy brought them in contact; and so much importance was afterwards attached to such descriptions, that upon the termination of an embassy, the ambassador's commentaries were deposited in the temple of Saturn for the instruction of posterity. If this regulation had been observed by men of our own, or recent times, we should perhaps have had more light, and certainly less trash, infused into history. For my own part, as I always from my youth took delight in observing the habits of foreigners both at home and abroad, it was a matter of cordial pleasure to me that my services were required in embassies, not only by that wise prince, Your Majesty's grandfather Maximilian, but by Your Majesty also, by whose command I more than once travelled through the countries of the north. To Russia in particular, which of all the countries of Christendom differs so much from us in its manners, laws, religion, and military discipline, I made a second expedition, on which occasion the Imperial ambassador, Count Leonhard von Nugaroli was alike the sharer of my dignity and the companion of my journey. Although, however, I had by command of the Emperor Maximilian gone as ambassador to Denmark, Hungary, and Poland; and after the death of His Majesty, had in the name of my country, travelled through Italy and France, traversing both sea and land, to Spain, on a mission to Your Majesty's brother, the most powerful and invincible Emperor Charles V; and subsequently, by command of Your Majesty, went as ambassador to the kings of Hungary and Poland, and lastly, in company with Count Nicolas von Salm, to the camp of Solyman, the prince of the Turks; in all which journeyings I had made numerous notes, doubtless worthy of being commemorated in print, both of what I saw and learnt by diligent inquiry: yet I was unwilling to spend such leisure as I could afford myself from public councils, in committing to print any relation of such matters as had been either treated of skilfully and carefully by others, or were already set before the eyes and daily observation of all Europe. The more intimate habits of the Russians, however, which have not been brought before the knowledge of the present age, I have here taken upon myself to bring forward and describe; in doing which, I have mainly relied upon two things, namely, diligence in investigation, and my knowledge of the Sclavonic language; both which have served me largely in the production of a narrative of this nature. While, therefore, several others have, in describing other countries, touched upon Russia; among the more ancient of whom is Nicolas Cusanus, and in our own time, Paulus Jovius (whose name I mention on account of his very great learning and wonderful affection for myself, and of whose elegance and great fidelity of description I speak, on account of the abundant use that he made of an interpreter), Johann Fabri, and Anton Bied, who have left both maps and commentaries; and while some, also, of the authors to whom I refer have not written of Russia specifically, but only incidentally, in describing neighbouring countries, — as for instance, Olaus Gothus, in his description of Sweden, Matthæus Mechovita, Albertus Campensis, and Munster,—yet such as these have by no means deterred me from my resolution of writing. And this resolution I hold, because while I was in the country I derived my information, not only from personal observation, but from accounts which were worthy of credit, and daily availed myself of every opportunity to converse much upon such matters with a great number of people, so that occasionally I have been obliged (and I hope my words will not give offence) to give a more copious and ample explanation of matters which have been exhibited by others obscurely and as it were through a lattice. In addition to this, I here give a description of subjects which have not been at all touched upon by others, and which no one but an ambassador could have become acquainted with. In this my purpose and labour, moreover, I have been encouraged by Your Majesty, who has from time to time exhorted me to bring the work which I had begun to a conclusion, and who has even (as the saying is) spurred an already willing horse; while on the other hand, various embassies and other labours in Your Majesty's service have very frequently called me off from this occupation, upon which I have been able hitherto to bestow less time than I had contemplated. Now, however, that I find myself able to enjoy somewhat of leisure from the daily business of the Austrian treasury, I return, in obedience to Your Majesty's command, to my interrupted task; and I pay but little regard to those inconsiderate readers of this most delicate age, who will perhaps look for greater refinement in my writing; it is sufficient for me that I have given proof by the fact itself (since I could not do so equally by my language), of my wish by any means to provide instruction for posterity, and of my desire to obey the commands of Your Majesty, than which I hold nothing in greater reverence. I therefore hereby declare to Your Majesty, that these Notes upon Russia have been dictated by me far more from a desire to investigate and elucidate the truth, than for the sake of talking; and I humbly dedicate and commend myself to the patronage of Your Majesty, in whose service I have grown old, and pray Your Majesty to deign to accept this book with the same clemency and kindness which Your Majesty has ever vouchsafed to its author himself.

Vienna, First of March 1549.

The same, Your Majesty's faithful Councillor and Chamberlain, and Governor of the Austrian Treasury,

SIGISMUND,

Baron of Herberstein, Neyperg, and Guettenhag.

TO THE READER.

In thus entering upon the description of Moscow, which is the capital of Russia, and which extends its sway far and wide through Scythia, it will be indispensable, candid reader, that I should in this work touch upon many parts of the north, which have not been sufficiently known either to ancient authors or those of our own day, and it will follow that I shall sometimes be compelled to differ from the accounts they give. And in order that my opinion in this matter may not be looked upon with suspicion, or considered presumptuous, I assert with all honesty, that not once only, but repeatedly, while engaged as ambassador for the Emperor Maximilian, and his grandson Ferdinand king of the Romans, I have seen and investigated Moscow, as it were under my very eyes (as the saying is); that I made myself acquainted with the greater part of the talented and trustworthy men of the place, and did not rely upon this or that man's account, but trusted only to the unvarying statements of the many; and having the advantage of knowing the Sclavonic language, which is identical with the Russian and Muscovitic, I have written these things and handed them down to the memory of posterity, not only as an ear, but as an eye-witness, and that not with any disguise in my description, but openly and freely.

But, in like manner as every nation has its own peculiar mode of pronunciation, so also the Russians connect and join together their letters in various ways, after a fashion to which we are quite unaccustomed; so that no one who did not pay particular attention to their pronunciation, would be able either conveniently to ask them a question, or to gain any intelligible reply. Since, therefore, in my description of Russia, I have, not without consideration, used Russian words in naming objects, places, and rivers, I have thought it right thus at the outset briefly to show the connexion and force of certain letters; by observing which, the reader will be enabled to understand many things more easily, and occasionally, perhaps, be induced to extend his inquiries.

The Russians write and spell Basilius with the consonant *w*;[1] yet as we have grown into the habit of writing and spelling it with a *b*, I have not thought it necessary to write it with the *w*; *c* placed before an aspirate, should not be pronounced *ci* or *schi*, as some nations are accustomed to write it, but *khi*, after the manner of the Germans, as in the words Chiovia, Chan, Chlinov, Chlopigorod, etc. But when a double *z* is prefixed, it should be pronounced in a rather more sonorous manner,—as Czeremisse, Czernigo, Czilma, Czunkas, etc. The Russians express *g* with an aspirated *h* more strongly than is the custom of other Sclavonians, and almost after the Bohemian fashion,—as when they write Iugra, Wolga, they pronounce Iuhra, Wolha.

The letter *i* receives the fullest force of a consonant,—as in Iausa, Iaroslaw, Iamma, Ieropolchus, etc.

Th is pronounced almost like *ph*,— thus, Theodore is called Pheodore or Feodore.

When *v* has the force of a consonant, I have put in the place of it *w*, which the Germans express by double *u*, as in Wolodimeria, Worothin, Wedrasch, Wisma, Wladislaus. But when the same letter is placed in the middle or at the end of a word, it receives the force or sound of the Greek letter *phi*,—as Oczakow [Ochakov], Rostow [Rostov], Asow [Azov], Owka [Ovka]. The reader will carefully observe the force of this letter, lest by a careless pronunciation one and the same word might seem to imply different things.

Moreover, in treating of the annals, origin, and deeds of the Russians, I have not used our number of years, but theirs;[2] lest in differing from their documents, I might seem to assume the character rather of a corrector than of a faithful interpreter.

---

[1] The reader is begged to observe that this is Herberstein's explanation of his own mode of expressing the force of Russian letters in Roman character. The Russians spell Basilius with a letter of the form of our *b*, and holding the third place in their alphabet, but having the sound of the English *v* and the German *w*. This accounts for Herberstein, who was a German, representing this sound by the letter *w*; but there is no *w* in Russian.

[2] The era of Constantinople, which was adopted by the Russians from the Greek church, and continued in use until the reign of Peter the Great, fixes the creation of the world in the 5508th year before Christ, the year of whose incarnation fell in the 5509th of this era.

NOTES UPON RUSSIA.

VARIOUS are the opinions entertained respecting the origin of the name of Russia. Some maintain that it is derived from one Russus, a prince of the Poles, and brother or nephew of Lech, as though he himself had been a prince of the Russians. Others again derive it from a certain very ancient town, named Russum,[1] not far from Great Novogorod. Some also derive it from the dark colour of the people; and some think that, by a change in the word, Russia has received its designation from Roxolania. The Muscovites, however, contradict those who maintain these discrepant opinions, and assert, that it was anciently called Rosseia, as a nation dispersed and scattered, which indeed the name implies. For Rosseia, in the language of the Russians, means a dissemination or dispersion; and the variety of races even now blended with the inhabitants and the various provinces of Russia lying promiscuously intermingled, manifestly prove that this is correct. It is well known also to those who read the sacred writings, that the prophets use a word expressing dissemination when they speak of the dispersion of nations.[2] There are not wanting those also, who by a somewhat similar process of reasoning, derive the name of the Russians from a

---

[1] Staraia Russa, Anglicè Old Russa, to the south of Lake Ilmen.

[2] Herberstein appears here to allude to Leviticus, chap. xxvi, verse 23, and Ezekiel, chap. xxii, verse 15, and other passages, where occurs the Hebrew root זרה, to scatter, probably connected with זרע, to sow.

Greek, and hence from a Chaldaic origin, viz., from the Greek word ῥοῦς, a flowing, or from a kind of dispersion, as it were, by drops, which is called by the Aramæans,[1] Resissaia or Ressaia ; just as the Galli and Umbri have received their appellations from the Hebrew words, Gall and Gallim, and from Umber, *i. e.*, floods, storms, and inundations ; which is as much as to call them an inconstant and stormy people, or a nation liable to burst out and run over. But whatever be the source from which Russia has derived its name, all the races using the Sclavonic language that observe both the faith and the forms of Christianity in accordance with the ritual of the Greeks, and are called in conventional language Russians, and in Latin Rhuteni, have increased to so great a multitude, that they have either driven out all intermediate nations, or have absorbed them into their own habits of living ; so that all may now be designated by one common word, Russians.

Moreover, the Slavonic language,—which, by a slight corruption of the word, is called Sclavonic at the present day,—has a most extensive range : for the Dalmatians, the Bosnians, the Croatians, the Istrians, and those who dwell along the Adriatic in a long tract of country as far as Friuli ; the Carni,[2] whom the Venetians call Charsi ; the Carniolians also, and the Carinthians, as far as the Drave ; the Styrians, like-

---

[1] The inhabitants of Syria and Mesopotamia, so named as the descendants of Aram the fifth son of Shem. The name of Aram, given in Genesis to Syria, extended itself also to Mesopotamia, Chaldea, Assyria, and Elam. The languages spoken in the ancient country of Aram,—viz., the Syriac and Chaldean,—are still called Aramæan languages.

[2] A people of Gallia Transpadana, whose boundaries are thus given by Pliny, Livy, and others : on the east, the river Formio, which divided them from the Istri ; on the north, the Julian Alps, by which they were separated from Noricum ; on the south, the Adriatic ; and on the west, the River Tagliamento, which divided them from the Veneti. Thus they occupied the country which now forms the eastern part of the province of Friuli and the county of Goritz. The capital was Aquileia, now Aglar, a small town lying about midway between Palma Nuova and the sea.

wise, below Gratz, who dwell along the Muhr, as far as the Danube; then the Mysians, Servians, Bulgarians, and others dwelling as far as Constantinople, all speak the Sclavonic language; add to these the *Bohemians, Lusatians, Silesians, Moravians, and those who dwell by the river Waag, in the kingdom of Hungary; the Poles also, and the widely ruling Russians, together with the Circassians, called the Quinquemontani, on the Black Sea; lastly, through Germany, the remains of the Vandals scattered here and there over the north beyond the Elbe. While these various nations pretend to be Sclavonians, the Germans promiscuously call all those who use the Sclavonic language, Wends, Winden, and Windisch,—a term taken only from the Vandals.

Russia extends near to the Sarmatian mountains, up to a short distance from Cracow; thence along the river Tyra, which the natives call Dniester, to the Black Sea, and across to the Dnieper. Some years since, however, the Turk took possession of Alba, otherwise called Moncastro [Bielograd], also situated at the mouth of the river Dniester, and under the dominion of the Waywode[1] of Moldavia. The king of Taurica likewise crossed the Dnieper, and laying waste the country far and wide, built two fortresses,—one of which, called Ochakov, situated not far from the mouth of the Dnieper, is still in the possession of the Turk: but the space between these two rivers is now a desert. Moreover, in ascending the Dnieper, we come to the town of Circas [Cherkasui], lying towards the west, and then to the very ancient city of Kiev, formerly the metropolis of Russia; and on the opposite side of the Dnieper, is the still inhabited province of Sewera; and from thence, directly eastward, we come to the sources of the Don. Proceeding then a long distance by the course of the Don, as far nearly as the

---

[1] The original is "Voyvoda", which, in Russian, signifies "leader of an army".

conflux of the rivers Occa and Volga, and crossing the Volga, a very long journey brings us at length to the Northern Ocean. Thence returning through the countries which are subject to the king of Sweden, by Finland, the Gulf of Livonia, Livonia, Samogithia, and Masovia, and lastly through Poland, the country is bounded by the Sarmatian mountains, two provinces only intervening,—namely, Lithuania and Samogithia,—which two provinces are intermixed with the Russians; and though they have their own dialects, and use the Roman ritual, the inhabitants are nevertheless for the most part Russian.

Of the princes who now rule over Russia, the first is the Grand Duke of Moscow, who holds the greatest part of it; the second is the Grand Duke of Lithuania; the third is the King of Poland, who now is sovereign both of Poland and Lithuania.

This nation possesses no information concerning its origin beyond the annals hereafter quoted, which state that this Sclavonic people were of the race of Japhet, and were formerly seated on the Danube, in that part which is now called Hungary and Bulgaria, and that they were at that time called Norici; that at length they were scattered and dispersed over various lands, and took the names of the places whither they went: as for instance, the Moravians took their name from the river Moraw; others called themselves Ozechi, *i. e.*, Bohemians; also Ghorwati,[1] Bieli, Serbli, *i. e.*, Servians; the Chorontani[2] also, who located themselves on the shores of the Danube; others being driven out by the Walachians, came to the Vistula, and took the name of Lechi, from one Lech, a prince of the Poles, from whom

[1] The Hungarian form for Croatians.
[2] The extent of Karantania, the country of the Chorontani or Karantani, is described by Schafarik, in his *Slawische Alterthümer*, as embracing Carinthia, Stiria, and part of Tyrol. It was thus bounded on the south by Lombardy, east by Pannonia, north by Lower Austria and Bavaria. The modern name of Karinthia is derived from it.

also the Poles are called Lechi. Others are called Lithuanians, Mazovians, and Pomeranians; others, taking their abode by the Dnieper where now Kiev is situated, were called Poleni; others Drewliani, dwelling in woods; others between the Dwina and Peti were called Dregowici; others called Poleutzani, on the river Polta, which flows into the Dwina; others about the Lake Ilmen, who took possession of Novogorod, and selected as their ruler a prince named Gostomissel; others, called Seweri or Sewerski,[1] dwelt on the shores of the rivers Desna and Sula;[2] others again named Chriwitzi, by the sources of the Volga and the Dnieper, whose capital and fortress is Smolensko. These things are testified by their own annals.

It is unknown who were the original sovereigns of Russia, for they had no characters in which their deeds could be written and transmitted to memory. But after that Michael, king of Constantinople, had sent the Sclavonian characters into Bulgaria in the year of the world six thousand four hundred and six [898],[3] then first, not only the occurrences of the period, but also those which they had heard from their ancestors and retained through long memory, began to be written and recorded in their annals. From these it appears, that the people of the Coseri had formerly exacted from some of the Russians a tribute of squirrel skins, to be delivered to them from each house, and also that the Waregi had been rulers over them. Concerning the Coseri,[4] I have

---

[1] *I. e.*, northern.

[2] Two rivers falling into the Dnieper.

[3] According to Nestor, the ancient Sclavonian chronicler, it was about the year 863, and not 898, as given by Herberstein, that Michael the Third sent into Bulgaria Cyrillus and Methodius, two brothers, natives of Thessalonia, who were distinguished for their learning and piety, to translate the Scriptures into the Sclavonian language of the country. They invented the letters known as the Cyrillic alphabet.

[4] The Khozars, or Khazars, a race of Turkish origin who inhabited for a long time the western shores of the Caspian. They were first called

been able to learn nothing from the annals, beyond the name, as to whence they came or who they were; and the same likewise with the Waregi;[1] but as they gave the name of Waregan Sea to the Baltic, and to that sea which divides Prussia, Livonia, and part of their own territory from Sweden, I have concluded from the vicinity that their princes were either Swedes or Danes, or Prussians. But since Wagria seems to have been formerly a most famous seat and province of the Vandals, near to Lubeck and the Duchy of Holstein, it would appear that the sea which is now called the Baltic took its name from it; and as that sea, together with the gulph which divides Germany from Denmark, and separates also Prussia, Livonia, and the maritime portion of the Russian empire from Sweden, was at that time called by the Russians Waretzokoie Morie, *i. e.* the Waregan Sea; and as in addition to this the Vandals were at that time powerful, used the language, and practised the manners and religion of the Russians, it appears to me more probable that the Russians called their princes from the Wagrii, or Waregi, than

Akazirs, under which name they in the year 212 made an irruption into Armenia. They were conquered first by Attila, and afterwards by the Bulgarians. After the death of Attila, they became free; and in the sixth century they had continual wars with the Persians, who, under Cosroes, erected a wall against them, known as the Caucasian wall, the ruins of which still exist. They subsequently carried on hostilities with the Arabs, invaded Hungary likewise, and made several princes tributary, so that their dominion extended from the Volga and the Caspian Sea to the Moldavia and Wallachia of the present day. At length their kingdom fell under the frequent attacks of the Russians about 1016; the name of *Chazars*, however, prevailed for a century or more afterwards. They were known under the name of *Kosa* to the Chinese themselves. For a summary of the history of this people, see Stritter, *Memoriæ Populorum Septentr.*, tom. iii, fo. 548; St. Petersburg, 1778, 4to.; Karamzin, tom. i, fo. 48; Paris, 1819, 8vo.; and De Guignes, *Hist. des Huns*, tom. i, part II, pp. 507-509.

[1] After a long controversy amongst the Russians, it seems to be very generally allowed by the best antiquaries, that the Waregi were Scandinavians or Northmen. For a detailed account of them, see Karamzin, vol. i, fo. 52, *et seq.*

that they conferred their government upon foreigners, who differed from them in religion, manners, and language. It happened, then, that as the Russians had contentions among themselves from time to time concerning the sovereignty, and the opposite parties, inflamed with hatred against each other, were carrying their quarrels to the highest pitch of malignity, one Gostomissel, a man of prudence and great authority in Novogorod, advised, as a conciliatory measure, that they should send to the Waregi, and request three brothers, who were there held in high estimation, to undertake the government. His advice meeting with a ready approval, ambassadors were sent to fetch the brother princes, who, upon their arrival, divided between them the government thus voluntarily conceded. Rurick obtained the principality of Novogorod, and fixed his residence in Ladoga, thirty-six German miles below great Novogorod. Sinaus settled himself at the White Lake [Bielosero] and Truvor, in the town of Svortzech [Isborsk], in the principality of Plescov. The Russians boast that these brothers derived their origin from the Romans, from whom even the present prince of Russia asserts that he is sprung. The entrance of these brothers into Russia took place, according to the annals, in the year of the world 6370 (862). Two of them dying without heirs, Rurick, the survivor, came into possession of all the principalities, and divided his fortresses among his friends and relatives. Upon his death-bed, he entrusted his youthful son, named Igor, together with the kingdom, to the care of one of his kinsmen, named Oleg, who increased the latter by the conquest of many provinces. Carrying his arms as far as Greece, he laid siege even to Constantinople, and after a reign of thirty three years, died of an injury caused by the bite of a poisonous snake, through accidentally planting his foot on the skull of his horse after it had been some time dead. Upon the death of Oleg, Igor, who had married a wife from Plescov, named Olga, took the reins of government. This prince proceeded with his forces still further than his predecessor, and reached Heraclea and Nicomedia; at length, however, he was overthrown in battle and fled. He met his death subsequently at the hand of Maldittus,[1] a prince of the Drevlians, at a place called Ciresti,[2] and was there buried. As his son Svyatoslav', whom he left an infant, could not reign on account of his tender age, his mother Olga became regent in the interim; and on one occasion, when the Drevlians sent twenty messengers to her with commands that she should marry their prince, Olga first ordered the messengers of the Drevlians to be buried alive, and then dispatched messengers of her own to them to say, that if they wished her to be their princess and mistress, they should send a greater number of wooers, and of higher rank: after this she scalded to death, in a bath, fifty picked men that had been sent to her, and again sent other messengers to announce their arrival, and ordered that they should prepare some aqua mulsa[3] and other things which were usually considered necessary in providing for the obsequies of a deceased husband. Moreover, when she came to the Drevlians, she held a mourning for her husband, and having made the Drevlians drunk, slew five thousand of them: she then returned to Kiev, raised an army, and proceeding against the Drevlians, oppressed them with a siege which lasted a whole year, during which she persecuted those who fled to her camp, and finally obtained the victory. Terms of peace being afterwards agreed upon, she demanded a tribute from

---

[1] Nestor calls this prince "Male".

[2] This is a misspelling for Korosten, the ancient capital of the Drevlians. It occupied the site of the present town of Iskorosk in Volhynia. A mound called the "Tomb of Igor" is still to be seen on a plain near the town by the banks of the river Oosha.— *Geographichesky Slovar Rossyeskago Gosoodarstva.* Moscow, 1804, 4to.

[3] Hydromel. Pliny, in his twenty-second book, says, "Mellis quidem ipsius natura talis est ut putrescere corpora non sinat". Columella (lib. xii, cap. 12, fo. 420) speaks of the preparation of aqua mulsa.

every house of three pigeons and as many sparrows, and upon receiving the birds, she sent them back with various combustible materials fastened under their wings; the birds being released, made their way for their accustomed homes, and flying back to the fortresses, set fire to them, while those who fled from the conflagration were either slain or taken prisoners, and sold. When she had taken possession of all the fortresses of the Drevlians, and revenged the death of her husband, she returned to Kiev. Proceeding subsequently to Greece, in the year of the world 6463 (955), she received baptism under King John of Constantinople, and changing her name of Olga for that of Helen, received large presents from the king upon the occasion of her baptism, soon after which she returned home. She was the first Christian among the Russians, according to their annals, which compare her to the Sun: for as the Sun illuminates the world itself, so also, say the records, she illuminated Russia with the faith of Christ. She could not, however, by any means persuade her son Svyatoslav' to be baptized, who on arriving at manhood proved to be strong and active, and shrunk from no warlike exertion or danger to which warriors were accustomed. He permitted his army to carry no baggage, not even cooking utensils, and himself ate nothing but roast meat, and was accustomed to sleep upon the ground with only a saddle for his pillow. He carried his arms as far as the Danube and conquered the Bulgarians, and fixed his court in the city of Pereaslav', saying to his mother and counsellors: "This is my capital, in the midst of my dominions; from Greece are brought to me Panodokhi[1] gold, silver, wine, and various fruits; from Hungary, silver and horses; from Russia, schora,[2]

---

[1] The editor is unable to offer any explanation of the meaning of this word, which on the following page is spelt panodochmi, beyond the suggestion that it may be derived from the Greek words $\pi\hat{a}\nu$ and $\delta\acute{e}\chi o\mu a\iota$, as implying the reception of "gifts of all sorts".

[2] A Russian word for harness.

wax, honey and slaves." To which his mother replied: "Now at length I am prepared to die, bury me wherever thou wilt." And at the end of three days she died, and was enrolled amongst the number of the saints by her grandson Vladimir, who had been already baptized. The 11th day of July is dedicated to her. Svyatoslav', who reigned after his mother's death, divided the provinces among his sons: to Yaropolk he gave Kiev, to Oleg he gave the Drevlians, and to Vladimir, Great Novogorod. Indeed, the Novogorodians were instigated by a certain woman named Dobrina, to request that Vladimir should be made their prince; for there was a certain man at Novogorod, called Calufcza the Little,[1] who had two daughters, Dobrina[2] and Malusha, and while Malusha was in the gynæceum of Olga she became the mother of Vladimir, by Svyatoslav'.

Meanwhile Svyatoslav', having an eye to the aggrandisement of his sons, proceeded to Bulgaria, laid siege to the city of Pereaslav', and took it. He then declared war against the kings Basil and Constantine; but they sent messengers to sue for peace, and promising, though deceitfully, that they would pay tribute according to the number of his army, desired that he would inform them of its extent; and after they had ascertained the number of his forces, they also levied an army. At length, when both were confronted, the Russians became terrified at the host of the Greeks, but Svyatoslav' seeing their fear, thus addressed them: "Since, O Russians, I see no place into which we can retreat with safety, and as at the same time it has never entered into my thoughts to surrender the soil of Russia to our enemies, I am resolved either to die or win renown by fighting bravely against them. For if I die fighting valiantly, my name will be immortal; whereas if I flee, I shall carry with me eternal disgrace. And since it is not possible

---

[1] Karamzin calls him Liubchanin.
[2] Karamzin describes Dobrina as the brother of Malusha.

for one who is surrounded by a host of enemies to escape, it is my determination to stand firmly, and at all risks to expose myself in the foremost rank for the sake of my country." The soldiers replied: "Wheresoever thou leadest we will follow.". Having thus restored the confidence of his army, he rushed upon the enemy with a terrific onslaught, and bore away the victory. Subsequently, while laying waste the country of the Greeks, the other princes of the country besieged him with presents of gold and panodochmi (so the annals have it); but all their gifts he slighted and refused, accepting the garments and arms which the Greeks afterwards sent to him. This manifestation of virtue on his part so moved the people of Greece, that they addressed their own sovereigns on one occasion when assembled together, to the effect, that that was the sort of king that they desired to serve—namely, one who preferred arms to gold. As Svyatoslav' was approaching Constantinople, the Greeks at last got rid of him from their country by the payment of a large tribute. Finally, in the year of the world 6480 (972), Cures, a prince of the Pieczenigi,[1] caught him in an ambush and slew him, and made a goblet of his skull surrounded with a golden rim, on which was engraved this sentence: "By seeking the possessions of others he lost his own." .

When Svyatoslav' was dead, one of his nobles named Svyadolt, went to Yaropolk at Kiev, and besought him with the greatest earnestness and pertinacity to thrust out his

---

[1] The Pieczenigi or Badjnaks were a tribe of Turkish origin constantly engaged in wars either with the Russians, the Hungarians, the Greeks, or the Khazars. They occupied an extensive territory, bounded south by Bulgaria and Servia, east by Hungary and Poland, north by the Grand Duchy of Kiev, and west by the Khazars. They gradually became weakened by their incessant wars, and were at length completely subdued by John II, Comnenus, since which time they ceased to be spoken of as an independent nation. For some details of their habits, see Von Hammer, *Sur les Origines Russes*. St. Petersburg, 1825, 4to., fo. 33 and 46.

brother Oleg from the kingdom, because he had put his son Lutas to death. Yaropolk, overruled by his persuasions, waged war against his brother, and routed his army of Drewlians; while Oleg himself, in endeavouring to escape to a certain fortress, was shut out from it by his own followers, and in the confusion of the flight was thrust over a certain bridge, and died a wretched death beneath the numerous bodies of those who fell upon him. Yaropolk, after having gained possession of the camp, sought for his brother, and when he found the body lying among the dead, he gazed upon his upturned countenance and exclaimed: "O Svyadolt, behold here the accomplishment of thy desire!" He then buried him.

When Vladimir heard that Oleg was slain, he left Novogorod and fled beyond the sea to the Waregi; upon which Yaropolk established a viceroy at Novogorod, and was made monarch of all Russia. After this, Vladimir, having procured the assistance of the Waregi, returned, drove out his brother's viceroy from Novogorod, and knowing that his brother was about to take up arms against him, was the first to make a declaration of war. In the interim he sent messengers to Rochvolochda, prince of Plescov', through whose country he had passed in his march from Wagria, to ask the hand of his daughter Rochmida in marriage. The maiden, however, knowing Vladimir was illegitimate, did not wish to be married to him, but rather to his brother Yaropolk, who she thought would be likely soon to prefer his suit. Vladimir, indignant at having suffered a refusal, waged war against Rochvolochda, and slew him and his two sons; but he took Rochmida the daughter to be his wife, and afterwards marched to Kiev against his brother. Yaropolk, however, not daring to engage in a battle against his brother, shut himself up at Kiev. While Vladimir was besieging Kiev, he sent a secret messenger to one Blud, the intimate counsellor of Yaropolk, and dignifying him with the appellation of father, begged him to suggest the means of killing his brother. When Blud understood the request of Vladimir, he promised that he himself would kill his master, but advised Vladimir to lay siege to the fortress; at the same time, however, he recommended Yaropolk not to remain within the fortress, alleging as a reason that many of his men had deserted to Vladimir. Yaropolk, confiding in his counsellor, fled to Roden, at the mouth of the Yursa,[1] imagining that he would there be safe against the violence of his brother. When Vladimir had subdued Kiev, he led his army against Roden, and pressed Yaropolk with a long and severe siege. Afterwards, when they were exhausted with long famine and could no longer endure the siege, Blud advised Yaropolk to make peace with his brother, he being by far the more powerful of the two. In the meantime, however, he sent a messenger to Vladimir, to say that he would soon bring his brother to him and deliver him up to him. Yaropolk followed the counsel of Blud, and submitted himself to the will and power of his brother, voluntarily avowing that he should be grateful for any concessions that he would be pleased to make in his favour.

These terms were by no means displeasing to Vladimir.

[1] Nestor calls this place Rodna on the Resa. Karamzin describes it as Rodnia, situated at the point where the river Ross falls into the Dnieper. In the *Geographichesky Slovar Rossyeskago Gosoodarstva*, Rodnia is given as the place to which Yarapolk fled, but is said to be on the Sula, a river which likewise falls into the Dnieper, and at a point not far distant from the embouchure of the Ross. After a fruitless examination of the best maps, both early and modern, the editor has concluded that it is a mistake to place the town in question on the Sula, since the Yursa of Herberstein, the Resa of Nestor, and the Ross of Karamzin, may easily be supposed to mean the same river, while they bear no resemblance to the name of Sula. Upon this subject, Scherbatov, after describing the town as Roden on the mouth of the Ursa, remarks that others call it Goroden, and place it on the Sula. It is remarkable that none of the various historians of Russia appear to have discussed this discrepancy as to the site of this town; and only one, as far as the editor has been able to discover, has even alluded to it.

Blud then recommended his master to go to Vladimir, though another counsellor of his, named Verasco, strongly advised him not to do so. Yaropolk, however, neglected the advice of the latter, and proceeded to his brother; and, as he was entering a gate, he was killed by two Waregi, while Vladimir himself was looking down upon the scene from a tower. After the commission of this crime, Vladimir debauched his brother's wife, a Greek woman by birth, whom Yaropolk also had got with child previous to marrying her, and at a time when she was a nun.

This Vladimir established many idols at Kiev: one of these was called Perun, whose head was of silver, but the rest of his body wood; the others were called Uslad, Corsa, Dasva, Striba, Simaergla, and Macosch. To these idols, which were also called Cumeri,[1] he offered sacrifices. His wives were numerous. By Rochmida he had Isoslaus, Yeroslas, Servold, and two daughters; by the Greek he had Svyatopolk; by a Bohemian he had Saslaus; and by another Bohemian, Svyatoslav' and Stanislaus; by a Bulgarian woman he had Boris and Glyeb. He kept, besides, in a high tower, three hundred concubines; in Bielograd, also three hundred, and in Berestov and Selvi, two hundred.

Now that Vladimir was become the undisputed monarch of all Russia, there came to him, from different quarters, ambassadors, exhorting him to join their respective sects; but when he saw that these sects differed from each other, he himself sent out messengers of his own to ascertain what were the requirements and ceremonies of each; and, finally making choice of the Christian religion, according to the Greek ritual, he sent ambassadors to the kings Basil and Constantine, at Constantinople, with a proposal, that, if they would give him their sister Anna to be his wife, he would embrace the Christian religion, with all his subjects, and would restore

---

[1] The Russian word for idols.

to them Corsun, and all the other places in Greece of which he had possession. This being agreed upon, the time was arranged, and Corsun selected as the spot for the celebration of the ceremony; and there, upon the arrival of the two kings, Vladimir was baptized, and received the name of Vasiley in lieu of that of Vladimir. After the celebration of the nuptials, he restored Corsun and the other places, as he had promised. These events took place in the year of the world 6469 (961), since which time Russia has continued in the faith of Christ. Anna died twenty-three years after her marriage, and Vladimir four years after the death of his wife. He built a city, situated between the rivers Wolga and Occa, which he called Vladimir, after his own name, and constituted it the metropolis of Russia. He is worshipped yearly among the saints, as an apostle, on the 15th of July.

After the death of Vladimir, his sons disagreed among themselves, and, preferring various claims to the succession, fought together, till the strongest overcame the weakest or less skilful and drove them from the kingdom. Svyatopolk, who had taken possession of the principality of Kiev by force, procured assassins to kill his brothers Boris and Glyeb, who, after death, were enrolled amongst the number of the saints under changed names, the latter being called David, and the former Romanus. The 24th of July is held sacred to them. But during these contentions among the brothers, no deed worthy of record was done by them, unless the reader wish to hear of treachery, ambuscades, deceit, and civil wars. Vladimir, the son of Levold, surnamed Monomach, again reduced the whole of Russia into a monarchy, and left behind him certain insignia which are used at the present day, at the inauguration of princes. Vladimir died A.M. 6633 (1125); nor did his children, or grandchildren after him, do any thing worthy of record till the times of Georgius and Vasiley, whom Bati, king of the Tartars, con-

D

quered and killed, and burnt and plundered Vladimir, Moscow, and a considerable part of Russia.

From that time, namely in the year 6745 (1237), up to the present Grand Duke Vasiley, not only were nearly all the princes of Russia tributaries of the Tartars, but every principality was deferred to the will of the Tartars when Russians were making any interest to procure them. Moreover, although the Tartars took cognizance of, and decided in, the quarrels that arose among them on account of their successors and inheritances, nevertheless wars often arose between the Russians and Tartars. Between brothers also there were sundry tumults, expulsions, and exchanges of kingdoms and dukedoms; for the Duke Andrew Alexandrovich obtained the Grand Duchy, and when Dimitry had taken possession of it, his brother Andrew requested, and obtained, an army of Tartars, drove him away, and committed many infamous acts throughout Russia. So also the Duke Dimitry Michailovich killed the Duke George Danielovich while he was among the Tartars. Asbech, king of the Tartars, seized Dimitry, and subjected him to capital punishment. There was a contention respecting the Grand Duchy of Tver, which, when the Duke Simeon Ivanovich begged of Zanabech, king of the Tartars, he demanded an annual tribute of him; but which the nobles, bribed with a large sum, successfully interceded for him that he should not pay. Afterwards, in the year 6886 (1378), the Grand Duke Dimitry overcame in battle the great king of the Tartars, named Mamaii, and three years afterwards again routed him, and that with such a slaughter that the ground for more than thirteen miles was covered with dead bodies. In the second year after that conflict, Tachtamich, king of the Tartars, came over and routed Dimitrye, and besieged and took possession of Moscow; those who were slaughtered were redeemed for burial at the rate of eighty bodies per ruble, and the total sum was computed at three thousand rubles. The Grand Duke Vasiley, who reigned in the year 6907 (1399), took possession of Bulgaria, which stretches along the banks of the Volga, and drove out the Tartars.

This Vasiley Dimitrievich left an only son, whom he did not love because he had suspected his wife Anastasia, who was this child's mother, of adultery; and therefore on his death-bed he left the Grand Duchy of Moscow, not to his son, but to his brother George. But as George observed that many of the Boyars[1] adhered to his son as the legitimate heir and successor, he hastened to the Tartars, and begged the king to summon Vasiley and decide to whom the Duchy lawfully belonged. The king, instigated by one of his counsellors who supported George, gave his opinion in favour of George in the presence of Vasiley; upon which the latter threw himself at the feet of the king, and begged permission to speak. On receiving the king's assent, he said: "Thou hast announced thy decision upon lifeless words, but I trust that the living documents which I possess, and which distinctly express, under the authority of thy golden seal, thy former wish to invest me with the Grand Duchy, may be held by thee to be of far greater weight and importance"; and he besought the king to hold his own words in remembrance, and graciously to adhere to the promise which he had given. To which the king replied: "That it would be more consistent with justice to keep the promises contained in living documents, than to admit the validity of dead ones." He ended by investing Vasiley with the Duchy, and dismissed him.

George, being very indignant at this result, levied an army and drove out Vasiley; but this he treated with the greatest unconcern, and retired to the Principality of Uglitz, which

---

[1] A title borne by the grandees or nobles of Russia. It is said to be derived from *boi*, a battle, the title being originally given to the chiefs who surrounded the prince on the field of battle. It was subsequently extended to all the chief dignitaries of state. In ancient days the boyars were always consulted by the czar in matters of importance.

had been left him by his father. George quietly enjoyed the Grand Duchy during his life time, and left it by will to his nephew Vasiley; but his sons Andrew and Dimitry, considering themselves deprived of their rightful inheritance, were greatly incensed at this, and laid siege to Moscow in consequence. When Vasiley, who had entered the monastery of St. Sergius, heard of these proceedings, he sent out scouts, and took the precaution of stationing outposts, that he might not be overwhelmed by a sudden attack. The two brothers, however, became aware of this, and laid a plot to fill certain waggons with armed soldiers, which they sent on as if they were loaded with merchandise; and being brought in at twilight, they attacked their enemies under cover of the night, and took them while unsuspicious of any danger. Vasiley was captured in the monastery, and having first had his eyes put out, was sent, together with his wife, to Uglitz. Shortly afterwards, when Dimitry saw that the generality of the nobles were hostile to him, and that they went over to the blind Vasiley, he fled to Novogorod, leaving behind him his son Ivan, who subsequently became the father of Vasiley Semeczitz, who was confined in prison at the very time that I was in Moscow: but of this more hereafter. Dimitry was surnamed Semecka, and hence all his descendants bear the cognomen of Semeczitzi.

At length the blind Vasiley Vasilievich obtained quiet possession of the Grand Duchy. From the time of Vladimir Monomach up to this Vasiley, Russia had no monarch. But Vasiley's son, who was surnamed Ivan, was most fortunate; for at the same time as he married Mary the sister of Michael, Grand Duke of Tver, he drove out his brother-in-law, and took possession first of the Grand Duchy of Tver, and then even of great Novogorod; and after that, all the other princes being either moved by the grandeur of his achievements or stricken with fear became subject to him. As affairs continued to prosper with him, he began to assume the title of

Grand Duke of Vladimir, Moscow, and Novogorod; and finally to declare himself monarch of all Russia. This Ivan had by Mary a son, also named Ivan, to whom he gave in marriage the daughter of Stephen the great Waywode of Moldavia, who had overthrown Mahomet king of the Turks, Matthew king of Hungary, and John Albert king of Poland. After the death of his first wife Mary, Ivan Vasilievich married Sophia, daughter of Thomas, who formerly had held wide sway in the Peloponnesus (I mean the son of Emanuel king of Constantinople, of the race of Palœologi): by her he had five sons, Gabriel, Dimitry, George, Simeon, and Andrew: and while living he divided their patrimony amongst them. To Ivan the eldest he reserved the sovereignty, to Gabriel he appointed Great Novogorod, and to the rest he made other allotments according to his pleasure. Ivan the eldest died, leaving a son, Dimitry; and his grandfather invested him with the sovereignty, according to custom, in the room of his late father. They say that this Sophia was a very artful woman, and had considerable influence over the actions of the grand duke. Among other things she is reported to have induced her husband to remove his grandson Dimitry from the sovereignty, and to elevate Gabriel to his place. For the duke, overruled by his wife, cast Dimitry into prison and kept him there, until at length on his death-bed he ordered him to be brought to him, and thus addressed him: " Dear grandson, I have sinned against God and thee, inasmuch as I have afflicted thee with imprisonment and have deprived thee of thy just inheritance; I beseech thee forgive me the injury I have done thee, depart in freedom and enjoy thy right." Dimitry, affected by this address, readily forgave his grandfather the injury; but as he went out he was seized by command of his step-brother Gabriel, and thrown into prison. Some think that he was murdered by starvation and cold, and others that he was suffocated with smoke. Gabriel acted as regent during the life of Dimitry, but after his death he retained the sovereignty without having been inaugurated, merely changing his name of Gabriel to that of Vasiley.

The Grand Duke Ivan had by Sophia a daughter, Helena, whom he united to Alexander, Grand Duke of Lithuania, afterwards proclaimed king of Poland. The Lithuanians hoped that the discords of these princes, which had already been very severe, would be arranged by this marriage; but far more grievous quarrels arose out of it. For at the nuptials it was agreed that a temple should be built in accordance with the Russian religion in an appointed spot in Vilna, and that certain matrons and virgins of the same religion should be attached to it; but as after some little time this was neglected to be done, Alexander's father-in-law took it up as a pretext of war against him, and having levied a triple army proceeded to attack him. The first army he sent southward, towards the province of Severa, the second westward against Toropetz and Bieloi, and the third he placed between them, towards Dorogobusch and Smolensko; thus supplying reserves for his army by which he could bring the most effective assistance to that portion of it against which he might observe a disposition in the Lithuanians to make an attack. But after both armies had reached a certain river called Vedrosha,[1] the Lithuanians under the command of Constantine Ostroski, who was surrounded by a numerous staff of noblemen and chiefs, gained information from some prisoners respecting the number of the enemy and of their leaders, and entertained great hope of routing them. Moreover, as the stream intercepted the conflict, both parties made search for a ford by which they could cross it. Some Russians, however, first reached the bank and challenged the Lithuanians to the combat; but the latter resisted, and routed them, and following in pursuit drove

[1] The Vedrosha is a very small river which flows into the Osma, an affluent of the Dnieper.

them back across the river. Both armies soon after met in a pitched battle, and a terrific engagement ensued. In the meantime, while they were keenly contending on both sides with equal fury, one of the armies which had been placed in ambush, though without the knowledge of many of the Russians, fell suddenly upon the main body of the enemy. The Lithuanians, stricken with fear, were routed, and the commander in chief, together with many nobles, taken; the remainder in terror yielded up their camp to the enemy, and surrendered themselves and the fortresses of Drogobush, Toropetz and Bieloi. The army, however, which had moved towards the south under the command of Machmethemin the Tartar king of Casan, made a vigorous attack on the governor (commonly called Waywode) of the city of Brensko, and took possession of that city. Afterwards, two brothers, cousins of Vasiley, the one named Staradub, the other Semeczitz, who were owners of a great part of the province of Severa, and otherwise subject to the dukes of Lithuania, surrendered themselves up to the government of Russia. Thus in one single conflict, and on one day, the Russians acquired what it had cost Vithold, Grand Duke of Lithuania, many years of the greatest exertion to gain possession of. The Russian monarch, however, behaved somewhat cruelly to these Lithuanian prisoners, and kept them confined in very severe bondage. He also made a stipulation with Constantine their general that he should desert his natural master and serve him; and as he had no hope of escaping by any other means, he accepted the condition, and after binding himself by a very strong oath, received his freedom; but although great estates and possessions were granted to him for the maintenance of his rank, he could not be reconciled or withheld from making his escape on the first opportunity through the intricacies of the woods.

Alexander, the king of Poland and Grand Duke of Lithuania, who always delighted more in peace than war, relinquished all the provinces and forts which had been taken by the Russians, and contenting himself with the liberation of his own people, made peace with his father-in-law.

This Ivan Vasilievich was so successful, that he overcame the people of Novogorod in battle at the river Scholona,[1] and reduced them to acknowledge him as their lord and prince, on certain proposed conditions. He granted them a large sum of money and then left them, after having first appointed a representative to supply his place; then again returning after the lapse of seven years, he entered the city with the cooperation of the Archbishop Theophilus, reduced the inhabitants to the most abject servitude, and seizing the gold and the silver and all the goods of the citizens, carried off more than three hundred waggons full of booty.

He himself was only once engaged in war, when the principalities of Novogorod and Tver were taken possession of; at other times he never used to go to battle, but nevertheless always carried off the palm of victory; so that Stephen the great Palatine of Moldavia would often say, when speaking of him at his banquets: "That he increased his dominion while sitting at home and sleeping, while he himself could scarcely defend his own boundaries by fighting every day." He even appointed and deposed the kings of Casan at his own pleasure; sometimes he threw them into prison, but at length, in his old age, received a severe defeat at their hands. He was the first who fortified his ducal residence at Moscow with a wall, as it is seen at this day. Moreover he was so hostile to women, that if any women met him by chance, they almost always fainted with terror at the sight of him. No access was allowed to him for poor men, who were oppressed by the more powerful or unjustly treated; he generally drunk so excessively at dinner as to fall asleep, and while his guests

---

[1] The river Chelon', which rises in the government of Pskov, and flowing in a north-east direction, falls into Lake Ilmen at its south-west corner.

were all struck with terror and sitting in silence, he would awake, rub his eyes, and then first begin to joke and make merry with them. But although this Grand Duke was so powerful a prince, he was nevertheless compelled to acknowledge the sway of the Tartars, for when the Tartar ambassadors were approaching, he would go forth from the city to meet them, and make them be seated while he stood to receive their addresses, a circumstance which so annoyed his Greek wife, that she would daily tell him she had married a slave of the Tartars, and to induce her husband to throw off this servile habit would sometimes persuade him to feign sickness on the approach of the Tartars. There was within the citadel of Moscow a house in which the Tartars lodged for the purpose of learning what was going on at Moscow, and as this also gave great offence to his wife, she sent messengers with liberal presents to the queen of the Tartars, begging her to give up that house to her; for that she had been admonished in a dream from heaven to build a temple upon that spot; at the same time she promised to allot another house to the Tartars. The queen granted her request; the house was destroyed and a temple was built on its site, and the Tartars thus driven out of the citadel have never been able to obtain a house from any subsequent Duke.

This Ivan the Great died A.M. 7014 [1506], and his son Gabriel, afterwards called Vasiley, succeeded him as Grand Duke, but kept his brother's son, Dimitry, in prison, who, according to the custom of the people, had been constituted the lawful monarch during the lifetime of his grandfather; for this reason Vasiley refused to receive the solemn investiture of the monarchy, not only while his nephew lived but even after his death. He imitated his father in many things; all the dominions that his father had left him he not only kept entire, but added thereto many provinces besides, not so much by war, in which he had but little success, as by industry. As his father had reduced Great Novogorod into subjection,

E

so did he with the confederate city of Plescov. He became likewise governor of the noble principality of Smolensko, which had been more than a century under the dominion of the Lithuanians; for when Alexander king of Poland died, Vasiley, seeing that Sigismund, who became king of Poland and Grand Duke of Lithuania, was rather inclined to peace than war, and that the Lithuanians were equally averse to fighting, although he had no ground of contention with him, found an excuse for a war in the following manner: he said that his sister, Alexander's widow, was treated with very great indignity by the Lithuanians, and also pretended that king Sigismund had provoked the Tartars against him. Upon this plea he declared a war, and bringing up his artillery laid siege to Smolensko, but without any success. Subsequently, however, Michael Lyncsky, who was sprung from the noble stock and of the family of the princes of Russia, and who had formerly held the chief management of affairs under Alexander, sent over to the Grand Duke of Muscovy, and managed so as to induce him to take up arms; he also undertook to carry Smolensko by storm if he would lay siege to it a second time, but with this stipulation, that the principality should be conceded to him. Vasiley consented to these conditions, and a second time pressed Smolensko with a heavy siege. Lyncsky having become possessor of the city by treaties, or more correctly by bribery, led all the officers of his soldiery with him into Moscow, with the exception of one, who, guiltless of the crime of treachery, returned to his master. The other officers, however, having been bribed with money and presents, did not dare to return into Lithuania; and to give a colour to their crime inspired fear into their soldiers, by saying, if we turn our steps towards Lithuania we shall from time to time be either plundered or killed; and by this process the soldiers becoming intimidated, went all of them into Moscow and received pay from the prince.

Vasiley, elated with this victory, ordered his army to proceed directly into Lithuania, but he himself remained in Smolensko. After some of the more neighbouring fortresses and towns had been received in surrender, then first did Sigismund, king of Poland, levy an army and send but too tardy assistance to those who were besieged in Smolensko. Afterwards, when Smolensko was taken, and when he saw that the Russian army was directing its march towards Lithuania, he himself fled to Borisov, which is situated near the river Beresina, and sent on his army thence under the command of Constantine Ostroski. When the latter reached the Dnieper, near the town of Orsa [Orcha], which is twenty-three German miles distant from Smolensko, he found that the Russian army, which was about eighty thousand strong, was not far from him. The Lithuanians, on the other hand, had not more than thirty-five thousand men, with the addition, nevertheless, of a few pieces of artillery. It was on the 8th day of September, A.D. 1514, that Constantine, seeing the state of affairs, threw a bridge over the Dnieper, and made his infantry pass over near the town of Orsa. The cavalry passed by a narrow ford under the very walls of Orsa. Presently, when half the army had crossed the Dnieper, Ivan Andryeevich Czeladin, to whom the chief command had been entrusted by the Grand Duke, received an intimation that he ought to attack this part of the army and overwhelm it. But he replied: " If we were to fall upon this part of the army, the other part, to which perhaps yet other forces may be added, will still remain, and thus a greater danger would threaten us : let us wait until the whole army has crossed, for our strength is such that without doubt we shall be able with but little exertion either to overwhelm this army, or to surround them and drive them like cattle to Moscow, and then it will only remain for us to take possession of the whole of Lithuania."

Meanwhile the Lithuanian army advanced, mixed with

Poles and foreign troops, and when they had arrived within four miles distance of Orsa both armies came to a halt. Two wings of the Russians had withdrawn to some distance in order to circumvent the enemy in the rear, but the main army stood drawn up midway, some advancing from the van to challenge the enemy to battle. On the other side the Lithuanian army was placed in a long array, drawn up according to their different nations, for each principality had sent troops and a captain from among its own people, and thus each had its allotted place in the body of the army. The legions being at length brought front to front, the Russians, sounding their clarions, made the first attack on the Lithuanians, who, however, met them vigorously and repulsed them. Presently others came to the assistance of the Russians, and in their turn put the Lithuanians to flight; and thus each side, assisted by new supplies, several times routed the other. At length came the greatest struggle. The Lithuanians purposely retreated towards the spot where their artillery had been placed, and then turning them upon the Russians who were in pursuit, struck their rear, which was placed rather closely together in reserve, and put them to utter confusion and flight. The Russians, who thought that those who fought with the enemy in the front ranks were the only men in danger, became terrified, and imagining that their van was already routed, fled in great confusion; upon which the Lithuanians turned and pursued them with all their forces, and put them to a terrific slaughter, which was checked only by the shades of night and the shelter of the woods.

Between Orsa and Dobrovna, which are four German miles distant from each other, there is a river called Cropivna, over whose slippery and steep banks so many fleeing Russians fell and were drowned, that the course of the river was stopped. All the captains and counsellors of the army were taken in that engagement, the chief of whom were received by Constantine with great honour on the following day, and sent to the king, and distributed among the fortresses of Lithuania. Ivan Czeladin, with two other captains, now of failing age, were kept in iron fetters at Vilna; and when I was sent into Moscow by the Emperor Maximilian, I visited them by the permission of King Sigismund, and offered them consolation. I gave them also some gold pieces.

When the prince heard of the slaughter of his soldiers, he instantly left Smolensko and fled into Russia, and ordered the fort of Drogobusch to be burned, lest the Lithuanians should take it. The Lithuanian army proceeded straight to the city of Smolensko, but could not take it, for it had been left under the protection of a strong garrison, and the approaching winter presented many obstacles to a siege; besides which, a great number of the soldiers, who had loaded themselves with spoil after the battle, thought that they had done enough, and returned home; and independently of these reasons, neither the Lithuanians nor the Russians were skilled in the method of besieging fortresses and taking them by storm.

King Sigismund regained nothing from that victory beyond three fortresses on this side of Smolensko. Four years after this battle the grand duke sent an army into Lithuania, which pitched their camp between the rivers Dwina and Poloczko, and sent out from thence a considerable portion of the army to lay Lithuania waste with plunder, slaughter, and fire. The Waywode Albert Gastold Polocski, however, went forth one night, and crossing the river, set fire to a great hillock of hay which the Russians had collected in preparation for a long siege, and fell upon the enemy, some of whom were killed by the sword, some drowned in their flight, and some taken prisoners. A small number escaped, while various detachments which were roving about laying waste Lithuania in various directions, were subdued or strayed into the woods, and were slain by the inhabitants.

At that time also the grand duke attacked the kingdom of Cazan both with a naval and military force, but returned unsuccessful, and with the loss of a large number of his soldiers. Although, however, the Prince Vasiley is thus most unsuccessful in war, he is, nevertheless, constantly being praised by his courtiers as if he had brought things to a happy issue; and on occasions when scarcely half his army has returned home, they have told him that not a man was lost in battle. In the sway which he holds over his people, he surpasses all the monarchs of the whole world, and has carried out his father's plan of ejecting all princes and others from the garrisons and fortified places. He certainly grants no fortresses to his relations, nor even puts them in charge of any, but oppresses nearly all of them with close confinement; and whoever receives his orders to attend at court, or to go to war, or upon any embassy, is compelled to undertake whatever it may be at his own expense, with the exception of the younger sons of nobles of slender fortune, whom he sends for every year, and maintains with a fixed but inadequate stipend. But such of these as receive six gold pieces yearly, forfeit the stipend every third year; and those who receive twelve gold pieces every year, are compelled to hold themselves in readiness, and fully equipped, for the performance of any duty, at their own expense, and with their own horses; and to the more distinguished among them, namely, such as undertake an embassy, or any office of a more weighty character, are assigned districts, or towns, or villages, which are allotted to them according to their respective dignity, or the task performed. From each of these governments, however, certain annual tributes are paid to the prince: the fines extorted from the poor who may chance to be guilty of any delinquencies, and some other perquisites, are all that these nobles receive. The Grand Duke grants tenures of this kind generally for a year and a half; but if he regards any one with unusual favour or goodwill, he adds a few months to the period, but when that time is elapsed, all favour ceases, and the service must be performed six years gratuitously. There was one Vasiley Tretyack Dolmatov, a favourite of the prince, and one of his private secretaries, who, when appointed ambassador to the Emperor Maximilian, and receiving orders to make his preparations, declared that he had not the means and appurtenances necessary for such a journey; upon which he was immediately seized in Bielosero, and thrown into prison for life. After his death, which was most miserable, his property, both real and personal, was seized by the prince for himself; and although he thus acquired three thousand florins in ready money, he did not give even a farthing to the brothers and heirs of the deceased. Independent of common report, one Ivan, a scribe, who was appointed by the prince to supply me with the daily necessaries of life, confessed that this was the case, and that he had him in his custody at the time that he was taken. The two brothers of Vasiley likewise, Feodore and Zacharias, who were appointed my purveyors on my return from Moscow to Smolensko, confirmed his statement.

Whatever articles of value ambassadors who have been sent to foreign princes bring back with them, the prince places in his own treasury, saying, that he will recompense them in some other manner, which manner is as I have described above. For when the ambassador, the Knes Ivan Posetzen Yaroslavski, was sent with Semen (*i. e.*, Simeon) Trofimov as his secretary, to the court of Charles V, they were presented by the emperor with heavy torques and chains of gold, and with Spanish money, and that in gold; and also by my master, the emperor's brother Ferdinand, Archduke of Austria, with cups of silver and baskets of gold and silver, and German money in gold; but when they returned with us to Moscow, the prince immediately on their arrival took away from them the chains and cups, and the greater part of the Spanish gold pieces. When I enquired of the ambassadors respecting the truth of this matter, one of them constantly denied it, from fear of compromising his prince; the other said, that the prince had ordered the royal presents to be sent to him that he might see them: as I alluded to the matter on frequent subsequent occasions, one of them, in order to avoid falsehood on the one side if he denied, or danger on the other if he were to confess the truth, ceased to visit me. The courtiers did not deny that it was the fact, but replied, " What then, if the prince repays them in some other kind?"

He uses his authority as much over ecclesiastics as laymen, and holds unlimited control over the lives and property of all his subjects: not one of his counsellors has sufficient authority to dare to oppose him, or even differ from him, on any subject. They openly confess that the will of the prince is the will of God, and that whatever the prince does he does by the will of God; on this account they call him God's key-bearer and chamberlain, and in short they believe that he is the executor of the divine will. Thus if at any time petitions are presented on behalf of any captive, or with reference to any important business, the prince himself is accustomed to reply, "when God commands, he shall be liberated". In like manner also, if any one enquires respecting some doubtful and uncertain matter, the common answer is, " God and the great prince know". It is matter of doubt whether the brutality of the people has made the prince a tyrant, or whether the people themselves have become thus brutal and cruel through the tyranny of their prince.

From the time of Rurick to this present sovereign, these princes have borne no other title than that of Grand Dukes, either of Vladimir or Moscow or Novogorod, etc., except Ivan Vasilievich, who styled himself Lord of all Russia, and Grand Duke of Vladimir, etc. But this Vasiley Ivanovich assumes to himself both the royal name and title thus. The Grand Duke Vasiley, by the grace of God King and Lord of all Russia and Grand Duke of Vladimir, Moscow, Novogorod, Plescov, Smolensko, Tver, Jugaria[1] [Jugra, Yugorski], Permia, Viackia [Viatka], Bulgaria, etc., Lord and Grand Duke of Nijni Novogorod and Tchernigov, Rezan, Volotkia [Vologda], Rschov,[2] Beloia,[3] Rostov, Yaroslav, Bielozeria, Udoria,[4] Obdoria,[5] Condinia,[6] etc.

Moreover, as all now call him emperor, it seems necessary that I should explain the title and the cause of this mistake. Czar in the Russian language signifies king, but in the common Slavonic dialect among the Poles, Bohemians, and all the rest, through a certain resemblance of sound in the last, which is the most important syllable, czar [or czeszar] would be understood as emperor or kaiser. In the same manner, all who are not skilled in the Russian idiom or mode of spelling, such as the Bohemians, Poles, and even the Slavonians who are subject to the kingdom of Hungary, call the king by another name, namely, kral, kyrall, or koroll.[7]

[1] An old province in the north of Russia, lying between Petchora and Condora. It still gives a title to the Emperors of Russia.
[2] Probably Rjer Vladimirov' is here referred to. This ancient town and district are situated in the government of Tver; but no town bearing any similar name supplies a title to the present Emperor.
[3] Perhaps White Russia is meant, the word meaning "white" in Russian.
[4] Now called in the titles of the Emperor Udorski, the ancient name of the country round Arkhangel, particularly the district of Mezen. It took its name from the River Udor which flowed through it.
[5] This name was anciently given to all the country in the north round the river Obi, and now comprehended in the government of Tobolsk in the district of Berezov'. The principal place is Obdorsk. Its name is still retained amongst the titles of the Russian sovereigns. In the dialect of the country it means "mouth of the Obi".
[6] The country through which the river Conda flows in the government of Tobolsk. It is still retained amongst the titles.
[7] The derivation of the word Tsar, or Czar, has been the subject of much discussion among etymologists. Constantine Oikonomos, in his

They think a kaiser or emperor only should be called Czar; and hence it came, that the Russian interpreters hearing their prince thus called by foreign nations, began themselves to call him emperor, and they think that the name of czar is more noble than that of king, although that is its real meaning. But if you examine all their histories and sacred scriptures, you will find everywhere that czar is put for "king", and kessar for "emperor". By the same mistake, the emperor of the Turks is called czar, though he has never borne any more distinguished title than that of king, viz., the ancient name of czar. Thus the European Turks who speak the Slavonic language call Constantinople Czarigrad, which means the royal city.

Some call the prince of Moscow Albus, or white. I have taken great pains to learn why he should be called the white king, since no prince of Moscow has hitherto borne that title; and, indeed, I have frequently, when occasion offered, told his counsellors themselves that we did not acknowledge him as king, but Grand Duke. Many have thought the reason of his bearing the title of king was because he had kings under his sway, but they supplied no reason for the name of Albus. My own belief is that in the same manner as they now call the Persian kisilpassa, that is, red head, on account of his red head-dress, these also are called white on account of their white garments. The Grand Duke, moreover, uses

Δοκιμιον περὶ τῆς πλησιεστάτης συγγενείας τῆς Σλαβονο-Ρωσσίκης γλώσσης πρὸς τὴν Ελληνικην, objects to the confounding what he calls the ancient Sclavonic word Tsar, with the much more recent Latin word Cæsar, and says that the mistake has arisen from the incorrect mode adopted by Europeans of representing the Russian word Tsar' by the ill-invented form of Czar. Reiff, on the other hand, in his *Dictionnaire Russe Français*, gives the word as a primitive, and describes it as expressed in Croatian by Czar and Czeszar, from the Latin Cæsar. The sentence in the original Latin is not very clear. The editor has inserted the Croatian form "czeszar" in brackets, by way of suggesting an explanation of Herberstein's meaning, when he speaks of the last syllable of a word, which would otherwise appear to contain but one.

the title of king to the Roman Emperor and Pontiff, the King of Sweden and Denmark, the Prince of Prussia and Livonia, and also, as I have heard, to the Sovereign of the Turks; but he is not called king by any of these, unless perhaps by the Prince of Livonia. In former times the Grand Dukes used to bear their titles on three circles included in a triangle, the first of which, on the topmost circle, was expressed in these words: Our God the Trinity, which was before all ages, Father, Son, and Holy Ghost,—not however three Gods in substance, but one God. In the second was the title of the emperor of the Turks, with the addition of the sentence: "To our beloved brother". In the third, the title of the Grand Duke of Muscovy, in which he declared himself king and heir and lord of all eastern and southern Russia, and in addition to the common formula we have seen added: "We have sent to thee our faithful counsellor". To the King of Poland the Grand Duke uses a title of this sort—"The great Lord Vasiley, by the grace of God, Lord of all Russia, and Grand Duke of Vladimir, Moscow, Novogorod, Smolensko, Tver, Jugaria, Permia, Bulgaria," etc., leaving out the title of king, for neither of these princes condescends to receive the letters of the other, if there is any addition of a new title. This happened once, indeed, while I was at Moscow, when the grand duke was highly indignant that the letters of King Sigismund should be sent to him with the addition of the title of Duke of Moscow. Some have asserted that the grand duke has requested that the style and title of king should be given him by the Pope and the Emperor Maximilian. I do not think this probable, especially as there is no one to whom he is more obnoxious than to the Pope, whom he does not condescend to designate by any title but that of Doctor. That he does not esteem the emperor to be greater than himself, is evident from his letters, in which he affixes the title of emperor to his own name.

The title of duke among these people, is given by the word

"knes";[1] nor, as I have already said, have they ever had any higher title than that, with the addition of the word "great", for all the other dukes who held only one principality, were simply called "knes"; but those who held several principalities and other "knesi" under their command, were called Veliki Knesi, that is, grand dukes. The lowest title or dignity amongst them, is that of the Boyars, who hold the rank of our nobles or knights. In Croatia, indeed, the superior nobles are likewise called Knesi; but with us, as also in Hungary, they only obtain the names of counts. Some gentlemen of princely rank have not hesitated to tell me, by way of casting it in my teeth, that the present Prince of Russia used to produce letters of the Emperor Maximilian of sacred memory, in which the name of king was given to his father Gabriel,— who subsequently changed his name, from preference, to that of Basil;—they say also, that he declares that I myself was the bearer of those letters to him; and on this ground he has desired that, in the recent negotiations with the King of Poland, he should be styled king, or else all treaties between them should be null and void. But although I ought to be by no means moved by these assertions, which are neither true nor probable, yet not so much for my own sake, as for that of my late excellent and most gracious prince, I am compelled to say a word in contradiction when I see that his sacred shade is thus cited upon an invidious question.

It is well known that there was once a quarrel between the Emperor Maximilian and Sigismund, king of Poland, viz., at the time when Sigismund took to wife the daughter of Stephen, Count of Scepus, *i. e.*, Zips; for some made it appear that the matter was so arranged, that John, the brother of the bride, was to receive in marriage Anne, daughter of Vladislav', king of Hungary, through the influence and management of his brother Sigismund; and by this means the right

---

[1] More properly represented by "knyaz". The correct meaning is "prince", not "duke".

of succession to the throne of Hungary, which appertained to Maximilian and his posterity, would be stopped, and become void. For this reason, Maximilian thought that it concerned his interests to make an ally of the Grand Duke of Russia, who was the perpetual enemy of the Lithuanians and Poles. But on a subsequent occasion, when a conference was held at Posen, between Maximilian and Vladislav', respecting the marriage of Anna, in the presence, and with the approval, of Sigismund, Maximilian met Sigismund, and unhesitatingly laying aside all appearance of suspicion or disagreement, embraced him so closely, that no one would doubt that he was ready to go either to heaven or hell with him. Although, therefore, there was a time when Maximilian wished the Grand Duke of Russia to be allied with him, yet he never gave him the title of king, which might be easily proved by letters and documents given and received on both sides, if there should be any one who thinks my testimony, true and faithful as it is, to be of too little weight.

But why should the Grand Duke ask this title from the Emperor Maximilian, since, before he had any communication with him, he would not only make himself appear his equal, but his superior, and always, whether speaking or writing, put the title of emperor after his name, and still retains it most tenaciously? Since my return from Moscow, however, he has assumed the title of King in writing to the King of Poland. Indeed, it is an acknowledged fact, that, in writing to the Emperor, or the Pope, he styles himself King and Lord of all Russia, nor does he refrain from using the title of emperor, if he chance to add any words from the Russian language, translated into Latin, inasmuch as the interpreters themselves change the word czar, which signifies king, into "Imperator". And in this manner he makes himself both king and emperor. But that he has been recognised as king by the Emperor Maximilian, or his successors, to the prejudice of the King of Poland, let no one believe. For why should he hesitate to seek the dignity of a king, as report says that he did, from the pope if he had received it already from the emperors?

I have said all this in the cause of my august master, Maximilian, who, as long as he lived, was a firm and faithful friend of King Sigismund. Why, indeed, should I speak of myself? How, I would ask, could I have presumed to go and return so often into Poland and Lithuania, to enter the presence of the two Sigismunds, father and son, kings of Poland, to take a part in public meetings of the Poles, and to look princes in the face, if I had compromised my prince in this matter, in whose name I have very often laid before the King and other persons of various ranks despatches couched in brotherly, kind and friendly terms, despatches that might well be sent from an excellent and most generous emperor in closest alliance with them. If there be nothing secret which shall not be revealed, it would certainly have come to light a long time ago, had I sanctioned anything unworthy of my office. But I comfort myself with the consciousness of rectitude, which is the strongest of all consolations; and I gratefully acknowledge that I never lacked the favour of the King of Poland, nor, indeed, the goodwill of persons of all ranks in that country. There were, perhaps, times when such things might occur without causing so much jealousy as now; but to promulgate them at this time, is only to seek the means of dissolving good feeling between princes who are most closely allied to each other,—a good feeling which has been cemented and consolidated by all kinds of obligations and good offices. Every thing which was generally regarded as of paramount importance towards preserving the remains of Hungary, and recovering what had been lost, seemed to have been done. But the very parties to whom this fact had already been of great service, and would have been of still greater service hereafter, under the influence of a Turkish or some other such perverse spirit, have ignored treaties and covenants, and plotted new injuries, without considering into what jeopardy they are about to bring themselves and the neighbouring provinces, especially Hungary, which has deserved so well of all Christendom.

Mode of Inaugurating their Princes.

The following formula, which I had some difficulty in obtaining, will depict to you the manner in which the princes of Russia are inaugurated, and which was adopted when the Grand Duke Ivan Vasileivich invested his grandson, Dimitry, as I have said above, with the Grand Dukedom and monarchy of Russia.

In the middle of the church of the Holy Virgin was erected a platform, on which three seats were placed,—one for the grandfather, one for the grandson, and one for the metropolitan. There was also placed on it a stage, upon which were laid the ducal hat and barma, which means the ducal ornament. The archbishops, bishops, abbots, priors, and the whole assembly of ecclesiastics, came in dressed respectively in their appropriate vestments. Then upon the entrance of the Grand Duke with his grandson into the church, the deacons sang, according to custom, "Long live the only Grand Duke, the great Ivan". The Metropolitan then began to sing, together with all the clergy, the prayer of the Holy Virgin, and of St. Peter the Confessor, whom, in their ritual, they call the Miraculous. Which done, the Metropolitan, the Grand Duke, and his grandson, ascended the platform, and sat on the seats placed for them; the grandson's seat being placed at the front of the platform. At length the Grand Duke spoke in these words: "Father Metropolitan, according to the custom anciently and until now observed by our predecessors the grand dukes, our ancestors the grand dukes have, by the grace of God, consigned the grand duchy to their eldest sons; and after their example the Grand Duke, my father, blessed me with the Grand Duchy in his own presence, so also I, in like manner, blessed my first-born son Ivan with the Grand Duchy in the presence of all. Since however it has happened by the Divine pleasure that my son is dead, but that his only son Dimitry, whom God gave me in the place of my son, survives, I likewise, in conformity with the same custom, bless him in the presence of all, both now and after my death, with the Grand Duchies of Vladimir, Novogorod, and all else with which I should have blessed his father."

Upon this, the Metropolitan desired the grandson to go to the seat which was assigned to him, and blessing him with the cross, ordered the deacon to repeat the Diaconal prayers; he himself meanwhile sitting near him with his head bowed, pronounced the following prayer: "O Lord our God, King of kings, Lord of lords, who by thy servant Samuel the prophet, didst choose David and anointed him to be King over thy people Israel, hear now the prayers of Thine unworthy servant, and look down from Thy sanctuary upon Thy faithful servant whom Thou hast chosen to exalt him to be King over Thy holy nations, and whom Thou hast redeemed with the most precious blood of Thy only-begotten Son; anoint him with the oil of gladness, protect him with the virtue of the highest, place upon his head a crown of precious stones, give him length of days and a royal sceptre in his right hand, place him on a righteous throne, surround him with all the arms of justice, strengthen his arm and subdue unto him all barbarian tongues; let his whole heart be in Thy fear, that he may humbly obey Thee, keep him from the false path and point out to him the true preserver of the commands of Thy holy universal Church, that he may judge the people in justice, and administer justice to the poor and preserve the children of the poor, and finally that he may attain the kingdom of heaven." He then said in a loud voice: "Even as Thine is the power and Thine is the kingdom, so be praise and honour to Thee, God the Father, Son, and Holy Ghost, now and for ever." When this prayer was finished, the Metropolitan ordered two abbots to bring the barma, which, together with the hat, was covered with a certain silk covering called schirnikoiu. He then delivered it to the Grand Duke, and marked the grandson with the cross, and the Grand Duke placed the barma upon his grandson. The metropolitan then said "Peace be with you all"; to which the deacon responded, "Let us pray". After which the Metropolitan said, "Bow yourselves with me, and pray to Him who governs all things," and pronounced the following prayer: "O Lord, we pray to Thee, the only King Eternal, to whom also is committed the sovereignty of the earth, uphold [the prince] under Thy protection; continue him in the kingdom, that he may always do that which is good and seemly, make justice to shine in his days; and in the enlargement and tranquillity of his dominion, let us live quietly and peaceably in all goodness and purity." This was said in a rather subdued tone. Then, in a loud voice, he said: "Thou art the King of the world, and Preserver of our souls; praise be to Thee, Father, Son, and Holy Ghost, now and for ever. Amen." At length he delivered to the Grand Duke the ducal hat, which had been brought to him, at his command, by two abbots. He then marked the grandson with the cross, in the name of the Father, Son, and Holy Ghost; and while the Grand Duke placed the hat upon the head of his grandson, the Metropolitan first, and the archbishops and bishops approaching afterwards, blessed him with the imposition of hands. When this was finished in due order, the Metropolitan and Grand Duke ordered the grandson to be seated by the side of the Grand Duke, and after a short pause they rose. Meanwhile the deacon began a litany (as they call it), "Have mercy upon us, O Lord", and named Ivan as Grand Duke Ivan.

Again a chorus, in response, mentioned Dimitry, the grandson, as grand duke; and then made allusion to others in the usual manner. When the litany was finished, the Metropolitan prayed, "O most holy Lady, Virgin mother of God", and after the prayer the metropolitan and grand duke sat down. The priest or deacon then pointed out the place selected for the gospel, and said, with a loud voice,—" Long live the Grand Duke Ivan, good and faithful, beloved of Christ, chosen of God, and to be honoured by God; long live the Grand Duke Ivan Vasilievich, monarch of Novogorod and all Russia." Then the priests before the altar sang, " Long live the Grand Duke"; and the deacons in the choir, on the right and on the left, in like manner sang, " Long live the Grand Duke". At length again the deacon cried out with a loud voice, " Long live the Grand Duke Dimitry, good and faithful, beloved of Christ, chosen and to be honoured of God; long live Dimitry Ivanovich, Grand Duke of Novogorod and all Russia." The priests also before the altar and in both choirs thundered out, "Long live Dimitry!" When this was done, the metropolitan, the archbishop, the bishops, and the whole congregation, approached the grand dukes in procession, and saluted them with an obeisance; the sons also of the grand duke approached, bowing and saluting the grand duke.

Ceremonies after the Inauguration of the Grand Duke.

After the inauguration, Simon, the metropolitan, said: "O lord my son Dimitry, by the divine will Grand Duke, the Grand Duke, thy father, hath shewn thee favour, and blessed thee with the grand dukedom; do thou also, O lord my son, have the fear of God in thy heart. Love justice and just judgment; obey the grand duke thy grandfather, and interest thyself with all thy heart about all the truly faithful. We bless thee also, O lord my son, and pray God for thy welfare. Then the metropolitan and the grand dukes arose, and the metropolitan praying, blessed the grand duke and his sons with the cross; and at length, when the liturgy—*i. e.*, the holy service—was finished, the grand duke, the grandfather, withdrew to his own dwelling; but Dimitry, wearing the ducal hat and barma, left the church of the Blessed Virgin, and proceeded, surrounded with a host of boyars and their sons, to the church of Michael the Archangel, at the entrance of which, upon the threshold, he was sprinkled by George, son of the Grand Duke Ivan, with three golden dengs (the deng is one of their coins); and when he had entered the church, the priests singing the litany according to custom, blessed him with the cross, and signed him with the sign of the cross at the tombs and monuments. Then, as he went out of the church, he was again sprinkled by George at the door with golden dengs. He next proceeded straightway to the church of the Annunciation of the Virgin Mary, where the priests in the same manner blessed him, and he was sprinkled by George with dengs as before. When all this was finished, Dimitry presented himself to his grandfather and to his mother.

This took place on the 4th of February, anno mundi 7006, anno Domini 1497. There were present at this installation by the grand duke and consecration by Simon the metropolitan—Tychon, Archbishop of Rostov and Yaroslav, Nyphon, Archbishop of Susdal and Toruski, Vasian, Bishop of Tver, Prothasius, Bishop of Rezan and Murom, Afranius, Bishop of Columna, and Euphemius, Bishop of Sarki and Podonski. There were present also many abbots and priors, among the most powerful of whom were Serapian, prior of the monastery of Saints Sergius and Makirius, under the invocation of the Holy Trinity, and the prior of the monastery of St. Cyril, and finally, a great assemblage of monks and ecclesiastics. While at dinner, a broad girdle worked with gold, silver, and precious stones, was brought [to the grand duke?] as it were by way of a present, with which he girded himself. Afterwards were brought to him some selgi of Pereaslav,—that is, little fishes from the Lake of Pereaslav, not unlike herrings, and indeed they are called by the same name. It is thought that the reason for presenting that kind of fish is, because Pereaslav was never separated from Russia or the monarchy.

The barma is a sort of collar of broad form, of coarse silk, beautifully worked on the outside with gold and all kinds of gems. It was taken by Vladimir from a certain Genoese named Capha.[1] The hat which Vladimir Monomach used and left behind him, and which is adorned with precious stones and plates of gold, and curiously worked with certain vibrating spirules, is called in their language Schapka. Hitherto, I have spoken of the prince who holds the greater part of Russia. The other parts of Russia are held singly by Sigismund King of Poland and Grand Duke of Lithuania. But in speaking of the kings of Poland who have derived their

---

[1] The *Sviatŭi Barmi*, *i. e.*, Holy Barmi, as it is called (spelt by Herberstein barma), was worn by the czars of Russia at their coronation up to the time of Peter the Great. It is now preserved in the Imperial Museum at Moscow. Various are the accounts given of its first introduction into Russia. Some say, though there is no certainty in the story, that in the year 1114, the Grand Duke Vladimir ravaged Thrace, and carried off a vast booty. The Emperor Constantine, alarmed at his progress, sent him many valuable presents, and among others the barmi. It appears, however, from printed state documents, that the barmi was certainly known in the fourteenth century. The Grand Duke John Danielovich Kalita, by his will in 1328, bequeathed it to his younger sons John and Andrew. It would seem from the wording of the various bequests of the barmi, that it was attached to the dress, and always kept with it. Antiquaries are at variance as to the origin of the word; some have derived it from the Greek $\beta\alpha\rho\eta\mu\alpha$—heaviness, as implying the burden of duty and responsibility undertaken by the newly inaugurated monarch; but this is mere conjecture.

origin from the Lithuanians, I think it right to subjoin some details of their genealogy.

A certain Prince Vitenen ruled over the Grand Duchy of Lithuania, whom, according to the Polish annals, Gedemin, his servant slew, and afterwards gained possession both of his duchy and his wife. By her he had several sons,—the two principal of whom were Olgird and Kestud. Kestud was the father of Vithold, otherwise called Vitowd, and Anna, the wife of Janusius, Duke of Masovia. Vithold left an only daughter, Anastasia, who was given in marriage to Basil, Duke of Muscovy, and was named Sophia. She was the mother of Vasiley, father of the great Ivan, and grandfather of Vasiley, prince of the Russians, to whom I was sent as ambassador.

Moreover, Kestud was thrown into prison by his brother Olgird, and died miserably. Vithold also, than whom Lithuania has never produced a greater man, and who took the name of Alexander at his baptism, died in 1430. Olgird, son of Gedemin, amongst other sons whom he had by his wife Maria, a Christian princess of Tver, had Jagelon. He in his lust of dominion not only affected the kingdom of Poland, but Hedwige herself also, who at that time wore the crown, and who was betrothed to William Duke of Austria, and with the consent of her relatives and the primates of both kingdoms, had, after the royal fashion, lain with him before attaining a marriageable age. Jagelon presently sends ambassadors into Poland and asks for the kingdom and the hand of Hedwige. Moreover, in order to obtain the concurrence of the Poles, and to constitute himself a proper candidate, he promised among other things, that he and his brothers, together with the duchies of Lithuania and Samogithia, would embrace the Christian religion; and with other promises of the sort, he so drew over the Poles to his cause, that Hedwige, overruled by their authority, and even against her own will, rescinded her former treaty of marriage and married him. Upon this, Jagelon was immediately baptized, and took the name of Vladislav', and was crowned king. He received Hedwige in marriage A.D. 1386, but she died not long after in her first child-bed. He then married Anna, Countess of Cilley, by whom he had an only daughter, Hedwige, who was espoused to Frederic the younger of Brandenburg. He married also a certain old woman, who likewise dying, he married Sonca, a Russian lady, daughter of Andrew Ivan, Duke of Kiev, who afterwards adopted the Roman ritual, and was called Sophia. By her he had two sons, Vladislav' and Casimir. Vladislav' succeeded his father in the kingdom, and was also crowned king of Hungary, having removed the lawful heir Ladislav', the posthumous son of the deceased king Albert. He was subsequently overthrown by the Turks at Lake Warna. Casimir, who then held the Grand Duchy of Lithuania, and who, influenced perhaps by his brother's example, wished to deprive the posthumous Ladislav' of the kingdom of Bohemia, succeeded his brother in the kingdom of Poland. He afterwards married Elizabeth, sister of that Ladislav', king of Hungary and Bohemia, and had by her the following sons:—Vladislav', king of Hungary and Bohemia; John Albert, Alexander, and Sigismund, kings of Poland; Frederick, a cardinal; and Casimir, who was enrolled amongst the number of the saints.

Vladislav' had a son Louis, and a daughter Anna. Louis succeeded him in the kingdom, and married the daughter of Philip, King of Castile and Archduke of Austria. He was overthrown by the Turks at Mohaez, in the year 1526. Anna married Ferdinand, king of Hungary and Bohemia and Archduke of Austria, and after giving birth to four sons and eleven daughters, died in childbed at Prague, A.D. 1547. John Albert died unmarried. Alexander married Helen, daughter of Ivan, Grand Duke of Muscovy; but died without children. Sigismund had by his first wife, Barbara, daughter of Stephen, Count of Zips, Hedwige, who became wife of Joachim, Elector of Brandenburgh. By his second, Bona, daughter of John Sforza, Duke of Milan and Bari, he had Sigismund, second king of Poland, Grand Duke of Lithuania, who married Elizabeth, daughter of the Emperor Ferdinand, king of Hungary and Bohemia, on the 6th of May 1543; who, however, died an untimely death, and without issue, on the 15th of June 1545. He then married, against the consent of his parents, Barbara, of the house of Radavil, who had previously been married to Gastold, the Lithuanian; but his subjects were so indignant at this marriage, that a rebellion, which had already sprung up amongst them, would have ended in a dangerous outbreak, had not King Ferdinand preferred burying his daughter's injuries in oblivion to revenging them: but she being dead, Sigismund, being desirous to reestablish his alliance and relationship with Ferdinand, took to wife Catherine, half sister of Elizabeth, widow of Francis, Duke of Mantua. The marriage was celebrated at Cracow, the 31st of July 1553. I myself, as master, or prefect of the court, conducted each of these sisters to her bridegroom.

Semovisten, Duke of Mazovia, had by Alexandra, the sister of Jagelon, many sons and daughters. The sons died childless. Of the daughters, Czimburgis married Ernest, Archduke of Austria, and had by her the Emperor Frederick, father of the Emperor Maximilian. Maximilian was the father of Philip, King of Spain; and Philip was father of the Emperor Charles Ferdinand.

Ovka was given in marriage to Voleslaus, Duke of Teschen.

Amelia married Voguslaus, Duke of Stolpen, who is now called Duke of Pomerania. Anne married Michael, Duke of Lithuania. Catherine died unmarried.

Moreover, if any one would review in order the brothers and nephews of Olgird and Jagelon, and the daughters' children of the latter, as well as the descendants of Kestud, Casimir, and the other kings, the enumeration of the race would extend beyond all bounds; yet rapidly as it increased, the male line, at the present day, survives only in the son of the late King of Poland, viz., Sigismund, the second King of Poland.

But since we have made reference to the posterity of Gedemin, and the kings of that race, it seems appropriate to lay before the reader the events which occurred during the reigns of Vladimir, king of Hungary and Bohemia, and his brother Sigismund, king of Poland, the sons of Casimir.

After Vladislav' had come into possession of Hungary by the concession of the Emperor Maximilian, who, however, reserved to himself the right of succession, Vladislav' being now an old man with only one daughter, Maximilian, with the view of strengthening the right of succession by a somewhat stronger bond, began to propose to Vladislav' a marriage between one of his grandchildren by his son Philip, king of Spain, and Anna, Vladislav's daughter. Now John Zapolski, son of Stephen, Count of Zips, whose influence with King Mathias, and consequently with Vladislav' himself, was very great, was extremely anxious to bring about a marriage between himself and Anne; and in his pursuit of this object was strenuously assisted by his widowed mother, who bribed all the leading men in the counties and provinces of Hungary with presents and annual stipends, called in their language Jargalass, and thus held them bound to perform any service which she might require at their hands, nothing doubting, that by their contrivances and influence, she might bring about this marriage for her son, and thus procure him the kingdom : to these woman-like machinations the marriage between her daughter, John's sister, and Sigismund, king of Poland, added great weight. Maximilian observing this state of affairs, and considering that it now became still more necessary for him to urge his proposition of a marriage between his grandson and Anna, and finding also that Vladislav' desired the same thing, but that he met with impediments from the plots and contrivances of those who were under the orders of John Zapolski, thought it necessary for his own interest to cast the die, and to put Hungary to the test by force of arms; in which war I made my first essay in the career of a soldier. But as it happened that Vladislav's son, Lewis, was born in the midst of this strife of arms, a truce was entered into, and hence a more solid peace was brought about, which ended in Vladislav's coming to Maximilian at Vienna, together with his son already crowned, and his daughter and his brother Sigismund, king of Poland. The nuptials with Anne were then solemnized at Vienna, and all the enmity and suspicious feeling which had been engendered by the ambition of John Zapolski being extinguished, these princes were united in a lasting bond of amity. So great was the mutual satisfaction occasioned by this union between King Sigismund and the Emperor Maximilian, that the latter has sometimes said, in my hearing, that he would willingly go to heaven or hell with such a king. It was a vulgar saying concerning Lewis, that he was immaturely born, came of age too soon, and was immaturely married; that he came too early to the throne, and met with an untimely death. To these sayings it may be added, that his death was as disastrous to his kingdom of Hungary, and all the neighbouring states, as it was immature. But although Lewis was not well advised, it is certain that he was excellently well disposed towards his country and his subjects, and sought every means of benefiting them; for when he became aware that Soliman, after the capture of Belgrade, was planning a new and formidable expedition against himself, he, being a young man, sent a Pole, the master of his household, named Trepca, to his uncle, King Sigismund, beseeching him in the most anxious and earnest manner not to consider it a hardship to come to meet him on the frontier of his dominions for the purpose of giving him his advice in this dilemma. But as this request met with a distinct refusal on the part of Sigismund, Trepca is said to have exclaimed to him, with tears in his eyes, " Never again, O king, shalt thou see thy nephew, nor receive another message from him"; which prophecy, in fact, came to pass; for as King Sigismund subsequently left the confines of Hungary, on a religious pretext, for Dantzic in Prussia, his nephew died, together with this same Trepca, in that most disastrous slaughter, which is named, from the place, " the slaughter of Mohacz". But now I return to the Russians.

While Vasiley Ivanovich was deliberating about his marriage, it struck him that it would be better that he should marry the daughter of one of his subjects than a foreigner, by which means he would not only spare himself very great expense, but also avoid having a wife accustomed to foreign habits and of a different religion. The suggestor of this idea was one George, surnamed the Little, the prince's treasurer and chief councillor, who thought it likely that the prince would marry his own daughter; but at length it happened that when at the public suggestion fifteen hundred daughters of the boyars were brought together into one place, that the prince might make his selection from their number, he chose for his wife, contrary to George's anticipation, Salomea, daughter of the boyar Ivan Sapur; but as after one-and-twenty years he had no children by her, chagrined at her barrenness, he thrust her into a convent in the principality of Susdal, in the same year that I came to Moscow, namely, 1526. When the metropolitan, upon her arrival at the convent weeping and sobbing, cut off her hair and then offered to put on the hood, she was so indignant at its being placed upon her, that she took it and hurling it to the ground, stamped upon it with her feet. One of the chief councillors irritated at the sight of this indignity, not only reviled her bitterly, but beat her with a scourge, and asked her, "darest thou resist the will of my lord? and delayest thou to obey his commands?" When Salomea in return asked him by what authority he beat her, he replied, "by the will of his lord"; upon which she, broken-hearted, protested in the presence of all, that she took the hood unwillingly and under compulsion, and invoked the vengeance of God on her behalf for so great an injury. After Salomea was thus cast into the convent, the prince married Helen, daughter of the blind Duke Vasiley Lintzki (now dead)—I mean the brother of the Duke Michael Lintzki, who was then in prison; but this had no sooner taken place than a report became current that Salomea was pregnant and near the time of her delivery. This report was confirmed by two matrons, the wives of the chief councillors, George the Little, the treasurer, and Jacob Mazur, chamberlain,—which ladies said that they had heard from the mouth of Salomea herself that she was pregnant, and near the time of her delivery. The prince when he heard this was much disturbed, and drove both of them from his presence; he even punished one of them, the wife of George, with stripes, for not having earlier informed him of the fact; he then sent the councillor Theoderic Rack, and one Potal, a secretary, to the convent in which Salomea was confined, and desired them to inquire diligently into the truth of the case. While I was at Moscow, some persons declared solemnly that Salomea had brought forth a son, named George, but that she would not show the infant to any one; she is said, however, to have replied to some persons who were sent to her for the purpose of ascertaining the truth of the matter, that they were unworthy to set eyes upon the infant, who, when he came of age to be king, would revenge the injury done to his mother. Some, however, constantly denied that she had had a child. Thus the reports about this business are doubtful.

I have heard that there were two reasons why the

prince should marry the daughter of Vasiley Lintzki, the fugitive from Lithuania, besides the hope which he had of having children by her: the first was, that his father-in-law derived his lineage from the family of Petrovitz, which was formerly of great distinction in Hungary, and professed the Greek faith; the second was, that his children would have for their uncle Michael Lintzki, a man of uncommon talent and distinguished valour,— for the prince had two brothers-in-law yet living, George and Andrew, and therefore he thought that if he were to have any children by another wife they would not be safe in the government, while those brothers were alive; but he did not doubt that if Michael were again received into favour, and released from prison, the children whom he might have by Helen would enjoy greater peace by means of the authority of their uncle. His liberation was spoken of in my presence, and after having first had his chains removed, and then being honourably set free on his parole, I at length saw him at full liberty, and enrolled by the prince among the other dukes by patent, and finally appointed tutor to his nephews Ivan and George. But subsequently, after the death of the prince, when Michael saw that his widow was constantly dishonouring the royal bed with a certain boyar named Ovczina, and that she showed implacable enmity against her husband's brothers, who had been thrown into prison, and that she otherwise governed with much cruelty, he, actuated purely by a sense of piety and honour, took occasion sometimes to admonish her to live a more worthy and religious life. She received his admonitions, however, with so much offence and indignation, that it was not long before she took counsel as to the best means of putting him out of the way. She soon found a reason, for they say that Michael was immediately arraigned for the crime of treason, and again thrown into prison, where he died a wretched death. It is also said that the widow not long after was carried off by poison, and that the adulterous Ovczina was cut to pieces. The eldest son Ivan, who was born in 1528, came to the throne after the death of his mother.

Religion.

As Russia began, so to the present day it continues to observe the Christian faith according to the Greek ritual. The metropolitan formerly resided in Kiev, afterwards in Vladimir, but now in Moscow. It was a custom of the metropolitans to pay a visit every seven years to that part of Russia which was subject to the Lithuanians, and to return after exacting sums of money from them; but Withold fearing that his territories would become exhausted of coin, would no longer permit this. He therefore called a convocation of bishops, and appointed a special metropolitan, who at this day holds his seat at Wilna, the metropolis of Lithuania, a city which though observing the Roman ritual, has more Russian than Roman churches in it. The Russian metropolitans hold their authority from the Patriarch of Constantinople.

The Russians openly boast in their annals, that before the times of Vladimir and Olha, the land of Russia was baptized and blessed by Andrew, the apostle of Christ, who came, as they assert, from Greece to the mouth of the Dnieper, and that he sailed up the river against the stream as far as the mountains where Kiev now stands, and there blessed and baptized all the country; that he planted his cross there, and preached the great grace of God, foretelling that the churches of the Christians would be numerous; that thence he went afterwards to the sources of the Dnieper, to the Great Lake Volok, and descended by the River Lovat to Lake Ilmen, and thence by the River Volchov', which flows out of the same lake, to Novogorod; thence by the same river to Lake Ladoga, and by the River Neva to the sea, which they call Varetzkoi, but which we call the German Sea [the Baltic], between Finland and Livonia, and so sailed to Rome. Finally, that he was crucified for Christ's sake in the Peloponnesus by Antipater. Such is the account given in their annals.

Metropolitans and bishops were formerly chosen at an assembly of all the archbishops, bishops, abbots, and priors of monasteries; a man remarkable for sanctity was sought for through monasteries and deserts, and was selected. But they say that it is the custom of the present prince to summon certain ecclesiastics to him, and choose one of their number according to his own judgment. When I was the Emperor Maximilian's ambassador at Moscow, Bartholomew, a man of holy life, was the metropolitan; and on one occasion, when the prince had violated an oath made conjointly by him and the metropolitan himself to the Duke of Semeczitz, and had made assertions which appeared to him to be contrary to truth, he went to the prince and said:—Since thou usurpest all authority to thyself, I find it impossible to retain the charge of my office; and tendering the staff which he bore, which was in the form of a cross, he thus resigned his office. The prince without hesitation accepted the staff, together with the resignation of the office, and immediately sent the poor man bound with chains to Bielosero. They say that he was there a long while in chains, but that he was afterwards liberated, and privately passed the rest of his life in a monastery. One Daniel succeeded him as metropolitan, a man of about thirty years of age, of a large and corpulent frame, and with a red face, who, lest he should be thought more given to gluttony than to fastings, vigils, and prayers, used on all occasions when he had to perform any public ceremony, to expose his face to the fumes of sulphur to make himself pale; and when he had by this means become thoroughly pale, he would present himself in public.

There are also two other archbishops in the Russian monarch's dominions in Novogorod, viz., the archbishop of Magrici and of Rostov'; also, the bishops of Tver, Resan, Smolensko, Permia, Susdal, Columna, Tczernigov', and Sari. All these are subject to the metropolitan of Moscow; but they have certain revenues of their own out of estates and other extraordinary accidentals (as they call them); they have, however, no forts, cities, or other secular administration (as they call it). They abstain constantly from meats. I only found two abbots in Russia, but very many priors of monasteries, all of whom are chosen at the will of the prince himself, whom no one dares resist.

The mode of electing the priors is described in the letters of one Varlamus, prior of the monastery of Hutten, established in the year 7034 [1525], from which I have only selected the leading particulars. In the first place, the brothers of any monastery beseech the Grand Duke to choose a fitting prior to instruct them in divine precepts. After the election, he is compelled, before he is confirmed by the prince, to bind himself by an oath and a bond, that he will live a pious and holy life in that monastery, according to the appointment of the holy fathers,—to appoint all officers with the consent of the elder brothers, according to the custom of their predecessors,—to advance such as are faithful in performing their duties, and to give diligent attention to the welfare of the monastery,—to consult three or four of the elders on important questions of business, and after deliberation to refer the matter to the whole fraternity, and to decide and settle according to their general opinion; not daintily to live in private, but constantly to be at the same table and eat in common with the monks; diligently to collect all the registers and annual returns, and deposit them faithfully in the treasury of the monastery. All these things he promises to observe under a heavy penalty, which the prince can inflict on him even to the deprivation of his office. The senior monks also bind themselves by an oath that they will observe all the aforesaid rules, and faithfully and diligently obey the prior who shall be appointed.

Those who are consecrated secular priests are for the most part such as have served a long time in the churches as deacons. But no one is consecrated deacon unless he be married, whence they are very often married and ordained deacons at the same time. But if the betrothed of any deacon is in bad repute, he is not ordained deacon: it is necessary that he should have a wife of unblemished character.

When the wife of a priest is dead he is immediately suspended from officiating, but if he live in chastity, he may be present in the choir as a minister with the other minister of the church, at the offices and other divine engagements. Indeed it was the custom formerly for widowers who lived in chastity to administer the sacraments without blame, but now the custom is introduced that no widower be permitted to perform the sacraments, unless he enter some monastery and live according to rule. If any priest who is a widower enter on a second marriage, which he is free to do, he has nothing in common with the clergy, nor does any priest whatever dare either to administer the sacrament, to baptize, or to perform any other duty, unless a deacon be present.

Priests hold the first place in the churches, and if any one of them on any account were to do that which is contrary to religion and the priestly office, he is brought to a spiritual tribunal; but if he be accused of theft or drunkenness, or fall into any other vice of that sort, he is punished by the *secular* magistrate as they call him. I saw some drunken priests publicly whipped at Moscow, whose only complaint was, that they were beaten by slaves, and not by a gentleman. A few years ago, one of the prince's deputies caused a priest who had been caught in theft to be strangled, at which the metropolitan was very displeased, and laid the matter before the prince. When the deputy was summoned to the prince, he replied, that "according to the ancient custom of the country a thief who was not a priest was hanged"; and so he was sent away unblamed. If a priest complain before a lay judge that he has been struck by a layman (for all kinds of assaults and injuries apply to the secular law), then the judge, if he happen to learn that the layman was provoked by the priest, or previously injured in any way by him, punishes the priest.

Priests are generally maintained from the contribution of people connected with the court, and have some small tenements allotted to them with fields and meadows, whence they derive their support by their own and their families' industry, like their neighbours. . They have very slender offerings. Sometimes the church money is put out at interest at ten per cent., and they give the interest to the priest from fear of being compelled to maintain him at their own expense. There are some also who live by the liberality of the princes. Certainly, not many parishes are found endowed with estates and possessions, except the bishoprics and some monasteries. No parish or priesthood is conferred on any one but a priest. In every church there is only one altar, and they do not think it right that the service should be performed more than once a day. A church is very seldom found without a priest, who is bound only to perform the services three times a week.

They wear nearly the same dress as the laity, with the addition of a small round skull cap to cover the tonsure, and a broad hat to keep off the heat and rain, or they use an oblong beaver hat of a grey colour. They all carry staves to lean upon, called Possoch.

Abbots and priors, as we have said, preside over monasteries,—the latter are called Igumens, the former Archimandrites.[1] Their laws and regulations are very severe, but

---

[1] Dr. King, in his *Rites and Ceremonies of the Greek Church in Russia,*

are gradually falling into disuse, and becoming obsolete. They dare not indulge in any sort of amusement. If any one is found to have a harp or any musical instrument, he is most severely punished. They constantly abstain from meat. They all obey, not only the commands of the prince, but all the boyars sent by the prince. I was present when my purveyor requested something at the hands of a certain prior, and finding that he persisted in refusing to comply with his request, he threatened to have him beaten, the hearing which immediately produced the desired effect. There are many who leave the monasteries and betake themselves into wildernesses and there build huts, in which they live sometimes alone and sometimes with companions. They seek their livelihood from the earth and the trees, eating roots and the fruits of the trees. These are called Stolpniki: for Stolp means a column: and their narrow little dwellings are raised up high in the air and supported on columns.

The metropolitan, the bishops, and archbishops, constantly abstain from all kinds of meat; but when they invite laymen or priests at seasons when meat is eaten, they have the prerogative of being permitted to place meat before them at their entertainment; but this is prohibited to abbots and priors.

The archbishops, bishops, and abbots, wear round black mitres; but the bishop of Novogorod alone wears a white two-horned mitre after our fashion. The daily garments of the bishops are like those of other monks, except that sometimes they have them of silk, especially the black pallium, which has three white strips waving, like the flowing of a river, from the breast in every direction, to signify that from their mouth and heart flow streams of the doctrine of faith

says: "The principal of a monastery is called either Archimandrite, from μανδρα, *a fold;* or Hegumen, from ἡγοῦμαι, *duco.* The former is equivalent to abbot or father, the appellation of him who has the government of the monks or friars, who are brethren. The Hegumen is much the same as prior, who is the chief of a smaller convent, of which he has the direction.

and good works. They carry a staff in the form of a cross, on which they lean, which in the common language is called Possoch. The bishop of Novogorod wears a white pallium. The bishops confine their attention entirely to matters of divinity and to the pious promotion and advancement of religion itself, and intrust the management of both private and public affairs to their officials.

They have in their list certain Roman pontiffs whom they venerate among the saints, but they execrate others who followed that schism as seceders from the ordinances of the holy fathers and the seven councils, and call them heretics and schismatics, and hate them even more than the Mahometans. For they say, that it was decided at the seventh general council, that those things which had been settled and determined upon in the previous councils should be maintained unalterably for ever, and that it was not lawful for any body thereafter either to summon or to attend at any other council, on pain of anathema; and this decision they themselves most rigidly observe. There was one metropolitan of Russia who, at the instance of Pope Eugene, went to a synod, where the two Churches were met in unison, but on his return to his own country he was seized, all his goods were confiscated, and he thrown into prison, from which, however, he after some time escaped.

What difference exists between our[1] creed and theirs may be learned from a letter addressed by John, metropolitan of Russia, to the Archbishop of Rome, as they call him, which is as follows:—

"I have loved thy glory, O lord and blessed father, most worthy of the apostolic seat and vocation, who from afar hast looked down upon our humility and poverty, and cherishest us with the wings of love, and salutest us as thine own in thy charity, and inquirest specially concerning our true and

[1] The reader will recollect that Herberstein was a member of the Roman Church.

orthodox faith, and when thou heardest admired, for so the bishop related to us of your blessedness. And since thou art such and so great a priest, I therefore in my poverty salute thee, honouring thy head and kissing thy hands and arms. Mayst thou be joyful and protected by the supreme hand of God, and may God Almighty grant good order to thee, thy spirituals, and us. I know not whence heresies have arisen respecting the true way of salvation and redemption; and I cannot sufficiently wonder what devil was so malignant and envious, so hostile to the truth, and such an adversary to our mutual good-will, as to alienate our brotherly love from the whole Christian congregation, by saying that we are not Christians; we for our parts have from the beginning acknowledged that by the grace of God ye are Christians, although ye do not keep the faith of Christ in all things, and are in many things divided,—a fact which I will show from the seven great synods by which the orthodox Christian faith has been established and definitely confirmed, in which also the wisdom of God has built herself a house as it were upon seven pillars. Moreover, all the popes who sat in these seven synods were held worthy of the chair of St. Peter, because they agreed with us. In the first synod was Pope Sylvester;[1] in the second, Damasus;[2] in the third, Celestinus;[3] in the fourth, the most blessed Pope Leo;[4] in the

---

[1] Sylvester held the first œcumenical Council of Nicæa, A.D. 325, against Arius, who ascribed different substances to the Trinity, and denied the divinity of the Word.

[2] Damasus held the first Council of Constantinople, A.D. 381, against Macedonius and Eudoxus, who denied that the Holy Ghost was God.

[3] Celestine held the first Council of Ephesus, A.D. 431, against Nestorius, Bishop of Constantinople, who declared that the Virgin was only the mother of Christ's manhood, and that the Word consisted of two persons, God and man.

[4] Leo the Great held the Council of Chalcedon, A.D. 451, against Eutyches, Abbot of Constantinople, who asserted that Christ, after becoming incarnate, had not two natures, but only the divine nature.

fifth, Vigil;[1] in the sixth, Oaphanius,[2] a venerable man, and learned in the Holy Scriptures; in the seventh, the holy Pope Adrian,[3] who first sent Peter as bishop and abbot of the monastery of St. Sabas, whence have subsequently arisen dissensions between us and you, which have principally prevailed in ancient Rana. Truly, there are many evil things done by you contrary to the divine laws and statutes, of which we will briefly write to thy charity. First, concerning the unlawful observance of fasting on the Sabbath; secondly, concerning the great fast from which ye cut off a week, and eat meats, and allure men to you by the gluttony of feasting. You reject also those priests who lawfully marry wives. Ye also anoint a second time those who have been anointed in baptism by the presbyters, and say that baptisms may not be performed by simple priests but by bishops only. So likewise with respect to unwholesome unleavened bread, which manifestly indicates Jewish service or worship. And, which is the chief of all evils, ye have begun to alter and pervert those things which were ratified by the holy synods, and say of the Holy Ghost, that he not only proceeds from the Father but also from the Son, with many more things, concerning which your Blessedness ought to refer to your spiritual brother, the Patriarch of Constantinople, and to use all diligence that such errors should be at some time removed, and that we should be united in spiritual harmony, as St. Paul says in his instructive words, 'I beseech you, therefore,

[1] Vigil held the second Council of Constantinople, A.D. 553, against Origen and Evagrius, who denied the Resurrection, and maintained that the soul is created before the body. In this synod it was ordered that the Blessed Virgin should be called Θεοτοκος, or Deipara, to express her being the mother of God as well as man.

[2] This Oaphanius must be Agathon, who held the sixth recognized œcumenical council of the Greek church—which was the third Council of Constantinople—A.D. 680, against the Monothelites, who asserted that Christ had only one will and one nature.

[3] Adrian I held the second Council of Nicæa, A.D. 787, against the iconoclasts.

brethren, by the name of our Lord Jesus Christ, that ye think and speak the same thing, and that there be no division among you, and that ye be joined together in the same mind and in the same judgment.'

"We[1] have written to you as much as we could of these six excesses; we will hereafter write to thy charity of other things also. For if it be true as we have heard, thou thyself wilt acknowledge with me that the canons of the holy apostles are transgressed by you, as well as the institutes of the seven great councils, at which all your first patriarchs were present, and united in pronouncing your doctrine to be vain. And that you are manifestly wrong, I will now plainly prove. In the first place, with reference to fasting on the Sabbath, you see what the holy apostles, whose doctrine ye hold, taught respecting it, as well as the most blessed Pope Clement, the first after the Apostle St. Peter, who thus writes concerning the Sabbath, from the statutes of the apostles, as it is given in the sixty-fourth canon:—If an ecclesiastic be found to fast on the Lord's day or the Sabbath, except the great Sabbath, let him be degraded; but if a layman do so, let him be excommunicated and separated from the Church. Secondly, with reference to general fasting, which ye corrupt. It is a heresy of the Jacobites[2] and Armenians, who use sheep's milk even on the great holy fast, for what true Christian dares so to do or to think? Read the canons of the sixth

---

[1] The indiscriminate use of "we" and "I" in this letter, is literally translated from the original.

[2] A religious sect in the east, whose leader was Jacob Zanzale, Bishop of Edessa in Mesopotamia in 541. They still exist in different parts of Asia, particularly in Syria, Ethiopia, and Armenia. Their chief resides at Kara-Amid, capital of Diarbehir. They only recognize one nature in Jesus Christ, namely, the divine nature, a dogma originated by Eutyches (respecting whom, see note at page 64), and of which, after being nearly extinguished by the decision of the Council of Chalcedon and by Imperial edicts, the Jacobites were but the revivers.

great synod, in which your Pope Oaphanius forbids these things. We indeed, when we learned that in Armenia and some other places they ate cheese made from sheep's milk at the great fast, ordered our people who were there to abstain from such food and from every sacrifice to devils; from which, if a man abstain not, he should be separated from the Church; and if he be a priest, he should be suspended from performing the sacred offices. Moreover, the third error and sin is very great, concerning the marriage of priests, for ye forbid those who have wives to receive the Lord's body; whereas the holy council, which was held at Gangra, writes in the fourth canon, 'He who despises a priest who has a wife according to law, and says that it is not lawful to receive the sacrament at his hand, let him be accursed.' The council also says, 'Every deacon or priest putting away his own wife shall be deprived of his priesthood'. The fourth sin is the anointment or confirmation. Is it not everywhere said in the councils, 'I acknowledge one baptism for the remission of sins'. If, therefore, there is one baptism, there will be also one anointing, and the virtue of the bishop will be the same as that of the priest. The fifth error is with reference to unleavened bread, which error indeed is the beginning and root of all heresy, as I will prove; and although it might be necessary to bring to the proof many Scriptures, yet I will do otherwise, and for the present will merely say: That the Jews make unleavened bread in memory of their deliverance and flight from Egypt; but we are once for all Christians—we never were in Egyptian bondage—and we have been commanded to omit this kind of Jewish observances with respect to the Sabbath, unleavened bread, and circumcision. And as St. Paul says, whosoever follows one of them is bound to keep the whole law; for the same apostle says, 'Brethren, I have received from the Lord, that which also I have delivered unto you, how that the Lord on the night on which he was betrayed, took bread, blessed, and sanctified it, broke it and gave it to the holy disciples, saying, Take and eat, etc.' Consider what I say: he did not say, 'The Lord taking unleavened bread', but bread. That on that occasion, no unleavened bread was used,—and that it was not the Passover,—and that the Lord was not then eating the Passover with his disciples, is probable from the fact, that the Jews' Passover was eaten standing, which was not the case at Christ's supper, as the Scripture says, 'While they were lying down with the twelve'; also, 'And the disciple lay upon his bosom at supper'. For when he himself says, 'With desire I have desired to eat this Passover with you', he does not understand the Jews' Passover, which he had often before eaten with them. Nor when he says, 'This do in remembrance of me', did he impose the necessity of doing as at the Jews' Passover. Nor does he give them unleavened bread, but bread, when he says, 'Behold the bread which I give you'; and likewise to Judas, 'To whomsoever I shall give the bread when I have dipped it in the salt, he shall betray me'.[1] But if ye argue, 'we use unleavened bread in the sacrament, because in divine things there is no admixture of the earthly', why then have ye forgotten divinity, and follow the rites of the Jews, walking in the heresy of Julian himself, of Mahomet, of Apollinarius,[2] and Paul[3] the Syrian, of Samosata, and Eutychius,[4]

[1] These passages are literally translated from the original, but the reader will see that though placed between inverted commas, they are not given strictly in the language of Scripture.

[2] There were two Greek rhetoricians of this name, in the fourth century, father and son, who taught at Berytus and Laodicæa. They embraced Christianity; and Apollinaris the younger, who is here alluded to, became a bishop. He originated a dogma that there was nothing human in the soul of Jesus Christ. He was condemned by many councils.

[3] Paulus Syrius Samosatensis, Bishop of Samosata in Syria, and afterwards Patriarch of Antioch about 262. He was the author of a heresy which consisted in denying the Trinity, and the divinity of Jesus Christ: he was excommunicated at the Council of Antioch, 270: his followers were named Paulinists.

[4] Eutychius, more properly Eutyches, was abbot of a monastery near

and Diasterius,[1] and others, who were pronounced at the sixth Council to be most depraved heretics, and filled with the spirit of the devil? For why do ye say, 'I believe in God the Father, and in the Son, and in the Holy Ghost, who proceeds from the Father and the Son'? Truly it is marvellous and horrible to speak of, that ye thus dare pervert the faith, while from the beginning it has been constantly sung in all Churches throughout the whole world, 'I believe in the Holy Ghost, the Lord, the Giver of life, who proceedeth from the Father, who, together with the Father and the Son, is worshipped and glorified'. Why then do ye not say as all other Christians do, instead of making additions, and introducing a new doctrine, while on the other hand the Apostle declares, 'If any man preach to you more than those things which we have declared to you, let him be anathema.' I hope ye may not fall under that curse, for it is a dangerous and a fearful thing to alter and pervert the Scripture of God, composed by the saints. Do ye not know how very great is your error? For ye

Constantinople at the time when Nestorius promulgated his heresy: he left his retreat in order to defend the faith, but fell himself into a new heresy, which he began to disseminate in 448. He taught that there was only one nature in Jesus Christ, namely the divine nature, in which his human nature was absorbed like a drop of water in the sea. His followers, many of whom still exist in the East, are called Eutychians, or Monophysites.

[1] The editor has sought in vain for information respecting this heresiarch. Neither Tillemont, Walch, Pluquet, nor Mosheim, make any allusion to the name of Diasterius. Possibly, by an error, this name has been written for that of Dioscorus, patriarch of Alexandria, who adopted the opinions of Eutyches. He supported those opinions at the Council of Ephesus, in 449; and, on his return to Alexandria, had the boldness to excommunicate the pope, Leo the Great; but in the following year he was deposed from his patriarchate, at the Council of Constantinople, and in 451 was deprived of his bishopric and priesthood at the Council of Chalcedon. He died in exile, A.D. 458, at Gangra, in Paphlagonia,—the place above alluded to, at p. 63, as the seat of a council which was held in the year 324.

introduce two virtues, two wills, and two principles, with reference to the Holy Spirit, taking away and making of small account his honour, and ye conform to the Macedonian heresy,[1] from which God preserve us. I bow myself at thy sacred feet, and beseech thee to cease from errors of this kind which are amongst you, and above all abstain from unleavened bread. I wished also to write something concerning strangled and unclean animals, and of monks eating meat, but if it please God, I will write of these hereafter. Excuse me of thy extreme charity that I have written to thee of these things. Examine the Scriptures and thou wilt find whether the things which are done by you ought to be done. I pray thee, my Lord, write to my Lord the Patriarch of Constantinople, and to the holy metropolitans who have in themselves the word of life, and shine as lights in the world. For it may be, that by their means God may inquire concerning errors of this sort, and correct and settle them. Afterwards, if it shall seem good to thee, write to me who am the least among all others. I, Metropolitan of Russia, salute thee and all thy subjects, both clergy and laity. The holy bishops, monks, kings, and great men, salute thee also. The love of the Holy Spirit be with thee and all thine. Amen."

Here follow the Canons of one John, a Metropolitan
CALLED THE PROPHET, WHICH I HAVE THOUGHT WELL TO SUBJOIN, ALTHOUGH COLLECTED AT INTERVALS AS I WAS ABLE TO OBTAIN THEM.

Children may be baptized in a case of necessity without a priest.

Animals and birds torn by birds or animals may not be

---

[1] Macedonius, Patriarch of Constantinople in the middle of the fourth century, did not believe that the divinity of the Holy Ghost was clearly declared in the Scriptures, but that they simply ascribed to him the characteristics of a creature.

eaten; but those who eat them, who celebrate the sacrament with unleavened bread, or who eat meat during Septuagesima,[1] or consume the blood of animals, shall be corrected.

Birds and animals which have been strangled may not be eaten.

The Russians may, in case of necessity, eat with the Romans, but by no means receive the sacrament with them.

Russians should convert to the true faith all Romans not rightly baptized (inasmuch as they have not been entirely immersed in water); and when they are converted, the Eucharist is not to be immediately administered to them, any more than to Tartars or others of a different creed.

Old images and pictures which have been consecrated may not be burned, but buried in gardens or some other honourable place, lest they should be injured or disfigured.

If you build a house upon a spot that has been consecrated, let the place where the altar has stood be left void.

If a married man enter a monastery and his wife marry another, let him be consecrated to the priesthood.

A prince's daughter shall not be given in marriage to one who receives the communion in unleavened bread, or uses unclean meats.

Priests should wear in the winter time leggings, made of the skins of the animals which they have eaten.

Those who have not confessed, nor made restitution of the property of another, shall not be admitted to the communion.

Priests and monks may not be present at weddings at the time of the dances.

If a priest shall knowingly perform the marriage service

[1] Septuagesima Sunday being the first term of preparation for Lent, it is customary in the Greek Church to announce the approaching fast to the people on that day, and hence the week following is called the week of prosphonesima, or week of publication.

for any one wishing to be married the third time, he shall be deprived of his office.

When a mother wishes her children to be baptized, and they are unable to fast, she shall fast for them.

If a husband leave his first wife and marry a second, or if the wife marry another, he shall not be admitted to the communion until he return into wedlock.

Let no one be sold to a strange faith.

Any one knowingly eating with the Romans must be purified by prayers of purification.

If a priest's wife be taken by the infidels, she should be redeemed, and be taken again into wedlock, because she has suffered violence.

Merchants and foreigners going into Roman parts shall not be deprived of the communion, but shall be admitted after making atonement by certain prayers enjoined as a penance.

No women shall be invited to any feast held in a monastery.

Marriages may only be contracted publicly, in churches.

Here follow the questions of one Cyril to Niphon,
BISHOP OF NOVOGOROD.[1]

What if a man after the communion vomit from a surfeit of meat and drink? *Answer:* He shall do penance by fasting forty days. If it be not from a surfeit, but from nausea, he shall fast twenty days. If from some other trifling cause, a shorter time. A priest doing such a thing, shall abstain

---

[1] Some of these being more interesting to the theologian than acceptable to the good taste of the general reader, the translator has thought proper to omit them, and to supply their place with asterisks.

from sacred functions, and fast forty days; but if it happen from some slight cause, he shall fast for a week, and abstain from mead, flesh, and milk. If a man vomit on the third or fourth day after communion, he shall do penance; but if any one vomit the sacrament, he shall do penance for one hundred and twenty days, unless it be through infirmity, when he shall do penance for three days, but he shall burn the vomit in the fire and say one hundred psalms; but if a dog devour the vomit, he shall fast one hundred days.

If vessels of earthen ware or wood be unclean, what is to be done? *Answer:* Let them be cleansed with prayers of purification.

What is to be done for the soul of a deceased person? *Answer:* Let one grifna[1] be given for five masses, with fumigations, loaves, and cooked barley, called kuthia; but let the priest have his own wine.

What if I were to give nothing to eat for twelve days to a sick monk wearing the seraphic vestment? *Answer:* It were well done, since he belonged to the angelic order.

What if a member of the Roman Church wish to be initiated into the Roman ritual? *Answer:* Let him enter our church seven days; let a new name be given him, and on each day four prayers be devoutly offered in his presence; let him then wash himself in a bath, abstain seven days from meats and milk, and on the eighth day after washing, let him enter the church; then let those four prayers be said over him; let him put on clean robes; let a crown or garland be placed upon his head; let him be anointed with the chrism, and a wax light be put in his hand. While the mass is being performed, let him receive the communion, and be accepted as a new Christian.

Is it lawful to kill birds, fishes, and other animals, on festivals. *Answer:* A man should go to church on Sunday,

---

[1] A coin, to be referred to hereafter, under the head of Russian money.

because it is a festival; but under the demands of human nature, these animals may be killed.

Is it lawful to preserve for a whole year the sacrament that has been consecrated in Passion week? *Answer*: Let it be preserved in a clean vessel; but when the priest administers it to a sick man, let him add a little wine to it.

Is it lawful, in administering the communion to the sick, to add water to the wine? *Answer*: The wine alone is sufficient.

Is it lawful to administer the sacrament to demoniacs and to insane persons? *Answer*: Let their mouths only be touched with the sacrament.

Is it lawful for a priest, who has a wife in child-bed, to repeat prayers over her as he would over the wives of laymen? *Answer*: No,—for that custom is not retained in Greece, unless in case no other priest can be found.

What should be eaten on the day of the exaltation of the holy cross? *Answer*: Monks may not eat fish; but laymen, who have that day kissed the holy cross, may eat meat, unless it happen to fall on Friday or Wednesday.

* * *[1]

Are little infants to receive the communion after baptism? *Answer*: They may receive it in the church during the performance of service, or while vespers are being sung.

What kind of food is to be eaten during the great fast? *Answer*: On Sundays and Saturdays, fish; but on other days, ikhri, that is, fishes' entrails. In the great week, monks should eat honey, and drink kwas, that is, acid water.

In the consecration of the Kuthia, how many wax-lights should be burned? *Answer*: Two for the souls of the dead, three for the health of the living.

How should Kuthia be made? *Answer*: Three parts should be of cooked barley, the fourth of peas, beans, and vetches, also cooked. It should be seasoned with honey and

---

[1] Seven lines are here omitted.

sugar; other condiments may also be used if they are at hand. This Kuthia is to be used in the church after the performance of funerals.

When may Bulgarians, Poles, and Czudi,[1] be baptized? *Answer*: After forty days' fasting, and prayers of purification being said over them; but if it be a Sclavonian, he need only fast eight days; but let the priest who baptizes a child well gird up his sleeves, lest while he dips the child anything from the baptismal font remain upon his vestment. A woman after child-birth shall not enter a church for forty days.

*   *   *
*   *   *

Is it lawful to enter the dwelling of a woman in childbed? *Answer*: No one must enter the place where a woman has been delivered till after three days, for as unclean vessels are carefully washed, so should that dwelling be first purified by prayers.

Should persons be buried after sun-set? *Answer*: No one should be buried after the setting of the sun; for it is the crown of dead men to see the sun before they are buried. But he is most deserving who buries the bones of the dead and ancient images under the ground.

*   *   *[2]

If any paper containing sacred writings happen to be torn and thrown upon the ground, is it lawful to walk over that spot? *Answer*: No.

---

[1] The north of Europe and also of Asia seem alike to be the country of the Czudi; at all events, one can recognize no essential difference between them and the Huns who came from Tartary under Attila and spread themselves over Western Europe. It is perhaps to this resemblance to the Huns that they owe the name given to them by all foreigners, that of Finns (in Latin, Fenni), but which they themselves do not recognize.—Schnitzler, *Essai d'une Statistique générale de l'Empire de Russie*.

[2] Eleven lines are here omitted.

Is it lawful to use the milk of a cow on the same day that she has calved? *Answer:* No; because it is mixed with blood; but after two days it may be used.

* * *

How is a man who has divorced his wife to do penance? *Answer:* Let him keep perpetual abstinence from the eucharist, except upon his death-bed.

Is it lawful to any one in life to undergo the ceremony of the burial of the dead for the health of his soul? *Answer:* It is lawful.

May husband and wife assist each other in performing penance. *Answer:* No; but a brother may assist a brother.

Ought a priest to undertake sacred duties on the same day that he has buried and kissed a dead person? *Answer:* He ought not.

Ought a woman in child-bed, whose health is despaired of, to have the communion administered to her? *Answer:* Only provided she be removed from the place where she was delivered, and be washed.

* * *[2]

Is it lawful to offer prayers in a church immediately after dinner or supper before going to sleep? *Answer:* Which is better, to sleep or to pray?

May a priest approach a sick man and administer the sacrament to him without wearing his sacerdotal robe? *Answer:* He may.

* * *[3]

May a woman take the advice of old women how she may conceive? *Answer:* Women, who by the advice of old crones, use herbs to produce conception instead of going to priests who might assist them with their prayers, shall do penance six weeks, and pay three griffnas to the priest. If

---

[1] Fifteen lines omitted.   [2] Five, ditto.   [3] Ten, ditto.

a drunken man injure a pregnant woman so as to produce miscarriage, he shall do penance half a year. Midwives also shall absent themselves eight days from church, and in the interim be purified by prayers.

Baptism.

The mode of baptizing is as follows:—When a child is born, a priest is immediately sent for, who, standing before the door of the child-bearing woman's dwelling, repeats certain prayers, and gives the child its name. Afterwards, generally on the fortieth day, if the child happen to be ill, he is brought into the church and baptized, and is dipped three times entirely into the water, otherwise they would not consider him baptized. He is then sprinkled with the chrism, which is consecrated in the holy week, and lastly he is sprinkled with myrrh, according to their account.

The baptismal water is consecrated for each separate child, and is always poured away after the baptism outside the door of the church. Children are always baptized in the church, unless the distance be too great, or the cold injurious to the child: they never use warm water, except for sickly children.

Sponsors are adopted at the choice of the parents; and while the priest precedes them with certain words, they spit upon the ground for every time that they renounce the devil. The priest also cuts off some hairs[1] from the child's head, and mixes them with wax, and lays them up in a certain spot in the church. They use neither salt nor saliva in the mixture.

[1] Dr. King, quoting from Simeon of Thessalonica says:—"The hair is offered by the baptized person to Christ, as a sort of first fruits, as the sacrifice of his body, the hair being as it were the exhalation of the whole body: the chief priest therefore does not carelessly throw it away, but lays it apart in a sacred place."

Here follows a Bull of Pope Alexander,

IN WHICH THE ORDINANCE OF BAPTISM AMONG
THE RUSSIANS IS FULLY DESCRIBED.

The Bishop Alexander, servant of the servants of God, for a perpetual remembrance. The loftiness of the divine wisdom, which no human reason can grasp, always originating out of the essence of its boundless goodness something for the welfare of the human race, produces and brings it to light at that convenient season which God himself, by a secret mystery, knows to be the suitable one ; in order that men may know that they can do nothing by their own merits as of themselves, but that their salvation and every gift of grace proceeds from the supreme God himself, and from the Father of light. Truly it is not without great and lively joy in our mind that we have heard that some Russians in the Duchy of Lithuania, and others living according to the Greek ritual, but in other respects professing the Christian faith, dwelling in the cities and dioceses of Wilna and Kiev, Lukov'[1] and Medniki,[2] and other places in the same duchy, have, by the illumination of the Holy Spirit working in them, expressed a desire utterly to reject from their minds and hearts some errors which while living in the ritual and custom of the Greeks they have hitherto observed, and to embrace the unity of the Catholic faith and of the Latin Roman Church, and to live according to the ritual of the said Latin and Roman Church. But as they have been

[1] A small town in Poland, six leagues south of Siedlec, and five northeast of Radzyn. Though it has only about twenty thousand inhabitants, of whom a large proportion are Jews, it contains a castle, several churches, and a college.

[2] A little town in the government of Wilna on the banks of the Varvitza. It is the residence of a Catholic bishop, who calls himself Bishop of Samogithia.

baptized according to the ritual of the Greeks,—namely, in the third person, and some assert that they ought to be baptized anew,—the aforesaid, who have hitherto lived, and still live, under the Greek ritual, refuse to receive baptism again, as though they had been already rightly baptized. We therefore, who, in the pastoral office committed to us from above, though insufficiently deserving it, desire to bring every sheep entrusted to us to the true fold of Christ, that there may be one shepherd and one fold, and to the end that the holy Catholic Church may have no discordant or unsightly members at variance with the head, but all in harmony therewith; and taking into consideration that in the council held at Florence by our predecessor, Eugene the fourth of blessed memory, at which were present Greeks and Armenians agreeing with the Romish Church, it was decided that the form of this sacrament of baptism should be, "I baptize thee in the name of the Father, and of the Son, and of the Holy Ghost. Amen": and also that by the words, "Let such a servant of Jesus Christ be baptized in the name of the Father, and of the Son, and of the Holy Ghost, or such an one is baptized by my hands in the name of the Father, and of the Son, and of the Holy Ghost", a true baptism is performed: for the main source from which baptism derives its virtue, is the Holy Trinity—the instrument is the minister, and the exposition of the sacrament is effected by his ministry, in his invocation of the Holy Trinity; we, therefore, having maturely deliberated upon the subject with our brethren, declare by these presents, in virtue of the apostolical authority delivered to us and the other Roman pontiffs by our Lord Jesus Christ himself through Saint Peter (to whom and his successors was committed the dispensation of the ministry), that the repetition of such sacrament thus administered in the third person is not necessary. We declare that each and all of those who have been baptized in the third person of the Trinity, and wish to leave the Greek ritual, and to conform to the forms and ritual of the Latin and holy Roman Church, are to be admitted in all simplicity, and without any contradiction, obligation, or compulsion to be rebaptized; it being moreover intended that such rites as they may have been accustomed to observe in the Eastern Church, may continue to be observed by them, provided there be no heretical depravity therein; always provided that they first solemnly abjure all errors of the Greek ritual, and such things as differ from the ritual and institutions of the Latin and Roman Church. At the same time we exhort by the bowels of the mercy of our God, that each and all of such as are so baptized, and who live according to the Greek ritual, repudiating the errors which they have hitherto held according to the custom and ritual of the Greek Church, and contrary to the immaculate and holy Catholic Latin and Roman Church and to the approved institutions of her holy fathers, do willingly conform to the said holy Catholic Church and to her wholesome doctrines, for the sake of the salvation of their souls and the advancement of the knowledge of the true God; and that their holy resolution may meet with no hindrance from any one, we now charge and enjoin upon our venerable brother the bishop of Wilna, by virtue of sacred obedience, that he receive and admit each and all who may be so baptized, and who wish to conform to the unity of the aforesaid Latin Church, and abjure the aforesaid errors either by themselves, or by proxy, or by committing the same abjuration to any of the secular prelates, ecclesiastics, or preachers, or to the learned and worthy professors of the regular observance of the minor orders, or any fitting persons to whom such abjuration might be entrusted. And by these presents we grant to all and singular of the aforesaid full and free liberty to induct, as often as may be expedient, any such, as aforesaid, who may have in any way incurred the sentence of excommunication, or any other sentence or penalties of the Church on account of the observance of such errors or any heretical depravity proceeding therefrom, and by the aforesaid apostolical authority to absolve them, and by way of exculpation to inflict a salutary penance, or to adopt any measures which may be deemed necessary in the cases described. But since it might perhaps be difficult to convey this our letter to all the places where it may be needed, we will and by the same apostolical authority decree, that the rescript of this our letter be re-copied by the hand of a notary public, and sealed with the seal of the aforesaid bishop of Wilna, or some other bishop, or ecclesiastical prelate; and that this copy, or transcript, shall have as much validity as would be given to the original in every tribunal, and in every place where it shall be exhibited or declared, notwithstanding any apostolical institutions, orders, or ordinances whatsoever. Be it understood, therefore, that it shall not be lawful for any one whatever to infringe, or by any bold act of temerity to contravene this our letter of constitution, declaration, exhortation, commission, mandate, concession, will, and decree: and if any one whosoever shall dare to attempt this, let him know that he will incur the indignation of Almighty God, and of the blessed apostles Peter and Paul. Given at Rome, at St. Peter's, in the year of the incarnation of our Lord, 1501, 10° Calend., Septemb. in the ninth year of our Pontificate.

Confession.

Although confession forms a part of their religious constitution, the common people nevertheless think it to be mainly the duty of princes, and to belong especially to noble lords and men of exalted rank. Confession is made about the feast of Easter with great contrition of heart and reverence. The confessor stands together with the person confessing in the middle of the church, with his face turned towards a certain image placed for that purpose. When the confession is finished, and penance enjoined according to the nature of the offence, they bow before the image, mark their foreheads and breasts with the sign of the cross, and lastly cry out with great wailing, "O Jesus Christ, thou Son of God, have mercy upon us". For this is their common prayer. Some are enjoined to fast by way of penance; some to say certain prayers (for very few know the Lord's Prayer); and those who have committed any rather serious offence, are washed with water. For at the Epiphany of our Lord, they draw water from a spring, and after it has been consecrated in the church for a whole year, they draw it off for cleansing and washing away the more serious sins. They also judge more leniently a sin committed on the Sabbath, and enjoin less penance for it. There are also many very slight causes for which they are not admitted into the church; but when they are shut out, they are accustomed to stand at many of the church windows and doors, and thence see and hear as well as if they were in the church.

Communion.

They communicate in both kinds, mixing the bread with the wine, or the body with the blood. The priest takes a small portion, in a spoon, out of the chalice, and hands it to the communicant. Any one may receive the Lord's body as often in the year as he will, provided he have confessed; otherwise they have a fixed time, at Easter. They administer the Sacrament to boys of seven years old, and say, that at that age man sins. If a boy happen to be sick, or near death, so that he cannot take bread, a drop is poured out for him from the chalice. The Sacrament is not consecrated for the Communion unless it be already sacred; but it is consecrated on Thursday in the Holy Week for sick people, and kept through the whole year; and when it is wanted the priest takes a small piece of it and places it in the wine, and when it is well soaked he hands it to the sick person, and then adds a little warm water.

No monk or priest prays the canonical hours, as they are called, except in the presence of an image, which nobody touches without great reverence; and he who carries it in public, bears it in his hand high raised in the air, and all who pass by it cover their heads, crossing themselves and bowing with the greatest reverence. They only place the books of the gospel in places of honour, regarding them as a sacred thing; nor do they touch them with the hand, unless they have previously protected themselves with the sign of the cross, and then they manifest their devotion by bowing with the head covered, and after that, with the greatest reverence, they take the book in their hands. The bread also, before it has been consecrated as with us, with the usual words, is carried round the church, and they worship and adore it with words conceived in their own minds.

Feast Days.

Men of superior rank observe the feast days by indulging, when the service of the church is over, in banquets, drunkenness, and elegant attire; the common people, the domestics, and the serfs, for the most part, work, and say that it is for their masters to make holiday and abstain from labour. The citizens and mechanics are present at the service, after which they return to their work, thinking it more holy to stoop to labour, than idly to waste their substance and their time in drinking, playing, and so on; for beer and mead are forbidden to the common people, except on some of the more solemn feast days, such as Christmas Day, Easter Day, Whit Sunday, and some others, when they are permitted to drink them, so that, on these days, they abstain from labour, not for divine worship, but rather for the sake of the drink.

They keep the feast of the Trinity on Monday during the feast of Pentecost, and on the eighth day of Pentecost they keep the feast of All Saints; but they do not observe the day of Corpus Christi as we do.

In taking oaths and swearing, they seldom use the name of God; but when they swear, they confirm what they have said or promised by kissing the cross. Their common imprecation is like that of the Hungarians, "May a dog defile thy mother", etc. Whenever they sign themselves with the sign of the cross, they do it with the right hand, that they may first touch the forehead, then the breast, then the right, and lastly the left side of the breast, in the form of a cross; but if any one guide his hand otherwise, they do not regard him as a follower of the same creed,[1] but as a stranger; for I remember that I myself, being ignorant of this ceremony, and guiding my hand otherwise, was noticed and reproached with this appellation.

Purgatory.

They do not believe in Purgatory, but say that every one who is dead receives a place according to his desert; that to the pious is ordained a bright abode with the peaceful angels, and to the ungodly, a gloomy place beset with black darkness, with the angels of terror, where they await the last

[1] Domestico fidei suæ.

judgment; and, that from the angelic realms of peace, the souls there experience the favour of God, and always long for the final judgment; but the others contrariwise. Nor do they think that the soul, when separated from the body, is exposed to punishment; for as the soul had contaminated itself in the body, they think it must be expiated with the body. They do, however, believe that, by performing sacred funereal rights for the dead, they may obtain a more tolerable place for their souls, in which they may, with the greater ease, wait for the judgment to come. No one sprinkles himself with holy water, but is sprinkled by the priest. They do not consecrate cemeteries for burying bodies in, but say that the earth itself is consecrated by anointed and consecrated bodies, and not the bodies by the earth.

The Worship of Saints.

They reverence Nicolas of Bari[1] as first among the saints, and preach daily of his numerous miracles, one of which, which happened a few years ago, I have thought right to relate. One Michael Kysaletski, a large and powerful man, in one of the engagements with the Tartars, pursued a certain renowned Tartar, who fled from him, and when he found he could not catch him, however much he spurred his horse, he said, "O Saint Nicolas, bring me up with this hound!" The Tartar hearing this, cried out in affright, "O Saint Nicolas, if this man catch me by thy assistance, thou wilt perform no miracle; but if thou rescuest me who am a stranger to thy faith from his pursuit, thy renown will be

---

[1] St. Nicolas, Bishop of Myra in Lycia, called by Herberstein, Barensis, from Bari in Apuglia, where he was buried, and where his body is said to be still preserved. He is the patron saint of Russia.

great." They say that Michael's horse immediately stopped, and the Tartar escaped; and that every year of his life afterwards the Tartar made an offering to Saint Nicolas of certain measures of honey on account of his rescue, and as many measures to Michael likewise in memory of his delivery, with the addition of a robe of honour made of marten skins.

Fasting.

They fast in Lent seven consecutive weeks. The first week they use preparations of milk or a sort of cheese, which they call Syrna, but in the other weeks they all, with the exception of foreigners, abstain even from fish. Some take food on the Sundays and Saturdays, and abstain from all food the other days: some take food on Sunday, Tuesday, Thursday, and Saturday, and abstain the remaining three days. There are many who content themselves with a piece of bread taken with water on Monday, Wednesday, and Friday. They do not observe the other fasts throughout the year so strictly, but they fast from the eighth day after Pentecost, which is their All Saints' Day, till the holidays of St. Peter and St. Paul, and this is called the fast of St. Peter. Then they have the fast of the Blessed Virgin from the first of August until the Assumption of the Virgin Mary. Also the fast of St. Philip, six weeks in Advent, which is called St. Philip's fast, because the beginning of that fast happens on the feast of St. Philip according to their calendar. Moreover, if the feast of St. Peter and St. Paul, and that of the Assumption, fall on Wednesday or Friday, then they do not eat meat on that day. They do not keep the vigil of any Saint with fasting except the beheading of St. John, which they observe yearly on the 29th of August. If, moreover, any Saint's day, such as the Annunciation of the Virgin Mary, happen in the great fast of Lent, they eat fish on that day. But the monks have many more severe and trying fasts imposed upon them, for they are obliged to content themselves with an acid drink, called kwas, and water mixed with yeast. The priests also are prohibited the use of warm water and beer at that time, although now all the laws and statutes are becoming lax and are abused. Moreover, besides the time of fasting, they eat meat on the Sabbath, but abstain on Wednesday. The teachers whom they follow are Basil the Great, Gregory, and John Chrysostom, whom they call Slatousta, *i.e.*, golden mouth. They have no preachers. They think it enough to have been present at the service, and to have heard the words of the Gospel, the Epistles, and other teachers, which the priest recites in the vernacular. For this purpose, as they think that they avoid various opinions and heresies which often arise out of sermons, the festivals of the following week are announced on the Lord's Day, and they repeat the public confession. Moreover, whatever they see that the prince himself thinks and believes, that they set down to be right, and to be followed in all things.

I heard at Moscow that the patriarch of Constantinople, at the request of the prince of Russia himself, sent a certain monk named Maximilian to reduce judiciously into order all the books and canons, and all the statutes appertaining to the faith; and when he had done so, and when having corrected many most serious errors, he pronounced in the presence of the prince, that he who did not follow the Roman or Greek ritual, was evidently a schismatic: when, I say, he said this, not long after (although the prince treated him with the greatest kindness) he is said to have disappeared, and many think he was drowned. It was in the third year of my residence at Moscow that one Marcus, a Greek merchant from Caffa, was reported to have said this, and he also was seized (although the Turkish ambassador at the time interceded for him even with somewhat unworthy petitions) and put out of the way. Georgius, a Greek, surnamed the "Little", who was the prince's treasurer, chancellor, and chief counsellor, was immediately removed from all his posts which he held, and lost the prince's favour, because he encouraged and defended the same cause. But as the prince could by no means dispense with his assistance, he was again restored to favour, and placed in a different office, for he was a man of remarkable learning and extensive experience. He had come to Moscow with the prince's mother; and the prince respected him so much, that on one occasion when he had summoned him, and found that he was sick, he ordered some of his counsellors of the first rank to fetch him in a sedan to his own residence. But when he reached the palace, he refused to be carried up so many steep steps, and being taken out of the sedan, he commenced ascending slowly up to the prince. When the prince accidentally saw this, he began to be extremely angry, and commanded that he should be brought up to him in a litter; and after he had consulted him, and his business was over, he ordered that he should be carried down the steps in a litter, and that he should be carried up and down ever afterwards.

The principal care of the monks is to convert all men whatsoever to their own creed. The hermit monks have already brought over to the faith of Christ a great part of those who were idolaters through daily and industriously disseminating the word of God amongst them. Even now they go to various countries in the north and east, which they can only reach by the greatest toil, at the risk of both fame and life, and without hope of the least personal advantage; nor do they seek it, for they have an eye to this one thing only, viz., that they may be able to do an acceptable service to God, and to recall into the right path the souls of many who have gone astray (sometimes confirming the doctrine of Christ by death), and to bring them in as gain to Christ.

The principal monastery in Moscow is that of the Holy Trinity,[1] which is twelve German miles to the west of Moscow, where St. Sergius was buried, and is said to perform many miracles. He is honoured by the prayers of a wonderful assemblage of nations and peoples. The prince himself often goes there and takes a meal at the expense of the monastery; but the common people only go on certain annual occasions. There is said to be a copper cauldron there, in which certain food—especially herbs—is cooked, and whether few or many go there, there is always enough food remaining in it to feed the inmates of the monastery, so that there is never either a deficiency nor a surplus.

The Muscovites boast that they are the only true Christians, and condemn us as deserters from the Primitive Church, and from the old sacred institutions. But if any one of our religion of his own accord goes over to the Muscovites, or even flees to them against the will of his master, as though for the sake of learning and embracing their religion, they say that he ought not to be let go or restored to his master, even if he should demand him back, a fact which came to my knowledge in a certain instance which I have thought right to insert here. A certain leading citizen of Cracow, when I was starting for Moscow, recommended and delivered to me, almost against my will, a not ill-educated young man named Erasmus, of the respectable family of the Bethmans. He was, however, so given to drinking, that he would sometimes be intoxicated even to madness, and compelled me, by his repeated drunkenness, to have him put in the stocks. Over-

---

[1] This monastery, which is named the "Laurel of St. Sergius, under the invocation of the Blessed Trinity", is the richest in all Russia, and perhaps in the whole world, and one of the most remarkable for the great historical events associated with it, both as to the important services rendered by it to the country, and the illustrious men it has produced.

come then by a sense of his error, he ran away from the city of Moscow one night, accompanied by three of the citizens and my Polish coachman. He swam across the river Occa, and proceeded towards Azov. When the prince learned this, he immediately sent his couriers, whom they call Gonecz, in every direction, to bring them back. These men fell in with the out-liers who were stationed in those parts to guard against the continual incursions of the Tartars, and explaining the case to them, made them also ride about in search of the fugitives; and they met a man who said that five men, availing themselves of the cover of the night, had compelled him to show them the right road for Azov. The out-liers, therefore, following close upon their footsteps, at nightfall saw a fire which they had lighted; and while their horses were wandering on the pastures in the neighbourhood of the place where they were about to spend the night, they crept up silently like serpents and drove them further away. When, therefore, my coachman rose up and went to bring back the horses which had strayed, the men rushed upon him from the grass, and threatened him with death if he uttered the least sound, and thus they kept him bound. Again they drove the horses farther, and as one and another and a third tried to bring them back, they were all by turns in the same manner taken in the snare, Erasmus only excepted, who, when they rushed upon him, drew his weapon and defended himself, and called to Stanislaus, which was the name of my coachman. When the latter answered that he was taken and bound, Erasmus said, "Since you are taken, I neither care for freedom nor life," and thus surrendered himself when only about two days journey from Asov. When the prisoners were brought back, I asked the prince to restore me my men, but he replied that it was not lawful for any one to render up a man who had gone over to the Muscovites for the sake of learning the true religion, which, as I have said, they preach that they alone maintain. He did, however, shortly afterwards restore me my coachman; and when he refused to give up Erasmus, I told the purveyor who had been attached to my household, and whom they call pristav', that men would both think and speak ill of the prince if he took away the servants of ambassadors. In order that neither the prince nor I should be blamed, I asked him to allow him to come before me in the presence of the prince's counsellors that I myself might understand his wish on the subject. The prince agreed to this, and it was done; and when I asked Erasmus whether he wished to remain with the prince on the score of religion, he answered, " Yes"; upon which I said, " If you have made your bed well, well may you lie on it." Afterwards a certain Lithuanian, who had attached himself to the family of Count Nugarol, dissuaded him from his purpose, when his reply was that he dreaded to encounter my severity. The Lithuanian then asked him if he would come back if the count would receive him into his family, to which he consented. When the count heard of the matter, he asked me if I would agree to the arrangement. I replied that he was free to act as he pleased in the matter for me; for I myself wished it to be so, lest the relatives of the young man should interpret the matter otherwise than as it really occurred.

However they seldom flee to the Russians unless when there is no place to live in, and no security elsewhere. Such was the case in my time with one Severinus Nordwed, admiral of the sea to Christian, king of Denmark, a warlike man indeed, but accustomed to invoke the auspices of the devil upon all his undertakings, of whom I have heard many things which in prudence I leave unsaid. When he saw that the king was hated on account of his cruelty at Holmia (which is the capital of Sweden, and called in their own language Stockholm), and that he of his own accord left his kingdom, Severinus took possession of a certain place in the island of Gothland (which is twelve German miles in extent), from which he daily infested the Baltic Sea, sparing nobody, and plundering alike both friends and enemies. At length being afraid that all would be opposed to him as to some common plague, and seeing that there was no place in which he could be safe from snares, he took to himself a certain number of freebooters and fled to the prince of Moscow, and came with certain ships into the river Narva to Ivanogorod, a fortress of the prince of Russia; thence by a land journey he came to Moscow the same year that I was there. Being discharged at the request of the emperor Charles V, he died in his service, pierced through with a cannon ball at the siege of Florence, a city of Italy.

Concerning Tithes.

Vladimir, who was initiated into the mysteries of the lifegiving font in the year 6496 (A. D. 987), instituted, in conjunction with the metropolitan see, tithes of all things to be given on behalf of the poor, orphans, the sick, the aged, strangers, prisoners, as well as for the burial of the poor; for the assistance also of those who had a numerous offspring, or who had lost their property by fire,—in short, for the relief of the necessities of all the wretched, for the churches of poor monasteries, and chief of all, for the solace of the dead and of the living. The same Vladimir subjected all abbots, presbyters, deacons, and the whole establishment of the clergy, to spiritual power and jurisdiction, as well as monks, nuns, and those women who make proscura for the services, and are called proscurnicæ,[1] also

[1] These words, proscura and proscurnicæ, appear to have been taken by Herberstein from hearsay, as from the description contained in the following paragraph, "proscura" is evidently written in error for "prosphora", the usual term for the loaves offered in the sacrament.

the wives and daughters of priests, physicians, widows, midwives, and those who have been the subjects of a miracle from any of the saints, or those who have received manumission for the salvation of any soul; lastly, all the servants of monasteries and hospitals, and those who make the clothes of the monks. Whatever difference or disagreement, therefore, arises among the aforesaid persons, the bishop himself has power, as a competent judge, to decide upon and settle it; but if any controversy arise between these and laymen, it is decided by common law.

The proscurnicæ are women who, being past child-bearing, make the bread for the sacrifice, which bread is called proscura.

It is the duty of the bishops to adjudge divorces, not only among the Knesi and Boyars, but all laymen who keep concubines. It also appertains to the episcopal jurisdiction to decide if at any time a wife does not obey her husband; if any one be taken in adultery or fornication; if a man marry a woman who is a blood-relation; or if any married person plot any injury to his or her husband or wife. Also in cases of divination, incantations, poisonings, quarrels about heresy or fornication; or if a son injure his parents, or beat his sisters too severely. Moreover, they have the punishment of sodomites, sacrilegious persons, spoilers of the dead, and of such as tear away anything from the images of saints or from crucifixes for the sake of incantations, as well as of persons who either bring a dog, a bird, or any other unclean animal, into any sacred edifice, or who eat such things. In these cases, they have the ordering and appointing the measure of punishment for each. Let no one, however, be surprised, if he find the foregoing details differ in any way from the canons and traditions themselves, for some of them have been changed in some respects, not so much from age as that they have been allowed to become corrupted and vitiated for the sake of money.

If at any time the prince receives a metropolitan at an entertainment, he usually gives him the first seat at table, when his own brethren are not present. At a funeral ceremony, when he invites the metropolitan and the bishops, he himself hands them both their meat and drink at the commencement of the dinner; afterwards he appoints his brother, or some person of princely rank, to supply his place till the end of the dinner.

I succeeded, indeed, in witnessing their ceremonies in the churches on one solemn occasion; and in each of my embassies, I went on the 15th of August, which is the feast of the assumption of the Blessed Virgin, into the great church in the citadel, which was strewed with boughs of trees, and saw the prince standing against the wall to the right of the door at which he had entered, with his head covered, leaning on his staff, called posoch, and one holding before him in his right hand a kalpak;[1] his ministers were standing against the pillars of the church, whither I also was conducted. In the middle of the church, upon a platform, stood the metropolitan in the sacred dress, wearing a round mitre adorned with images of saints on the upper part, and on the lower with ermine. He leaned on a posoch in the same manner as the prince did, and while some were chanting he prayed, accompanied by the priests who attended him. Afterwards, advancing towards the choir, he turned to the left, after our own fashion, and went out by a smaller door, preceded by the choristers, priests, and deacons, one of whom carried on his head in a patera the bread already prepared for the sacrifice; another carried the chalice uncovered; the rest followed promiscuously, bearing images of St. Paul, St. Peter, St. Nicolas, and the Archangel, the people around making great acclamations with obeisances. Some of the bystanders cried, "Lord, have mercy upon us!" others,

---

[1] A Tartar hat.

after the fashion of the country, touched the ground with their foreheads, and wept. Finally, the crowd followed the emblems, which were carried about with various manifestations of devotion. After the circuit was completed, they entered by the middle door of the choir, and the service or highest office (as they call it) began to be performed. It is the custom, however, among them to perform the whole service or mass in the vulgar or vernacular tongue. Moreover, the Epistle and the Gospel for the day are read in a clear voice outside the choir to the people who stand round, in order that they may more distinctly hear them. In my first embassy, I saw on the same festival above a hundred men working in the moat of the citadel; for, as we shall have occasion to say hereafter, only the princes and boyars are accustomed to make holidays.

Their mode of contracting Marriages.

It is held to be dishonourable and a disgrace for a young man to address a girl, in order that he may obtain her hand in marriage. It is the part of the father to communicate with the young man upon the subject of his marrying his daughter. It is generally the custom for them to use such words as the following: "As I have a daughter, I should wish to have you for a son-in-law." To which the young man replies: "If you desire to have me for a son-in-law, I will, if you think fit, have a meeting with my parents, and confer with them upon the subject." Then, if his parents and nearest relatives agree, a meeting is held to treat of the sum which the girl's father is willing to give by way of dowry. After the dowry is settled, a day is appointed for the wedding. Meanwhile, the young man is forbidden the house of his betrothed; so strictly indeed, that if he should happen to try to get a sight of her, the parents usually reply: " Learn what she is from others who have known her." Certainly, unless the espousals have been first confirmed with very heavy penalties, so that the young man who is betrothed could not, if he would, repudiate her without a heavy punishment, no access is permitted to him. Horses, dresses, weapons, cattle, servants, and the like, are generally given as dowry. Those who are invited to the wedding, seldom offer money, but send presents to the bride, each of which is carefully marked and put away by the bridegroom. When the marriage is over, he again arranges them in order, and examines them, and sends such of them as please him, and as he thinks likely to be of use to him, to the market, and orders them to be valued by the appraisers; he then sends back all the other things to their respective donors, with an expression of thanks. He makes compensation in the course of the following year, either in money or in something else of equal value, for those things which he has kept. Moreover, if any one make out his gift to be of greater value, the bridegroom then sends back immediately to the sworn appraisers and compels the party to stand by their valuation. Also, if the bridegroom should not make compensation when a year has elapsed, or restore the accepted gift, then he is bound to return double. Finally, if he should neglect to send any one's gift to be valued by the sworn appraisers, he is compelled to repay according to the will and decision of the party who gave it. And this custom the common people themselves are wont to observe with all liberality, as a kind of donation.

They do not contract marriages within the fourth degree of consanguinity or relationship. They think it heretical for brothers to marry their sisters. Also, no one dare take to wife the sister of his kinsman. They likewise most rigidly observe that no marriage take place between those who are connected by the spiritual relationship of baptism. If any one marry a second wife, and become a bigamist, they allow it indeed, but scarcely think it a lawful marriage. They do not permit a third marriage, except for some weighty cause; but a fourth they allow to nobody, and do not even consider it Christian. They admit divorces, and grant a writ of repudiation, but they mostly conceal it, because they know it to be contrary to religion and the statutes.

We have said a little before, that the prince himself repudiated his wife Salomea on account of barrenness, and thrust her into a convent, and married Helen, daughter of the Knes Basil Lynski. Some years ago, a certain Duke Basil Bielski had fled from Lithuania into Moscow, and his friends detained his wife, who was young and recently married, a long time at his own house (for they thought that he would return again from love and desire of his bride). Bielski referred the case of his absent wife to the council of the metropolitan. After receiving the result of their deliberation, the metropolitan gave for answer: "Since the fault was not yours, but rather your wife's and your relations', that you could not have her company, I will give you the benefit of the law, and release you from her." On hearing this, he soon after married another woman, daughter of the princely race of the Resanenses, by whom he had some sons, whom we now see in great authority about the prince.

They do not call it adultery unless one have the wife of another. Love between those that are married is for the most part lukewarm, especially among the nobles and princes, because they marry girls whom they have never seen before; and being engaged in the service of the prince, they are compelled to desert them, and become corrupted with disgraceful connexions with others.

'The condition of the women is most miserable; for they consider no woman virtuous unless she live shut up at home, and be so closely guarded, that she go out nowhere. They give a woman, I say, little credit for modesty, if she be seen by strangers or people out of doors. But shut up at home they do nothing but spin and sew, and have literally no authority or influence in the house. All the domestic work is done by the servants. Whatever is strangled by the hands of a woman, whether it be a fowl, or any other kind of animal, they abominate as unclean. The wives, however, of the poorer classes do the household work and cook. But if their husbands and the men-servants happen to be away, and they wish to strangle a fowl, they stand at the door holding the fowl, or whatever other animal it may be, and a knife, and generally beg the men that pass by to kill it. They are very seldom admitted into the churches, and still less frequently to friendly meetings, unless they be very old and free from all suspicion. On certain holidays, however, men allow their wives and daughters, as a special gratification, to meet in very pleasant meadows, where they seat themselves on a sort of wheel of fortune, and are moved alternately up and down, or they fasten a rope somewhere, with a seat to it, in which they sit, and are swung backwards and forwards; or they otherwise make merry with clapping their hands and singing songs, but they have no dances whatever.

There is at Moscow a certain German, a blacksmith, named Jordan, who married a Russian woman. After she had lived some time with her husband, she one day thus lovingly addressed him: "Why is it, my dearest husband, that you do not love me?" The husband replied: "I do love you passionately." "I have as yet," said she, "received no proofs of your love." The husband inquired what proofs she desired. Her reply was: "You have never beaten me." "Really," said the husband, "I did not think that blows were proofs of love; but, however, I will not fail even in this respect." And so not long after he beat her most cruelly; and confessed to me that after that process his wife showed much greater affection towards him. So he repeated the exercise frequently; and finally, while I was still at Moscow, cut off her head and her legs.

All confess themselves to be Chlopos, that is, serfs of the prince. Almost all the upper classes also have serfs, who either have been taken prisoners, or purchased; and those whom they keep in free service are not at liberty to quit at their own pleasure. If any one goes away without his master's consent, no one receives him. If a master does not treat a good and useful servant well, he by some means gets a bad name amongst others, and after that he can procure no more domestics.

This people enjoy slavery more than freedom; for persons on the point of death very often manumit some of their serfs, but they immediately sell themselves for money to other families. If the father should sell the son, which is the custom, and he by any means become free or be manumitted, the father can sell him again and again, by right of his paternal authority. But after the fourth sale, the father has no more right over his son. The prince alone can inflict capital punishment on serfs or others.

Every second or third year the prince holds a census through the provinces, and conscribes the sons of the boyars, that he may know their number, and how many horses and serfs each one has. Then he appoints each his stipend, as has been said above. Those who have the means to do so, fight without pay. Rest is seldom given them, for either they are waging war against the Lithuanians, or the Livonians, or the Swedes, or the Tartars of Cazar; or if no war is going on, the prince generally appoints twenty thousand men every year in places about the Don and the Occa, as guards to repress the eruptions and depredations of the Tartars of Precop. He generally summons some also every year by rotation out of his provinces, to fill the various offices in his service at Moscow. But in war time, they do not serve in annual rotation, or by turns, but each and all are compelled, both as stipendiaries and as aspirants to the prince's favour, to go to battle.

They have small gelded horses, unshod, and with very light bridles, and their saddles are so adapted that they may turn round in any direction without impediment, and draw the bow. They sit on horseback with the feet so drawn up, that they cannot sustain any more than commonly severe shock from a spear or javelin. Very few use spurs, but most use the whip, which always hangs from the little finger of the right hand, so that they may lay hold of it and use it as often as they need; and if they have occasion to use their arms, they let it fall again so as to hang from the hand. Their ordinary arms are a bow, a javelin, a hatchet, and a stick, like a cæstus,[1] which is called in Russian, kesteni; in Polish, bassalich. The more noble and wealthy men use a lance. They have also suspended from their arm oblong poignards like knives, which are so buried in the scabbard, that they can scarcely touch the tip of the hilt, or lay hold of them in the moment of necessity. They have also a long bridle perforated at the end, which they attach to a finger of the left hand, so that they may hold it at the same time as they use the bow. Moreover, although they hold the bridle, the bow, the short sword, the javelin, and the whip, in their hands all at the same time, yet they know how to use them skilfully without feeling any incumbrance.

Some of the higher classes use a coat of mail beautifully worked on the breast with a sort of scales and with rings; some few use a helmet of a peaked form like a pyramid.

Some use a dress made of silk stuffed with wool, to enable them to sustain any blows. They also use pikes.

They never have infantry or artillery in an engagement; for whatever they do, whether they are attacking, or pursu-

---

[1] This instrument is more fully described in the German edition as a stick having a thong attached to it, from which depends a knot or ball covered with spikes.

RUSSIAN EQUIPMENTS.
From Herberstein.

ing, or fleeing from the enemy, they do everything suddenly and rapidly, so that neither infantry nor artillery can be of any use to them. Both infantry and artillery have however been used by the present Prince Vasiley, for when the King of Precop, on his return from investing his nephew with the sovereignty of Kasan, had pitched his camp at thirteen miles' distance from Moscow, the Prince Vasiley in the following year pitched his camp by the River Occa, and then for the first time made use of infantry and artillery, perhaps with the view of displaying his strength, or to blot out the disgrace which he had incurred the year before from a most disgraceful flight, in which he was said to have hidden himself some days under a hay stack; or possibly he may have done so with the intention of ridding his territories of a king whom he thought likely to invade his throne. It is certain that he had to my knowledge, for I saw them, nearly fifteen hundred infantry, consisting of Lithuanians, and a host of men of various nations.

They make the first charge on the enemy with great impetuosity; but their valour does not hold out very long, for they seem as if they would give a hint to the enemy, as much as to say, "if you do not flee, we must". They seldom take a city by storm, or by a sudden assault, but prefer a long siege, and to reduce the people to surrender by hunger or by treachery. Although Vasiley besieged the city of Smolensko with cannon, some of which he had taken with him from Moscow, and some he had founded there during the siege, and though he battered the city to pieces, he accomplished nothing. In like manner he besieged Kasan with a large force of men, and brought up some cannon against it, which he had conveyed thither by the river, but on that occasion also he produced no beneficial result; for such was the cowardice manifested on this occasion, that during a lapse of time while the citadel was in flames and was burning down to the ground—aye, and even might have been completely built a second time—not a single soldier had the courage to scale the naked hill to take possession.

The prince has now German and Italian cannon-founders, who cast cannon and other pieces of ordnance, and iron cannon balls such as our own princes use; and yet these people, who consider that everything depends upon rapidity, cannot understand the use of them, nor can they ever employ them in an engagement. I omitted also to state, that they seem not to comprehend the different kinds of artillery, or rather I should say, what use to make of them. I mean to say, that they do not know when they ought to use the larger kind of cannon which are intended for destroying walls, or the smaller for breaking the force of an enemy's attack. This has occurred on several occasions, but especially at the time when the Tartars were said to be on the point of besieging Moscow, for on that occasion the officer to whom the command was deputed, to the amusement of a German bombardier, ordered one of the largest cannons to be placed under the gate of a fortress, where it could scarcely be brought in the space of three days, and with only one discharge of it he would have blown the gate to pieces.

There is a great difference and variety of conduct amongst men in fighting as well as in other things. The Russian, for instance, when he once takes flight, thinks there is no safety beyond what flight may obtain for him; and if he be pursued or taken by the enemy, he neither defends himself nor asks for quarter. The Tartar, on the contrary, if he be thrown from his horse and stripped of all his weapons, and be even very severely wounded, will generally defend himself with his hands, feet, and teeth, when and how he can, as long as he has any breath in his body. The Turk, when he finds himself beyond the reach of all help, and has no hope of escaping, suppliantly begs pardon, and throwing down his arms, holds out his hands to his conqueror joined together ready for binding, and hopes that by captivity he may secure his life.

They select a very extensive space for pitching their camp, where the leading men erect tents, others make a sort of arch of bushes on the ground, and cover it with wrappers, and under these they place their harness, and bows, etc., and protect themselves from the weather. They drive their horses loose to pasture, which is the reason of their having their tents so wide apart. They never fortify their camp with their chariots, or with a ditch, or any other impediment, unless the place itself happen to be naturally defended either by woods, or rivers, or marshes.

It may appear wonderful to anybody that they can support themselves and their people so long on so little pay as I have stated above. I will therefore briefly describe their frugality and parsimony. A man who has six or perhaps more horses, only uses one of them as a sumpter horse to carry the necessaries of life. In the first place he has some ground millet in a bag two or three palms long, then eight or ten pounds of salt pork, with some salt in a bag, mixed, if he be rich, with a little pepper. Besides this, every man carries with him a hatchet, some fuel, and a kettle or a copper porringer, so that if he chance to come to a place where he finds no fruits, or garlic, or onions, or game, he then lights a fire and fills his porringer with water, into which he throws a spoonful of millet with some salt, and boils it, and both master and serfs live content with this fare. Moreover, if the master be very hungry, he eats it all, and the serfs thus undergo a severe fast sometimes for two or three days. If in addition to this the master wish to indulge in a more luxurious repast, he then adds a very small portion of pork to the meal. I do not say this of the superior classes, but of men of middle condition. The generals of the army and other military officers sometimes invite such as are poorer, who, after they have had one good dinner, sometimes abstain from meat for two or three days. Also when they have fruits, or garlic, or onions, they can easily dispense with everything else.

When they are about to go into an engagement, they place more reliance in their numbers, and the amount of forces with which they may be able to encounter the enemy, than in the strength of their soldiers, or any degree of discipline in their army. They fight much more comfortably at a distance than hand to hand, and therefore their principal aim is to circumvent the enemy, and attack him in the rear. They have a great many trumpeters, and when they blow their trumpets all together, as is the custom of the country, and play in unison, you hear a remarkable and most uncommon kind of melody. They have also another sort of musical instrument, which in the common language they call szurnu. When they use this, they will by some means blow it for an hour more or less, apparently without any respiration or inhalation of air. They first fill their cheeks with air, and then being trained to draw in their breath at the same time through the nostrils, they are said to pour out the voice through the tube without any cessation.

They all use the same kind of dress and body-gear; they wear oblong tunics without folds and with rather tight sleeves, almost in the Hungarian style, in which the Christians have buttons to fasten the breast on the right side; but Tartars, who wear a similar garment, have the buttons on the left side. They wear boots of a colour approaching to red, and rather short, so as not to reach the knees—the soles are protected with iron nails. They nearly all have shirts ornamented round the neck with various colours, fastened with necklaces, or with silver or copper-gilt beads, with clasps added for ornament's sake.

They never gird in the belly, but they gird the thighs, and then fasten the girdle as low as their middle to give prominence to the belly. Moreover, the Italians and Spaniards, nay, even the Germans, have now accustomed themselves to the same habit.

Both young men and boys are alike accustomed to meet

on holidays, but in some large and well-known place in the city, where they can be seen and heard by a great number whom they muster round them together by hisses or some other signal. When they are assembled, they run towards each other and wrestle; they then engage in boxing matches, and afterwards promiscuously kick each other with great force with their feet on the face, throat, breast, and belly, etc., or in any other way they can, they throw each other down, struggling for conquest, so that they are often carried away lifeless. He then who conquers the greatest number, stays longest on the field, and endures blows with the greatest fortitude, receives the highest praises, and is accounted a distinguished conqueror. This kind of contest was instituted in order that young men might be able to sustain blows and to endure strokes of any kind.

Justice is carried out very strictly against thieves; when they are caught, the order is, that they shall first have their heels broken, and then rest two or three days while they swell, and then while they are yet broken and swollen they make them walk again. They employ no other method of torturing malefactors to confess robberies or to inform against their accomplices. But if a man, when brought up for examination, be found to deserve death, he is hanged. Criminals are seldom punished with any other kind of punishment, unless they have committed some uncommonly heinous crime. Thefts, and even murders, unless they have been committed for the sake of gain, are seldom visited with capital punishment. If, indeed, a man catch a thief in the act and kill him, he can do so with impunity, always provided however that he bring the man that he has killed to the prince's palace, and explain how the matter occurred.

*   *   *[1]

Few magistrates have authority to inflict capital punish-

---

[1] A sentence is here omitted for the sake of propriety.

ment. No subject dares to put another to the torture. Most malefactors are brought to Moscow or the other principal cities, but convicts are generally punished in winter time, for in summer military pursuits preclude the opportunity of attending to these matters.

The following are Ordinances made by the Grand
DUKE IVAN VASILEIVICH, ANNO MUNDI 7006 (1497).

When a culprit is condemned one ruble, he must pay two altins to the judge and eight dengs to the notary. But if the parties come to terms before they reach the place of contest, they are to pay no less to the judge and notary than if judgment had been passed. But if they come to the place of contest, which can only be decided by Ocolnick and Nedelsnick,[1] and there come to terms, they are to pay as above to the judge, fifty dengs to the Ocolnick, and likewise fifty dengs and two altins to the Nedelsnick, and four altins and one deng to the scribe. But if they come to the contest, and one be overcome, then the guilty man must pay to the judge as much as is demanded by him; he must give a poltin and the arms of the conquered man to the Ocolnick, fifty dengs to the scribe, and a poltin and four altins to Nedelsnick. But if the duel is undertaken on account of an act of incendiarism, the slaying of a friend, plunder, or theft, then the accuser, if he conquer, may take from the guilty man whatever he sought; a poltin and the arms of the vanquished are to be given to the Ocolnick, fifty dengs to the scribe, a poltin to the Nedelsnick, and four altins to the veston (the veston is he who arranges the duel for both parties under the prescribed conditions), and whatever property the guilty man has left, is to be sold and given to the judges, and he is to receive corporeal punishment according to the character of his offence.

[1] For an explanation of these offices see *post*, page 106.

Men who slay their masters, betrayers of the camp, church robbers, kidnappers, and also those who secretly introduce things into another man's house, and then say that they have been stolen from themselves (whom they call podmetzchek), as well as incendiaries, and such as are evident malefactors, are liable to capital punishment. He who is convicted of theft for the first time, unless perhaps he be accused of sacrilege or kidnapping, is not to be punished with death, but to receive public correction, that is, he is to be beaten with rods and to be fined in money by the judge. If he be caught a second time in theft, and have not wherewith to satisfy his accuser or the judge, he must suffer death. If otherwise a convicted thief have not wherewith he can satisfy his accuser, he must be beaten with rods, and delivered to his accuser.

If any man be accused of theft, and any person of respectability declare with an oath that he has also been convicted of theft before, or has been reconciled to another on the score of theft without a judicial verdict, he must suffer death, and his goods are to be disposed of as above.

If any man of low condition or suspected life be charged with theft, he must be summoned to an examination. But if he cannot be convicted of theft, he is remanded on bail for further inquiry.

For the giving sentence or delivering judgment in an arbitration of one ruble, ten dengs are to be paid to the judge, one altin to the secretary who has the seal, and three dengs to the notary.

Governors who have no authority, on hearing a case, to decide or give a verdict, may condemn either party in so many rubles, and then send the case for judgment to the ordinary judges; and if the sentence seem to them just and according to equity, then for every ruble one altin must be paid to the judge, and four dengs to the secretary.

Whoever wishes to lay an accusation against another for

theft, plunder, or manslaughter, goes to Moscow and asks that such an one be summoned to justice. Nedelsnick is given to him, and he appoints a day, which he announces to the man against whom the accusation is laid, and on that day he brings him to Moscow. Afterwards, when the guilty man is brought to judgment, he often denies the crime which is laid to his charge. If the prosecutor produces witnesses, then both parties are asked whether they will stand to their words. The common reply to that is, "Let the witnesses be heard according to justice and custom." If they bear witness against the guilty man, he immediately objects, makes exceptions against themselves and their testimony, saying: "I demand an oath to be administered to me, and I commit myself to the justice of God, and desire a fair field and a duel." And thus, according to the custom of the country, a duel is adjudged to them. Either of them may appoint any other person to take his place in the duel, and each may supply himself with what arms he pleases, except a gun or a bow. But they generally have oblong coats of mail, sometimes double, a breast-plate, bracelets, a helmet, a lance, a hatchet, and a peculiar weapon in the hand, like a dagger sharpened at each end, which they use so rapidly with either hand as never to allow it to impede them in any encounter, nor to fall from the hand; it is generally used in an engagement on foot. They commence fighting with the lance, and afterwards use other arms. For the last many years the Russians, in fighting with foreigners, whether Germans, or Poles, or Lithuanians, have generally been beaten. But on a very recent occasion, when a certain Lithuanian of twenty-six years of age encountered a certain Russian (who had come off conqueror in more than twenty duels), and was killed, the prince in a rage immediately ordered him to be sent for that he might see him; and when he saw him he spat upon the ground, and ordered that in future no duel should be adjudged to any foreigner against his own subjects. The

Russians load themselves, rather than protect themselves, with a great number of different kinds of weapons, but foreigners go to an attack trusting to judgment rather than arms. They take especial care not to let their hands join, for they know that the Russians are very strong in their arms, and it is only by wearying them by perseverance and activity that they in most cases conquer them. Each side has many friends, abettors, and spectators of the contest, who are quite unarmed, except with sticks, which they sometimes use. For if any unfairness seem to be practised upon either of them, the friends of that one immediately rush to avenge his injury, and then the friends of the other interfere, and thus a battle arises between both sides, which is very amusing to the spectators, for the hair of their heads, fists, clubs, and sticks burnt at the points, are all brought into play on the occasion.

The testimony of one nobleman is worth more than that of a multitude of low condition. Attorneys are very seldom allowed: every one explains his own case. Although the prince is very severe, nevertheless all justice is venal, and that without much concealment. I heard of a certain counsellor who presided over the judgments being apprehended, because in a certain case he had received bribes from both parties, and had given judgment in the favour of the one who had made him the largest presents: when he was brought to the prince he did not deny the charge, but stated that the man in whose favour he had given judgment was rich, and held an honourable position in life, and therefore more to be believed than the other, who was poor and abject. The prince revoked the sentence, but at length sent him away with a laugh unpunished. It may be that poverty itself is the cause of so much avarice and injustice, and that the prince knowing his people are poor, connives at such misdeeds and dishonesty as by a predetermined concession of impunity to them.

P

The poor have no access to the prince, but only to the counsellors themselves; and indeed that is very difficult. Ocolnick holds the place of a prætor or judge appointed by the prince, otherwise the chief counsellor, who is always near the prince's person, is so called. Nedelsnick is the post of those who summon men to justice, seize malefactors and cast them into prison; and these are reckoned amongst the nobility.

Labourers work six days in the week for their master, but the seventh day is allowed for their private work. They have some fields and meadows of their own allowed them by their masters, from which they derive their livelihood: all the rest is their master's. They are, moreover, in a very wretched condition, for their goods are exposed to plunder from the nobility and soldiery, who call them Christians and black rascals by way of insult.

A nobleman, however poor he might be, would think it ignominious and disgraceful to labour with his own hands; but he does not think it disgraceful to pick up from the ground and eat the rind or peeling of fruits that have been thrown away by us and our servants, especially the skins of melons, garlic, and onions; but whenever occasion offers, they drink as immoderately as they eat sparingly. They are nearly all slow to anger, but proud in their poverty, whose irksome companion they consider slavery. They wear oblong dresses and white peaked hats of felt (of which we see coarse mantles made) rough from the shop.

The halls of their houses are indeed large and lofty enough, but the doors are so low, that in entering, one must stoop and bend one's self.

They who live by manual labour and work for hire, receive a deng and a half as one day's pay; a mechanic receives two dengs, but these do not work very industriously unless they are well beaten. I have heard some servants complain that they had not received their fair amount of beating from their masters. They think that they have displeased their master, and that it is a sign of his anger if they are not beaten.

Of entering another Man's House.

In all houses and dwellings they have the images of saints, either painted or cast, placed in some honourable position: and when any one goes to see another, as he enters the house, he immediately takes his hat off and looks round to see where the image is, and when he sees it he signs himself three times with the cross, and bowing his head says, "O Lord, have mercy." He then salutes the host with these words, "God give health." They then shake hands, kiss each other, and bow, and then each looks at the other, to see if he have any more bowing to do, and thus bowing their heads three or four times alternately, and paying their respects to each other, they by some means come to an understanding. They then seat themselves, and after their business is settled, the guest walks straight into the middle of the dwelling, with his face turned towards the image, and again signing himself three times with the cross, bows his head and repeats the former words. At length when they have saluted each other with the above-mentioned words, he departs. If he be a man of some authority, the host follows him to the steps, but if he be of a superior position in life, he accompanies him further, due respect being observed for the rank of each person. They are wonderfully ceremonious, for no man of small fortune is permitted to ride within the gate of the house of one of higher rank. The poor and obscure classes also find access difficult even to the common nobles, who walk out but seldom in public, in order that they may retain greater authority thereby, and have more respect paid to them. Likewise no nobleman who is moderately rich walks on foot so far as the fourth or fifth house from his own without his horse being led in attendance. In winter time, however, when they cannot use their horses without danger on account of the ice, for they are unshod, or on occasions when they may have to go to the prince's palace, or to the temples of the saints, they generally leave their horses at home. Gentlemen always sit within their own houses, and seldom or never transact business walking. They used to wonder extremely when they saw us walking in our hotels, and frequently transacting business while we were walking.

The prince has post stations in all parts of his dominions, with a regular number of horses at the different places, so that when the royal courier is sent anywhere, he may immediately have a horse without delay; and the courier has authority to choose any horse he pleases. When I was making a rapid journey from Great Novogorod to Moscow, the post-master, who in their language is called jamschnick, would have sometimes thirty and occasionally forty or fifty horses brought out to me the first thing in the morning, when there was no need of more than twelve. Each of my people, therefore, took the horse which he thought would best suit him, and when they were tired we constantly changed them on reaching another inn on the road (they call their inns jama), but kept the same saddle and bridle. Every one is at liberty to ride at full speed, and if his horse happen to fall, or can go on no longer, he may take another with impunity from the first house he comes to, or from any one he may chance to meet, the prince's courier alone excepted. If, however, a horse be exhausted and left on the road, the jamschnick requires restoration; and it is customary to give another to him from whom it was taken, or to pay a price according to the length of the journey. Six dengs are generally reckoned for from ten to twenty wersts.[1]

[1] The werst is equal to $1166\frac{2}{3}$ English yards, or somewhat less than two-thirds of an English mile.

On one occasion, a servant of mine rode on such post horses from Novogorod to Moscow, a distance of six hundred wersts, that is, a hundred and twenty German miles, in seventy-two hours, which is the more remarkable, because they are small ponies, and far less carefully tended than ours, and yet such is the work that they will perform.

Of their Money.

They have four kinds of silver money,—that of Moscow, of Novogorod, of Tver, and of Plescow. The money of Moscow is not round, but oblong, and of a sort of oval form, called a deng. It has different impressions, the old deng having on one side the figure of a rose, and the later one the figure of a man sitting on horseback; both of these have an inscription on the reverse. A hundred of them go to one Hungarian gold piece; six dengs make an altin; twenty a grifna; one hundred a poltin; and two hundred a ruble.

There are new coins now struck, with characters on both sides, forty of which are worth one ruble.

The coin of Tver has an inscription on both sides, and is of the same value as that of Moscow.

The coin of Novogorod has on one side the figure of the prince sitting on his throne, and a man opposite him making his obeisance; on the other it has an inscription, and is worth twice as much as that of Moscow. Moreover, the grifna of Novogorod is worth fourteen rubles, and the ruble of Novogorod two hundred and twenty-two dengs.

The coin of Plescow has the head of an ox crowned, and an inscription on the other side. They have also a copper coin called polani; sixty of these are worth one deng of Moscow.

They have no gold money, nor do they themselves coin any, but mostly use Hungarian, and occasionally Rhenish money. They often change their valuation of these coins, especially when a foreigner wishes to purchase anything with gold, for then they immediately depreciate its value; but if any one is about to go anywhere on a journey and wants gold, they then raise the price again.

They use the rubles of Riga on account of its proximity, one of which is worth two of those of Moscow. The money of Moscow is of pure and good silver, although that is also adulterated now. Yet I never heard of any one being reprehended for this misdemeanour. Nearly all the goldsmiths of Moscow coin money; and when any one brings masses of pure silver and asks for money for them, they weigh both the money and the silver and balance it equally. There is a small fixed price above the equal weight to be paid to the goldsmiths, who otherwise charge but little for their labour. Some have written[1] that in some very few spots in this country there is an abundance of silver, and that the prince forbids its exportation. The truth is that the country contains no silver, except (as I have said) what is imported; but the prince may rather be said to guard against than to forbid its exportation, and to that effect orders his subjects to barter their commodities, and to give and receive some articles in exchange for others, such as skins (in which they abound), or anything else of the kind, so as to keep their gold and silver in the province. It is scarcely a hundred years since the silver money which they used was principally of their own coining. When silver was first introduced into the province, they used to cast little oblong pieces of silver without any impression or inscription, of the value of one ruble, not one of which is now to be seen. Money was also coined in the principality of Galicia; but as that had no constant value,

---

[1] Myechov, in his *Tractatus de duabus Sarmatiis* (*Tractatus* ii, lib. 2), says, "Estque terra dives argento et custodia undique clausa."

it disappeared. In early times, moreover, before they had money, they made use of the snouts and ears of squirrels and other animals, whose skins are brought to us in lieu of coin, and bought the necessaries of life with them as with money.

They use such a kind of reckoning that they count or divide things by sorogh or devenost, that is, either by the number forty or ninety, in the same manner as we do by a hundred. So that in counting they repeat and multiply by two sorogh, three sorogh, four sorogh, that is, forty; or two, three, or four dewenost, that is, ninety. A thousand in the vulgar tongue is tissutzæ; ten thousand is expressed in one word, tma; twenty thousand by dwetma; and thirty thousand by tritma.

When any one brings any articles of merchandize to Moscow, he is compelled to declare them, and show them immediately to the gate-keepers or officers of the customs; and these latter examine them at a stated hour and put a value on them; and when they have been valued, no one dares either to sell or buy until they have been reported to the prince. Moreover, if the prince should wish to buy anything, the merchant is not allowed to show his goods, nor propose a price for them, to any one; and hence it sometimes happens that merchants are detained a considerable time.

Nor is it allowed to every merchant to come to Moscow, but only to Lithuanians, Poles, or persons subject to those governments. For Swedes and Livonians and Germans from the maritime states may only go to Novogorod; and Turks and Tartars are permitted to traffic and carry on business in the town of Chlopigrod, whither at the time of the markets men congregate from the most distant places. But when legates and ambassadors go to Moscow, then all merchants from all places who have been taken under their countenance and protection are accustomed to enter freely into Moscow, and can pass without paying custom.

The principal part of their merchandize consists of masses of silver, cloths, silk, clothes of silk and gold, clasps, jewels, and gold in filagree; and sometimes, at its proper season, they bring some things of a paltry character from which they derive no little profit. It often even happens that every one is anxious to buy a certain article, and he who becomes the first possessor of it makes more than a fair profit by it. Then when several merchants bring a great quantity of the same articles, the price will fall to such an extent, that he who sells his goods for the highest price will buy them again when the price has fallen, and carry them back again to his own country after having made a large profit. The articles of merchandize which are exported from Russia into Germany are skins and wax; into Lithuania and Turkey, leather, skins, and the long white teeth of animals which they call mors,[1] and which inhabit the northern ocean, out of which the Turks are accustomed very skilfully to make the handles of daggers; our people think they are the teeth of fish, and call them so. Into Tartary, moreover, are exported saddles, bridles, clothes, and leather; but arms or iron are not exported to other places towards the east or north, except by stealth, or by the express permission of the officers. They take, however, cloth and linen dresses, knives, hatchets, needles, mirrors, and purses, or anything of that sort. They traffic most deceitfully and craftily, and not with few words, as some have stated that they do. Moreover, when they are bargaining and bating down an article to less than half its value, in order to cheat the seller, they will sometimes hold the merchants in suspense and uncertainty for a month or two, and indeed lead them on to the point of desperation. But any one who is aware of their habits and the cunning language with which they depreciate the value of an article and lengthen out the time, makes no to-do or dissimulation, but sells his goods without any abatement. A certain citizen

---

[1] The morse, walrus, or sea-horse.

of Cracow had brought two hundred-weight of copper, which the prince wished to buy, and he detained the merchant so long, that at last he became weary of the delay, and started to take the copper back to his own country. But when he was at some miles' distance from the city, some underlings pursued him, and stopped his goods, and put him under an interdict, under pretence that he had not paid duty. The merchant returned to Moscow and laid a complaint before the prince's counsellors of the injury that had been done to him. When they had heard the case, they immediately of their own accord took upon themselves to be mediators, and promised that they would arrange the matter if he would ask it as a favour. The crafty merchant, who knew that it would be a disgrace to the prince if such goods were to be taken back from his territory and no one be found to buy and pay for them, would ask no favour, but demanded that justice should be done to him. At length, when they saw that he was so determined, that he could not be turned from his purpose, and that he would not yield to their trickery or cheating, they bought the copper in the name of the prince, and having paid the just price they sent him away.

They sell everything dearer to foreigners, so that what might be bought elsewhere for one ducat they mark at five, eight, ten, and sometimes twenty ducats; although they themselves in their turn sometimes buy a rare article from foreigners for ten or fifteen florins, which is scarcely worth one or two florins. Moreover, in making bargains, if you happen to say or promise anything somewhat imprudently, they carefully remember it, and urge its performance; but if they themselves in their turn promise anything, they do not hold to it at all. Whenever, also, they begin to swear and protest, you may know for a certainty that there is some trick underneath, for they swear with the very intention of deceiving and overreaching.

I once asked a certain counsellor of the prince to assist

me, that I might not be deceived in buying certain skins, and he so readily promised me his assistance, that he again threw me for a longer time into a state of doubt. He wished to obtrude his own skins upon me; and, moreover, other merchants came to him, promising him douceurs if he would sell their goods to me at a good price. For it is the custom of the merchants to constitute themselves go-betweens in buying and selling, and to receive presents from both parties under the promise of their faithful assistance.

There is a spacious walled building not far from the citadel, called the "Hall of the Master Merchants", in which the merchants live and store their goods, and where are sold pepper, saffron, silks, and that sort of merchandize, at a far lower price than in Germany. But this is to be attributed to the bartering of goods. For while the Russians put a high price upon skins purchased cheaply elsewhere, foreigners in their turn, perhaps influenced by their example, offer goods also bought for a small sum, and quote them at a higher price; the result is, that as each makes an equal barter of commodities, the Russians can sell goods, especially such as they receive in exchange for skins, at a low price, and without profit.

There is a great difference in the skins. In sable skins, the blackness, length, and thickness of the hair, argue full growth. If also the animal be taken at a fitting season, they raise the price, a rule which is also observed with reference to other skins. The sables are found very seldom on this side of the Ustyug and the province of Dwina, but more often, and of a finer sort, about Petchora.

Marten skins are brought from different parts; good ones from Sewera, better from Switzerland, and the best from Sweden.

I have sometimes heard of sable skins being seen at Moscow, some of which have been sold for thirty, and some for twenty gold pieces. But I never had the good fortune to see any such skins myself. Ermine skins also are brought from various places turned inside out, by which, however, many buyers are imposed upon. They have certain marks about the head and tail, by which they are known whether they have been caught at the proper season. For directly this animal is caught it is skinned, and the skin is turned inside out, lest it should be injured by the hair being rubbed. If one of them be taken at an unseasonable time, and the skin be deficient in its natural good colour, they then pull out and extract (as it is said) certain significant hairs from the head and tail, lest it should be known that the animal was caught at the wrong time, and so they deceive the purchasers; they are mostly sold, however, for three or four dengs a-piece; those which are a little larger are deficient in that whiteness which is otherwise seen pure in the smaller ones.

Fox skins, and especially black ones, which they usually make into caps, are valued very highly, for sometimes ten of them are sold for fifteen gold pieces. Squirrel skins also are brought from different parts, but the greater number from the province of Siberia; but those of the finest quality from Schvwaii [Svhajsk?], not far from Kazan. These skins are brought also from Permia, Viatka, Ustyug, and Vologda, always bound up in bundles of ten; in each of which bundles there are two best, which they call Litzschna; three, somewhat inferior, which they call Crasna; four, which they call Pocrasna; and the last one, called Moloischna, is the worst of all. These skins are sold for one or two dengs a-piece.

The merchants take the best and picked ones into Germany and other parts, and derive great profit therefrom.

Lynx skins are of little value, but wolves' skins, since they began to be held in esteem in Germany and Moscow, have a very high price attached to them; but wolves' skins are much less costly here than with us.

Beavers' skins are held by them in high esteem, and nearly

all have the borders of their garments made of this fur, because it is black, which is the natural colour.

The women use the skins of domestic cats. There is a certain animal, which in their common language they call pessetz,[1] the skin of which they use on a journey or in expeditions, because it generally gives most warmth to the body.

The customs or duty on all goods, either imported or exported, is carried into the treasury. Seven dengs are levied on everything of the value of one ruble, except wax, on which the duty is demanded, not only according to its value, but also its weight. Four dengs are levied on a certain weight, commonly called pud.

I shall give a full description below in the "Chorography of Russia", of the roads which the merchants take in importing and exporting their merchandize, and also through the different districts of Russia.

Usury is prevalent; and although they acknowledge it to be a great sin, yet scarcely any one refrains from it. Moreover, it is absolutely intolerable, for it is always taken at one in five, that is, twenty per cent. They seem to treat the church more leniently (as it is called), and accept from it ten per cent. (as they term it).

[1] Canis lagopus. The arctic fox of Pennant.

END OF THE FIRST VOLUME.

ERRATA

Introduction, page vi, line 8, for "1599-60", read "1599-1600".
,, ix, 30, for "Royal", read "Royale".
,, xxi, 14, for "Aut.", read "Ant."
,, xxviii, Note, for "Humbolt", read "Humboldt".
,, lxxi, 12, for "Weid", read "Wied".
,, lxxxviii, 3, for "Polschaftn", read "Potschaftn".